MAYAN CALENDAR

BIRTHDAY BOOK

Ephemeris/Guide

Easy reference handbook
for finding and understanding
your birthday solar glyph and tone

by **Mary Fran Koppa** (Ahau/2)

This Book is dedicated to my son Chris (Ahau/6),
who has given me the example of freedom and
following your own dream.

Special thanks to José Argüelles for introducing me to the
Mayan Calendar symbols in his wonderful book, *The Mayan Factor*.

Cover Art *Solar Glyph 20, AHAU*, pastel drawing by Mary Fran Koppa

Mayan Calendar Art Publishing
P.O. Box 1833, Cottonwood, AZ 21044-1229 USA

INTRODUCTION

Dear Reader,

My work on the Mayan Calendar started in 1987 with a near-death experience. When I returned to consciousness, I had a new clarity about spiritual energy. I was led to the Mayan Calendar as a tool for spiritual development.

I learned that the Classic Mayans created a sacred calendar about 1,400 years ago. This calendar had symbols for 20 solar glyphs, 10 planets and 13 numbers, called tones. Each of these symbols represented a specific energy.

I learned that these symbols had been hidden all these years in the jungles of Mexico and Central America, only to be discovered by this generation, in our time of great need.

I wanted to make the energy of the symbols easier to understand and feel. Being an artist I created a pastel drawing for each of the 43 calendar symbols. I was successful in translating the energy of the symbols into colors and shapes.

I have learned many things about the energy of the Mayan Calendar through the artwork. I feel that I understand the purpose of life and spirituality more clearly than ever before. In this book I share some of the things I have learned.

When I began my study of the Mayan Calendar I found the written information hard to understand. Since I like to understand things clearly, I began writing and publishing articles to simplify the information. I decided to organize an easy- to-follow birthday chart to go with it. Then it seemed natural to put all the information in a book.

In this *Mayan Calendar Birthday Book*, there is a set of simple charts for *finding the solar glyph and tone for any day of any year*. I have summarized the meanings of the solar glyphs, tones and planets to help you understand your Mayan birthday symbols. This information is significant because it can help you with your life's purpose. It is also important because the symbols of the Mayan Sacred Calendar represent the actual energy of creation. This energy is the same energy that you use every single day of the year to achieve things in your life. Once you understand it you can use it more effectively.

I hope you have fun using this book for years to come!

In love and light,

Mary Fran Koppa

TABLE OF CONTENTS

Mayan Astrology 1

Sample Calendar 2

The Solar Glyphs and Tones 3

The 20 Solar Glyphs 6

Solar Glyphs Work with These Issues 13

The 13 Tones of Creation 15

The 7 Practical Tones 16

The 6 Cosmic Tones 19

Energy Supplied by the Tones 24

The 10 Planets of the Mayan Calendar 25

Correlations of the Planets and Solar Glyphs 27

Resource Energy of the Planets 27

Creation, Frequency and the Symbols of
the Mayan Calendar 30

How to Use the Charts in This Book 34

Birthday Charts 36

ILLUSTRATIONS

The 20 Solar Glyphs of the Mayan Calendar 5

The 13 Tones of the Mayan Calendar 14

The 10 Planets of the Mayan Calendar 25

MAYAN ASTROLOGY

Mayan astrology involves finding your Mayan birth signs and learning how they affect your life. You can start by finding the solar glyph and tone that were on the calendar the day you were born. You will need the day, month, and year of your birth. Look through the simple charts in this book to find the solar glyph and tone that correspond to your birthday.

After you know your personal solar glyph and tone, you can refer to the next section of this book to see what they represent.

> · **The solar glyphs symbolize the area that the soul wishes to focus on in this life.**

> · **The tones describe the quality of energy you carry in your body to help you understand reality and help you attain your life's purpose**

You will find a description of each of the solar glyphs and tones, including an explanation of what they mean on a cosmic level. When you know your birthday solar glyph, you can refer to the chapter on *The 10 Planets of the Mayan Calendar* to see which of the planets correlates to your solar glyph. This will give you another interesting aspect of your birthday sign.

The information on the symbols of the Mayan Calendar has been given to facilitate your soul development. Mayan astrology is interested in the evolution of the soul.

SAMPLE CALENDAR

SUN	MON	TUES	WED	THUR	FRI	SAT
1	2	3	4	5	6	7

You may use the information from the charts in this book to convert any calendar into a Mayan Calendar. Simply find the solar glyphs and tones for any given month and pencil them into your everyday calendar. This will help to familiarize you with the energy of the solar glyphs and tones.

Another way to do it is to pencil in just the solar glyph and tone for the day. That way you become very aware of the predominant energies of the day and you can work with them to help your life go more smoothly.

The 20 solar glyphs rotate and repeat every 20 days. In the sample above, you see *Manik, Lamat , Muluc, Oc, Chuen, Eb* and *Ben.* These solar glyphs will always appear on the calendar in this order, taking their place as part of the 20.

The tones also rotate and they repeat every 13 days. The ones in our sample calendar are tones *two, three, four, five, six, seven* and *eight.* Remember that in the Mayan numbering system a dot is *one* and a bar is *five.*

You might be interested to know that the same combination of solar glyph and tone appear on the calendar only once every 260 days. Any combination of solar glyph and tone will fall on the same birthday only once every 52 years.

Don't worry if your drawings of the solar glyphs on your calendar aren't exact. They are for you. Just have fun with it!

THE SOLAR GLYPHS AND TONES

On the Mayan Calendar there is **one solar glyph and one tone for each day of the year**. There are 20 solar glyphs and 13 tones.

You can learn about your life's purpose and the quality of energy you carry in your body by knowing the solar glyph and tone that were on the calendar on the day you were born.

The twenty solar glyphs symbolize the 20 levels of wisdom of the soul. Each person has to complete all 20 levels in order to be fully enlightened. Your birthday solar glyph is the level you chose to focus on in this life. You wanted to learn the lessons of this particular area of wisdom.

You will also be working on the other 19 levels. Every day on the calendar you can find the solar glyph energy that predominates. This cosmic energy will always provide experiences for you to understand the wisdom contained in the daily solar glyph. That is what life experiences are!

Some people have already completed the level of wisdom that they chose as their birthday solar glyph. Many others are still working on their birthday solar glyph, gradually completing the step. If you feel that you are still working on the level of wisdom described by your birthday solar glyph, remember to **pay attention when that solar glyph is the energy of the day on the calendar**. This will occur every 20 days. On these days you will be given special help, through your daily experiences and insights, to complete this step.

On any given day, everyone on the planet will be having experiences related to the solar glyph energy of the day. Sometimes the experiences will seem difficult, but they provide information that you need.

You may be consciously working on a level of wisdom that is *not* your birthday solar glyph, but it is symbolized by a different solar glyph. You can receive the energy needed to help complete *any of the 20 steps of the soul* on the day that its solar glyph is on the calendar. The energy of each day is always working with you to help you complete that particular step of the soul, whether you are aware of it or not. It is happening all the time, even at this very moment.

How to proceed

It is sometimes a good idea to sit quietly and meditate with the solar glyph that represents the level of wisdom you want to attain. The symbol will help you on the subconscious or telepathic level. Feel free to meditate with any of the solar glyphs that appeal to you. Follow your intuition as you move around through the 20 steps of the soul. You have been doing just that without realizing it your entire life.

The 20 solar glyph energies have been rotating since this world was created. That is why no two days are the same. You have been gaining your wisdom using this energy intuitively. Now you can take charge and work with these issues on a conscious level. It will speed up your progress.

The following is information about the individual solar glyphs as steps of the soul. Be aware that there are many correct ways of interpreting and using the symbols. Be open to *your own* insights as you work with these galactic energies. Your own insights will be the most important ones for you.

1. Imix	2. Ik	3. Akbal	4. Kan
5. Chicchan	6. Cimi	7. Manik	8. Lamat
9. Muluc	10. Oc	11. Chuen	12. Eb
13. Ben	14. Ix	15. Men	16. Cib
17. Caban	18. Etznab	19. Cauac	20. Ahau

THE 20 SOLAR GLYPHS OF THE MAYAN CALENDAR

THE 20 SOLAR GLYPHS

1. IMIX *Loving and nurturing yourself and others.*
There is both a Father and Mother aspect to God. Imix is God as Mother, the one who nurtures and who creates form. You will feel a cosmic closeness to the feminine aspect of God. You are interested in what that means and will explore the possibilities of being **a gentle and nurturing person**. You enjoy making things. You might be dealing with issues around **the value of your feminine side**. Meditating with this glyph can help restore health lost through self-hatred. Self-acceptance is the first step to perfect health and emotional balance.

2. IK *Seeing the big picture with compassion, love and humor.*
This is the symbol for God as Father, who blows life and humor into the forms with his breath. God as Father is the thought, the idea to create, the one who knows you. He represents truth. You will have a cosmic closeness to the masculine aspect of God, knowing what that means. You really enjoy and appreciate **humor**. You might be dealing with issues around **the value of your masculine side**. Meditating with this glyph can help you **bring your masculine and feminine sides into perfect balance**. This is necessary for becoming fully enlightened.

3. AKBAL *Creating a peaceful home and environment.*
The forms of creation take on an appearance and become the temple, or dwelling place of God. You will have a cosmic understanding of what it means to be the expression of divine energy in form. **The symbol of home is important for you.** and you will explore the meanings and spiritual aspects of home. You want to make it a **place of peace**. The concept of home expands to include your environment and your planet. You have a strong desire for balance and peace.

4. KAN *Appreciating the value and connectedness of all things.*
God's creations change and evolve continuously. You have a cosmic interest in the mysteries of creation. How does that miracle happen? This symbol portrays the dynamic and ongoing nature of creation. It speaks about reproduction, growth and change. You begin to **see all creation as an expression of Divine Love**. This step is necessary for becoming fully enlightened, because you need to **feel the oneness running through all life** in order to love all things. Everything that has ever

been created is a child of God, made from divine energy, and **we are all loved equally**. You can meditate with this glyph to help heal issues around bigotry or racial injustice. If God is present in all things, and we are loved equally, there is no point in making comparisons.

5. CHICCHAN *Having the courage to be yourself.*
At this step you become very aware of **your separateness as an individual**. The mind becomes your tool for separation. You are a separate consciousness, an individual, one who can think. Only when you complete the concept of yourself as being separate from God and other people can you experience who you really are. Who am I as I stand alone? What does that feel like? You will gain an appreciation for **your own value and worth**. You will experience your power and abilities more clearly. Then you can start the exciting journey back to the oneness of all things. You can experience your connectedness more profoundly. You might be dealing with issues around loneliness and a strong desire to be loved and accepted as you are. Meditating with this solar glyph can be helpful in moving through feelings of despair, knowing that your feelings of separation are a part of the lesson, but they are temporary.

6. CIMI *Appreciating and making the most of your life.*
Awareness of the concept of time. The realization that a lifetime is finite and has more to do with cycles of experience than endings. You know that you are making your way back to divinity and then choosing your next arena of experience. You become aware of the preciousness of life here on Earth, and you **want to make the most of your life**. You have a strong desire to understand the things of this Earth and you have **great courage and daring**, which move you into new experiences.

7. MANIK *Learning to make wonderful things, and to enjoy being alive.*
You attain the ability to make things. You begin to **understand how things work** on this planet. You also learn about how other people operate. You become successful. You learn how to make changes in your life smoothly. You enjoy creative abilities. Basically, you **enjoy being alive**. Meditating with this solar glyph can be helpful if you are dealing with issues around control. Is someone controlling you? Do you need to control others? Remember that the need to control springs from a lack of trust. Allow yourself to trust.

8. LAMAT *Loving yourself and others unconditionally.*
The Mayan Star. This step is basically about **learning to love. You develop a tolerance and a compassion for yourself and others**. The ability to love yourself is very important in attaining wisdom, and it is perfected at this step of the soul. You begin to feel a profound sense of your own value and a love for yourself exactly as you are. You evolve this self-love into a deep love for humanity and a love and caring for planet Earth. Meditating with this solar glyph will help you to remember and hold the vibration for unconditional love. Lamat portrays our coming forth into being from love when we awake, creating our bodies out of light, then our return back to love, which we all do each time we fall asleep. It is the symbolic portrayal that **love is what we are**.

9. MULUC *Having a cosmic understanding of life.*
Very clear awareness of your spiritual nature. Opening to a more vivid realization of the existence of God. You have a great desire to understand your divine nature on a **cosmic level**. You want to know about other levels of creation. Who are the angels? Why do they come here? You stand easily in the doorway between different worlds, seeing both sides. Meditating with this solar glyph will create **an opening to other dimensions of reality** when you do it with a pure intention to understand more and to grow in holiness.

10. OC *Healing emotional turmoil and balancing the passions.*
This symbol helps you **balance the emotions**. Your emotions may be vivid and scattered, and the job here is to make some sense of it all. You must keep the strong emotions, for they are needed in telepathy, but you arrange them in a more comfortable order. Passion is necessary on the higher levels of understanding, so you learn to calm yourself without stifling your passion for life. Sexuality is a big issue with this step of the soul. The goal is **integrating sexuality into your life and recognizing it as something of God**. As such, it is something to be appreciated and respected. Meditating with this solar glyph can help bring wild emotions into balance. It can also help you come to a place of peace around sexual issues, healing past wounds. This glyph will help on a telepathic level. No words are needed. Just state an intention as you begin your meditation.

11. CHUEN *Knowing what JOY really is.*

The gift of originality is received. God creates new things through you. This step of the soul portrays the loving recognition that everything you are and all that you do is of God. This is the step of the soul that has to do with **fun and playfulness.** You know that you are a co-creator with God and responsible for your own happiness. Nobody else can make you happy, so you learn how to do it for yourself. It starts with being true to yourself. Meditating with this solar glyph can put you into contact with the fact that you are a living reflection of the Creator. This knowledge will make you more powerful. It can help you resolve issues of powerlessness that sometimes create unwanted addictions.

12. EB *Balancing a deep love of God with success in the world.*

Realizing God's presence inside oneself, life takes on a more spiritual orientation. There is **a very close connection with God,** a deep love given and received. The temptation here is to spend most of your time in meditation and prayer, forgetting about your physical obligations. This needs to be brought into balance in order to attain the wisdom of this step. Most of the spiritual energy is concentrated from the heart to the top of the head, so feelings of bliss are easy to attain. Another challenge of this step is to avoid judgment and scorn for others who do not feel the close connection with God that you do. Meditating with this solar glyph can help balance spiritual and physical needs. It can help you allow others to be exactly what they want to be, knowing that every experience is wisdom gained.

13. BEN *Wanting peace and being willing to work for it.*

Awareness of God moving through all things. The longing for peace and harmony. Wanting to unite the pillars of heaven and earth. Thirteen is God's number. It was held in reverence by the Mayans and many other ancient civilizations. In this step of the soul the Divine energy assists you to create peace in your relationships and your environment. You become very uncomfortable with conflict. **You are the peacemaker.** If there is a tendency to "turn the other cheek" and allow others to take advantage of you, this needs to be brought into balance. Meditating with this solar glyph can bring the strength and courage necessary for honoring yourself and your needs. You learn what feels good and what doesn't. You learn to protect yourself by avoiding abusive situations. You learn that gentleness is a form of inner strength, and you honor yourself enough to stop any form of disrespect in your life.

14. IX *Having great power and learning to stay humble.*
This symbol teaches wisdom, the **power** to perform miracles, and the ability to create with thought. You receive the power to heal yourself and others. There may be a tendency to become the "teacher" because you seem to know more than others, and others are often eager to give their power to you as a way of avoiding responsibility. At this point in the soul's journey there is the danger of egotism. Humility is needed to complete this step. This solar glyph is all about power and **learning to combine power with humility**. The secret here is loving yourself. When you truly love yourself, you never need to be egotistical. Meditating with this solar glyph can help you deal with issues of power or ego.

15. MEN *Having telepathic connection with higher knowledge.*
This symbol is about learning through your own thoughts. You can access knowledge and wisdom from within yourself.

You will become very **telepathic** and be able to solve problems, then wonder where the answer came from. It came from someone else who knew the answer, and you reached out telepathically and picked it up. At this level of wisdom you are wise enough not to read people's minds. That would be an invasion of privacy. Here the pillars of heaven and earth are united as you grow in understanding. Activation of higher and higher frequencies in your physical body becomes routine as you expand into the highly evolved human.

16. CIB *Communicating between dimensions of reality to stabilize the Earth.*
This symbol will help you experience yourself as a member of the universe, and feel a sense of finally being at home here on Earth. You attain an ability to use and understand telepathy with ease. You become familiar with and **communicate with other life forms**, such as angels and space beings. You will be adjusting your physical body to the higher frequencies to make such communication possible. One lesson of this step of the soul is to stay out of awe or worship for other seemingly more powerful life forms. Just recognize them as brothers and sisters, and as equals. They will enjoy your company more if you have dignity.

17. CABAN *Holding the higher energy in the physical body as conduit for the new frequencies on Earth.*

This symbol shows planet Earth evolving to nurture a greater spirituality. More complex energy patterns from our Creator are now available to transform the planet to one of peace. You will be very interested in this process, becoming involved in **assisting the shift to the higher frequencies.** You will facilitate the shift in others by holding within yourself the "love/trust" vibration. This is the unwary heart, keeper of the wisdom. You will have to stay centered and very focused during this planetary transition period, especially during difficulties. Avoid the lower vibrations. Meditate with this solar glyph to help stabilize the new energies. You can also use it to tune into the Earth to find out what is going on.

18. ETZNAB *Understanding the deeper meanings and being at peace.*

This symbol gives the ability to be fully focused on what is in front of you. You learn to stop thinking so much about the past or worrying about the future. Your ego is centered and disciplined. You become **fully present in the** *now.* Your mind becomes peaceful, with no urge to complain or worry. Loving and allowing all things, you **allow life to be easy.** Meditate with this solar glyph if you are tired of complaining and worrying, and want to learn how to become content.

19. CAUAC *Cleaning out old energy patterns to make room for better things.*

This symbol represents the **last shedding of the tears** as you heal all past, present and future wounds of the body, mind and spirit. Your emotions are cleaned and purified. You have a complete and total trust in God and yourself. Your body is prepared for the final step of the soul. This is the solar glyph that directly assists in healing. Meditating with it or wearing it will help you release decayed energy that has been locked in the cellular mass of your body. This obsolete energy needs to get out to make room for more light to come into the body. Crying may help it to move out, but don't think of yourself as a victim when you do this. You are **taking charge of your body and your life**. If you want to cry, do it with the purpose of moving the old energy out of your body. This step of the soul is the final purification of the body and spirit, prior to full enlightenment, and is extremely important.

20. AHAU *Expressing a divine nature in all thoughts and actions, you transform the Earth.*

This symbol brings the spiritual energies from the head and the heart down to the base of your spine. You become aware that everything you do is a divine act. You easily **express God in all your actions and thoughts:** kind actions and loving thoughts, enjoying fun and humor. You become the purified human vessel for divine love expressing on Earth. You become the mind and body of light, the fully enlightened person. This step integrates all the other 19 steps into the physical body, and completes them. You will be very interested in the other 19 levels of wisdom and be actively working to finish them all! When you attain this 20th level of wisdom you will **feel your divinity** in the physical body. It will be allowed, acknowledged, and reclaimed.

The word *enthusiasm* comes from an ancient Greek word meaning, *To be filled with God*. When the Ahau step is completed, you will experience a great enthusiasm for life. You will have created a heaven on Earth.

SOLAR GLYPHS WORK WITH THESE ISSUES

1. Imix: Feminine energy

2. Ik: Masculine energy

3. Akbal: Importance of a peaceful home

4. Kan: Oneness of all things

5. Chicchan: Loneliness and feelings of abandonment

6. Cimi: Lack of direction or purpose

7. Manik: To become more skillful and to understand others

8. Lamat: To love yourself and others unconditionally

9. Muluc: To move between dimensions of reality

10. Oc: Emotional issues and sexual issues

11. Chuen: To learn to relax and play; also to overcome addictions

12. Eb: To balance spiritual and physical needs

13. Ben: To create peaceful relationships; also to overcome abuse

14. Ix: To balance great success with great humility

15. Men: To learn telepathy

16. Cib: To learn the languages of other worlds

17. Caban: To understand the frequency shift and help planet Earth

18. Etznab: To stop worrying and complaining, and find peace of mind

19. Cauac: To release old, obsolete energy patterns in the body

20. Ahau: To bring the spiritual light throughout the whole body

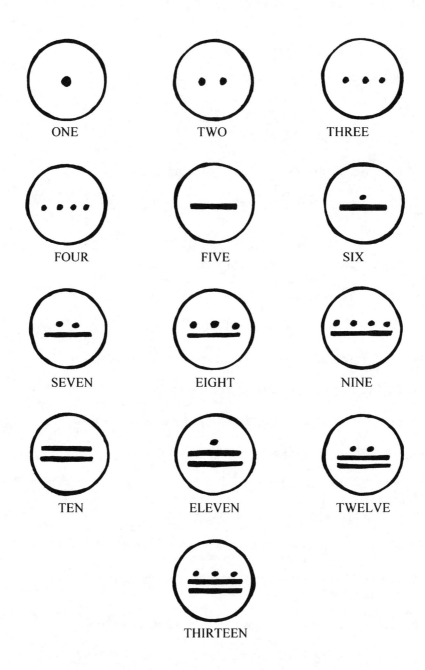

THE 13 TONES OF THE MAYAN CALENDAR

THE 13 TONES OF CREATION

The 13 tones on the Mayan Calendar are a symbolic depiction of the energies that were used to create our world.

In the Mayan numbering system a dot stands for *one* and a bar stands for *five*. These Mayan number-tones have been coded with the creative energies that they represent. This means that if you look at any of the Mayan numbers from one through thirteen you may be able to feel that particular creative energy, actually experience the feeling of it in your body.

The Mayan numbers are called tones because they are energy vibrations. Visualize something like the tone from a tuning fork being their song. There are thirteen different tones on the calendar because thirteen is God's number and is the spiritual totality. Tone thirteen encompasses and encloses all the spiritual energy that made creation.

The tones rotate on the calendar, repeating every thirteen days. On any given day, one of these tones will be the predominant energy of the day. We can consciously use the tone of the day to help in our lives by just being aware of it and asking for what we need. Also, it is important to remember that all the tones are present *every day* because they are the actual energies that sustain and evolve our world. They are all around us at this very moment.

We have been using them on an intuitive level to create everything in our lives. Now that we have more information about them, our creations can become less haphazard and more satisfying.

The tone that was on the calendar on your birthday will be the predominant energy in your body.

Your birthday tone will affect everything you do. It is the energy you use to express yourself in the world. You chose this particular energy before you were born because you thought that it would be the best one to help you attain your life's purpose, and it probably is.

If you become aware of what your tone energy is, you can work with it. You can stop questioning why you are the way you are. Then your life will flow more easily.

There are 7 practical tones and 6 cosmic tones. The 7 practical tones are doing specific jobs in this reality. People carrying one of the practical tones are anchoring energy and helping to establish it on the planet.

The six cosmic tones are related to cosmic purpose. Those born on days with cosmic tones are also anchoring the energy, but it is more complex because it reaches out and is working far beyond our reality as well as here on Earth. In both cases, the human body is a conduit for a specific type of energy. This energy can be easily observed in the style any person uses in living their life. Their style or approach to life is seen as their particular tone energy.

THE 7 PRACTICAL TONES

1. *The energy that loves to create.*

This is the tone for creation. It comes in on a straight line and will not waver. There is a lot of power behind the tone one energy. It moves fast and it is very direct. It is going to create one way or another, so people coming in with tone one birthdays need plenty of outlets for all this **creative energy**. If you have children or friends with tone one energy, you would be wise to support their positive creative endeavors, because if this energy is discouraged or blocked, it can create ill health or havoc for tone one people. This is a very powerful creative energy and people with this tone have the potential for creating great and wonderful things. The rest of us can access this energy every 13 days when it is the predominant energy of the day on the calendar.

2. *The energy that breaks up the old to make a space for the new.*

This is the tone that **challenges old, stagnant patterns of behavior**. It wants to see things change for the better. There is great force and power behind tone two energy, especially now that the Earth is in such desperate need of change. People coming in with two energy will feel a great dissatisfaction with those things that are not creating peace and harmony in their lives and in the world. They will be putting a lot of energy into solving these problems, not to control others, but in an effort to change things for the better for all concerned. The emphasis for tone two energy is to **break down the frequency** or the energy that supports the old, obsolete patterns. Tone two energy challenges the things that aren't working, and paves the way for improvement. If your birthday is on a tone two energy day you may feel that you run into resistance from other people much of the time. This is because most people resist change, and you are the **facilitator of change**. You will do your best work on the telepathic level, just knowing intuitively what things need to change. You don't have to convince anybody of anything. Just go about your business in a quiet way and watch things change for the better around you. You are a gift to the planet! Those who do not carry tone two energy in their bodies can get help in making needed changes by taking advantage of the days on the calendar where tone two energy is the energy of the day. This energy will always help you make changes.

3. *The energy that loves to play and be happy.*

Tone number three energy is **playful**. It is the energy which supports fun and joy and happiness on this planet. It is a light-filled frequency, and is always looking for ways to be happy. People with tone number three energy in their birth sign will tend to ignore the problems of life, or at least put them into perspective and not be dragged down by them. Tone three people have a great impetus for feeling light hearted and for sharing happy feelings with others. They are very valuable to others because they know how to lighten the darker energies that we live with today. **They are the restorers of spirit.** If you are planning a party, and you have a choice of days, make it a tone three day, and invite some tone three people!

4. *The energy that knows how to heal.*

Tone number four energy is **a healing energy**. It gives the ability to understand problems of the mind, body and spirit and bring comfort to the suffering. Tone four energy is a calm energy. It is balancing. Anybody who is sick can spend some time meditating with tone four. Try to relax and listen. Then you may feel some intuitive suggestions about what to do to heal yourself. Listen very quietly and decide what you want to do. Tone four is a gentle energy and tone four energy people will have a calming effect on others. Much of their help to others is done quietly with no words spoken or actions taken. Just being there is enough. **Remember that healing always rides on love**, because all healing has its source in our Creator.

5. *The energy that amplifies the positive.*

The number five tone energy comes in with a large splash. It is a happy, dynamic energy. It amplifies colors and sounds. It is **an exciting energy**. It loves to create variety and end dullness. It doesn't worry too much, but enjoys the good things that are here. People carrying tone five energy will sometimes run into resistance from people in their lives who enjoy suffering and who like to be negative. The best advice is, "Be with people who make you feel good about yourself and stay away from those who don't." That is good advice for anybody, but especially for tone five people who are carrying such a strong energy in their bodies that **wants to be positive and bright**.

6. *The energy that stabilizes change.*

Tone number six is a calming, steadying energy. It works to balance the more dynamic, creative energies. **It is responsible for the slow, steady process that we term "growth" on this planet.** Tone six energy is one of the major influences on planet Earth. People coming in with tone six energy usually prefer slow, anticipated change in their lives. You may resist ideas that demand a rapid shift in direction. While this energy is extremely important for stabilizing and balancing creation, realize that some rapid change is necessary and okay. All the creative energies work together to weave the pattern we term *reality*. Tone six people will be very skillful at keeping long range projects on course.

7. *The energy that sees into other worlds.*

Tone number seven is magic. It sees beyond what is real to create from the unknown. People coming in with tone seven energy will have a fascination with the mysterious. They want to figure it out. The main job of the tone seven energy is to create the portal to the unknown, allowing us to stand in a doorway to different thought. This energy provides **access to worlds beyond worlds**. Tone seven people have been known to look through that doorway, see something interesting and then create it for the rest of us on this planet. It is what we call *inventing things*. Tone sevens bring in concepts and tools for the rest of humanity to play with. Because of the **great power and mystery** that is associated with "the unknown", tone seven people need to be careful not to intimidate others with their knowledge. Their greatest challenge is to stay humble.

THE 6 COSMIC TONES

8. *The energy that holds reality in place.*

Tone number eight establishes patterns. It is a resonance signal that moves to the planet in a **golden spiral**. It sets the mold for creation. Tone eight works in conjunction with the other tones to keep a creation in form. All of the 13 number tones work together in various combinations, in the larger understanding. Tone eight works most easily with all the rest. When the other tones combine to create something, tone eight **moves an electrical pulse through the creation that holds it together**. Tone eight energy is everywhere you look on this planet. It is sometimes called *the golden spiral of creation*. People born on days with tone eight energy are helping to hold creation in place. You will be using this energy in your daily life by stabilizing change as it occurs. You will be very aware of patterns of behavior and the various patterns that exist in reality in general. You can help others to see through the confusion of modern living in order to facilitate needed change.

9. *The energy highway that links all things.*

Tone number nine energy is our direct link to the higher frequencies of the other realms of existence. You can ride out on tone nine energy all the way up the frequency hierarchy to our Source, God. Tone nine is an integral part of the planetary grid system and the cosmic grid system. **It is the grid system!** It is the interconnecting network that the other tone energies ride on. Tone nine energy is a part of everything in creation; it is in the electrical makeup of all that is. Just as we use a soft blanket to wrap a new baby, our creator uses tone nine energy to wrap and snuggle all of creation. It is a comforting energy and it is the reason we remember that we have a creator. It directly connects us to God.

Connections also run in many different directions along this master gridwork, and because of the way the gridwork is designed, beings from other dimensions can use tone nine energy to contact planet Earth. They simply ride down along the gridlines that extend out from Earth into the cosmos. Tone nine energy, from our standpoint, is associated with angels, extraterrestrials and the like.

When we meditate with tone nine energy, we may be invited to contact a being from another dimension. This is especially easy for people with a tone nine birthday. Be selective about who you communicate with if you want to try doing this! Remember that the master gridlines lead everywhere. If the contact doesn't feel like pure love, clap your hands and tell it to, **"Go away!"** You wouldn't invite just anybody into your home, so be selective when it comes to beings from other dimensions. At the start of your meditation state an intention that you want to contact only those beings of the highest light. Many angels and beings of the highest light want to help planet Earth at this time, and would be happy to communicate with you. Use the tone nine energy and the communication will be easy.

10. *The energy that creates beauty.*

Tone number ten energy is responsible for beauty. It places **our ability to like things** in creation. The ability to like things or to find things beautiful or attractive or pleasing is one of the most important attributes of life. Without this energy, life would seem empty and dull. Why is one thing beautiful and another not? It has to do with tone ten energy, which comes and goes. This energy is as ephemeral as the scent of a rose. That is because we humans have the power to call in the tone ten energy or send it away. This energy is not a permanent fixture. In these dark days on planet Earth, tone ten energy has been manipulated. Beauty has been very defined for us and very limited.

Know that beauty is always available to you, and **every single object in creation, being beautiful in God's eyes, has the potential to radiate tone ten energy.** When we, as observers, allow this beneficent energy to exist in the things and people around us, we will have created a paradise on Earth.

People born on tone ten energy days will be very aware of beauty around them. It will be important for them to have beautiful things, because this will feel very nurturing. It will resonate with the energy they carry in their bodies. Tone ten people will be happiest if they can have their own ideas about what is beautiful, and not be forced to accept the tastes of others. Tone ten energy people will be very motivated to create a beautiful environment for themselves. They can easily create something beautiful out of somebody else's old castoff. In fact, they can turn anything into something beautiful.

11. *The energy that holds the potential for change.*

Tone number eleven energy is **interested in change**. It is like a light switch because it holds that space between *what is* and *what will be*. Tone eleven energy always works in conjunction with one of the other streams of tone energy that is in the process of creating something. Since evolution is a continual, ongoing process, you can see that tone eleven energy is always holding millions of spaces. It is working throughout all creation, as are all the 13 number tones. **From our perspective on Earth, tone eleven creates the link between *now* and *then*.** If you are sitting motionless and you move slightly, tone eleven energy has provided the space between *still* and *move*. It is always involved with motion. It is also involved with the motion we call thought. It **provides the void** which allows our thoughts to change. Inside our bodies, tone eleven energy is the connection between all the parts and it links the movement of the chemicals. It also creates links in the motion of the electrical patterns of the nervous system. Tone eleven is involved with motion and evolution.

People carrying tone eleven energy in their birth signs will have a deeper perspective about reality than most others. They can easily see how things are connected. That is because the tone eleven energy in their bodies resonates with connectedness. There will be a certain restlessness in tone eleven people because this energy that they carry pervades all creation and it is always involved with change. Change may seem very attractive to people who are tone eleven, but it would be a good idea to sit and meditate before making a drastic change. Do not change for change's sake. That won't help your restless feelings. Know that on some level you are participating in great cosmic change. You are very important because you ground this cosmic energy here on the planet. **You do a great service to humankind.**

12. *The energy that stores all knowledge.*

Tone number twelve energy is the **teaching energy**. It is the *continuity of wisdom* energy. What is true? What works? What feels good? Once this wisdom is gained in an individual soul, it is added to the greater knowing of all, and becomes a part of the **ever expanding tone twelve energy**. This energy can be likened to a great library of information which is the wisdom of our Creator, gained through the experiences of all that has ever been created. (This has been going on a long time.) It is not a static body of knowledge. It is dynamic, and **it is enlarging and expanding moment by moment as the creations everywhere move through new experiences**. The tone twelve energy is available to everyone. We need only say, "I want to understand." This can be spoken telepathically to access the wisdom from tone twelve energy. We already do this all the time without knowing that we did it. This is how we get our ideas.

All experiences on every level of existence are recorded in the ephemeral swirl of tone twelve energy. This energy cannot be described except to say that it is always changing. Its job is to contain the knowledge and wisdom of all that is. **It can also be called the mind of God.** Tone twelve energy pervades all creation because it is keeping tabs on everything. Meditate with tone twelve briefly if you want to feel the enormity of the mind of God.

People born on a tone twelve energy day will have an interest in learning and teaching. They will be the great teachers because they will allow their students to teach them. There won't be any competition for status. Tone twelve people can access the vast body of wisdom that extends to other levels of existence, and bring back information for the rest of us. Tone twelve people are asked to stay in their integrity and assist in bringing peace to this planet.

13. *The energy that creates the other twelve.*

Tone number thirteen is **pure creator energy.** It is the energy stream that represents God. It is the spark of understanding in all people that knows their source is love. It is hard for us to talk about this because the concept of love on planet Earth has been distorted, so we really don't know what it means. But it is **a pure vibration of loving intent and loving concern**. It does not judge or condemn. It only loves and allows. On other planets, this tone thirteen energy is easier to feel. On planet Earth we have had too much evil and violence and this signal has been partially blocked from our awareness.

Tone thirteen takes part in all the tones of creation. But since our creator allows all things, Lucifer's game and the great forgetting that took place on planet Earth so long ago was allowed. At that time, Lucifer's game was considered wisdom to be gained. But, tone thirteen is our trump card, waiting to be played on the last trick, to win the game. We lost our purity for awhile, behind some of the other cards in our hands, but it has been found at last.

Since **our creator is love**, we will be drawn back into the remembering and experiencing of that love. Tone thirteen energy is Divine Love. This love is what allows the other twelve tones their play. It watches and loves and allows. It is the foundation energy for each of the other twelve tones of creation. It sends lines of divine energy running into and along with each of the other twelve. This energy is sometimes called *cosmic glue*.

Meditate with tone thirteen when you want a quick connection with Father/Mother/God. It will always be there for you. Always. It is fast because it is you. From an energy standpoint tone thirteen energy pervades and engulfs everything. **It is everything.** It is so gentle and so subtle and so integrated with all things that it has been overlooked by most people.

There is nothing that exists outside the vibrations of the thirteen tones of energy, symbolized by the thirteen numbers on the Mayan Calendar. It couldn't happen. Each of the thirteen tones work together to initiate and expand creation. They are pure energy with consciousness. They are aware of what they are doing. They are creative energy, performing a specific task in cooperation with divine thought.

People born on tone thirteen days will be able to utilize all the first twelve energy tones at will. They can be gentle one day and forceful the next. The advantage here is that they have it all. The disadvantage is that their behavior may seem somewhat erratic and unpredictable. **It is helpful to know it if you are carrying tone thirteen energy in your body.** Consider yourself normal and healthy, but having a greater selection of energy to work with than most other people. Find and choose the energy appropriate for any situation and you will enjoy incredible success in life. You have it all!

ENERGY SUPPLIED BY THE TONES

1. Energy to create something new

2. Energy to change obsolete patterns

3. Energy to play and be happy

4. Energy to heal

5. Energy to be positive and bright

6. Energy to stabilize change

7. Energy to see into other realities

8. Energy that establishes patterns

9. Energy of the interconnecting grid system

10. Energy that radiates beauty

11. Energy of motion and evolution

12. Energy of all knowledge

13. Energy of pure love for all things

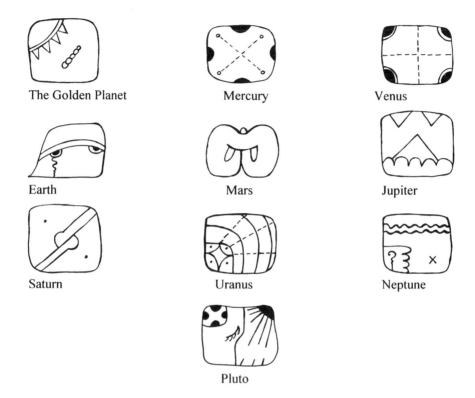

The Golden Planet   Mercury   Venus

Earth   Mars   Jupiter

Saturn   Uranus   Neptune

Pluto

THE 10 PLANETS OF THE MAYAN CALENDAR

The planets of the Mayan Calendar correlate to specific solar glyph birthdays. You will have a telepathic connection to the energy of your birthday planet. This means you will resonate with and learn from the information that is broadcast out from the energy field of your planet.

The location of any planet will affect its energy. Also, be aware that planets go through experiences and are affected by them. Planetary energy is influenced by natural phenomena such as the shifting of continents. But the thoughts and actions of its inhabitants and occasional visitors from other star systems will also have a profound effect. The energy and intentions of these beings will always be remembered in the host planet's energy field. There is a kind of energy language that each planet feels and remembers over the passage of time. Nothing is ever lost, energetically speaking. Be aware that the energy of the people influence the atoms of our Earth. Low vibrations will reduce the frequency in the

Earth's atoms. High vibrations will help raise the frequency. Earth's frequency is in a continual state of flux and juggling to balance and survive.

Have you ever heard of body language? ESP? How are they transmitted? The answer is energy. It is important to realize that everything is connected by an invisible grid system. This is a complex energy network that connects all things. As an example, the violence and cruelty that are commonplace on our television have a profound effect on the planetary energy system. When these programs are broadcast simultaneously in millions of homes across the surface of the planet, it is like an energy beating for our Earth. This is because the people watching these programs are responding with fear, indignation, or sadistic enjoyment in their bodies. Emotions always emit energy. Inhabitants are connected energetically to their planets. So, the net effect in this situation is that all this crude emotion given out from millions of people lowers the frequency of the planet even further. This is a daily occurrence.

A planet's history, combined with its geological makeup and location in the solar system will produce the character of that planet's energy field. This energy field is not a static thing. It is continually evolving. We humans are connected to all the planets, and to our birthday planet in particular, through the universal grid system that connects all things. There is an invisible energy link that connects everything in creation.

Each of the planets in our solar system has its own energy personality and its own gifts to offer. **You can connect to the energy of any planet by just thinking about it.** That is how the grid system works.

Each of us has a special connection to our birthday planet. We have had this connection since our birth. Our planet is linked to us through our solar glyph, and provides a resource energy that dovetails with our life's purpose.

Once you are aware of the resource energy that it supplies, you can tap into this energy by calming your thoughts and asking for it. Then wait a few moments to allow the connection. It is very easy to do. This is sometimes called *telepathy*, which means *creating an energy link using intention*. You may have been connecting to the energy of your planet intuitively your whole life. You just didn't realize that it was the great energy from your birthday planet that has been helping you.

There is an important shift in frequency occurring on planet Earth. It is a change to a higher vibration in the atoms that make up our world. When the shift is complete we will experience the meaning of *Peace on Earth*. This change is so vast that all the planets of our solar system are involved with it. Because everything in creation is connected, our entire solar system is being altered by this shift. That is called *evolution* on a grand scale.

CORRELATIONS OF THE PLANETS AND SOLAR GLYPHS

The Golden Planet- *Oc and Chuen*

Mercury- *Muluc and Eb*

Venus- *Lamat and Ben*

Earth- *Manik and Ix*

Mars- *Cimi and Men*

Jupiter- *Chicchan and Cib*

Saturn- *Kan and Caban*

Uranus- *Akbal and Etznab*

Neptune- *Ik and Cauac*

Pluto- *Imix and Ahau*

RESOURCE ENERGY OF THE PLANETS

The Golden Planet **(Solar Glyphs Oc and Chuen)** *The energy for healing.* The sun gives birth to new planets. When a new planet is created it moves out from the sun and takes its orbit nearest the sun. The other planets move out farther from the sun to make room for a new planet, bringing the energy of the solar system into balance. The Golden Planet is the newest child of our sun. It brings a fresh energy, called the gold frequency, to the entire solar system. The gold frequency is a healing vibration. If this is your birthday planet, you will carry healing energy in your body. You will be able to help those around you by just being there. You are capable of a deep loving connection with all creation. You are learning the lessons of compassion.

Mercury (Solar Glyphs Muluc and Eb) *The energy to create new things.*
Buzzing and zipping with very rapid rotation, Mercury is energetic and full of creativity. If this is your birthday planet, you will have a lot of energy to create new things.

Venus (Solar Glyphs Lamat and Ben) *The energy to love unconditionally.* Loving, peaceful and kind, Venus reaches out to the other planets to help balance them. If this is your birthday planet, you are capable of unconditional love for all things, including yourself.

Earth (Solar Glyphs Manik and Ix) *The energy to change for the better.* Earth is currently in a state of turmoil and imbalance. This state of confusion always occurs when systems break down. It precedes the transition to a higher frequency which will bring balance and harmony. There will be a new planetary energy grounded in peace, love and higher intelligence. If this is your birthday planet, you will feel a strong connection to the Earth and you will want to protect the environment. You may also be interested in the well being of humanity, knowing that this will help the planet.

Mars (Solar Glyphs Cimi and Men) *The energy to learn from mistakes.* Mars has a history of war and destruction. It is a place of desolation, and the original inhabitants are gone. It is currently used as a space station. New energy is now coming into Mars from our Creator to restore balance and peace. If this is your birthday planet, you will be very aware of the dangers of nuclear war. You will be actively working to promote peace.

Jupiter (Solar Glyphs Chicchan and Cib) *The energy for wealth and success* Jupiter is influenced by crystal energy. It knows the lessons of great power and strength. It understands influence and wealth. If this is your birthday planet, you are capable of achieving great material success and balancing it with your highly evolved spiritual nature.

Saturn (Solar Glyphs Kan and Caban) *The energy of wisdom and peace in the soul.* Knowing the lessons of wisdom and peace, Saturn is a place to restore peace in the soul. It knows unconditional love. If this is your birthday planet, you will be able to bring peace into any situation. Just connect with your planet and tap into that energy to remember how to do it.

Uranus (Solar Glyphs Akbal and Etznab) *The energy for higher intelligence.* Holding the energy of higher forms of intelligence, Uranus represents ideals and powers that will be in Earth's near future. If this is your birthday planet, you will be capable of knowing and creating on a higher level of understanding. You may be ahead of your time now, but you pave the way for a better life on Earth.

Neptune (Solar Glyphs Ik and Cauac) *The new energy that transforms the Earth.* Speeding up of frequencies. Expanded understanding of love. Wisdom. Awareness of Earth's transition. Assistance to planet Earth via an energy connection. If this is your birthday planet, you will probably be very uneasy in modern society. You will want something better. You are tapping into a very high vibration and anchoring it for this planet. Part of your life's purpose is to help bring in, and then stabilize the new energies. You are very important for bringing peace to the planet.

Pluto (Solar Glyphs Imix and Ahau) *The warrior energy that defends and protects.* Very high frequency vibrations. Altered magnetics. Pluto is a magnet for frequencies beyond our solar system. Sometimes called *Silver Shield Protector of the Solar System.* If this is your birthday planet you are one of the warriors. You have come in to help transform the Earth. You will be confronting the lower vibrations in your life, and your job is to teach by example. You may not use methods of war. Use your energy connection to Pluto and you will know how to proceed. This is the time for peace, but the warriors are needed here for their courage and steadfastness. This means *you are willing to do the job and you won't give up.* The situation on Earth is a great challenge for you, so you can be very proud of the good work you are doing.

CREATION, FREQUENCY AND THE SYMBOLS OF THE MAYAN CALENDAR

There is a connection between the human body's genetic coding and the larger frequencies portrayed by the 13 tones of the Mayan Calendar. Our genetic coding is the connecting point in the human body that acts as a beacon and a transmitter of energy on the cosmic level. This is how we communicate with and are influenced by the creative energies. You might say that this is how God talks to us. We are connected through every cell in our body.

What is this creative energy that is portrayed by the 13 tones on the Mayan Calendar? Visualize an enormous swirl of particles of energy. It casts a soft, shimmering glow as it moves. This energy pervades and engulfs our solar system, our planet and our bodies. It is this electrical/magnetic force that brought creation into being. It sustains the creation moment by moment.

Exactly what is this creative energy and how does it affect our daily lives? This is a very good question and the answer can be given on many levels of understanding. This creative energy is composed of 12 tones or vibrations called *streams of energy from God*. Each stream has a different value or purpose. There is a larger tone called tone 13 which is superimposed throughout the entire creative energy swirl, running along and within each of the 12 streams. It describes itself as *the totality of the 12 tones*. Thirteen is God's number. It is Father/Mother/God present in all things. As tone 13 moves throughout the energy swirl, it gives and receives information.

Information as we know it is a very simplified and primitive form of the information that moves throughout the larger creative energy. The **creative information** is understood without words. It is an elegant telepathy of consciousness that exists and evolves on a much higher frequency than is available on planet Earth.

Each of the 12 streams of energy is actually a child of God, no more, no less important in God's eyes than we are. Just different. And much older.

"In the beginning...". We can call it the beginning, but it was really just **our beginning**. Anyway, in the beginning, God had the idea to create a world. The world was to include land masses, water, atmosphere, light and inhabitants. When this idea registered in the divine energy we call our creator/God, a shudder moved throughout the sparkling *supporting curve of life*, from which all things originate. This shudder was a form of communication on an energy level. It triggered a response.

The response was to call forth the energy required to create a world. One by one the 12 tones of creation woke up and knew what was required. They had done this before.

On the telepathic level, via an electrical/chemical rush initiated by God, these 12 tones of creation were told what they could do to allow a new world into existence. Being children of God themselves, and having a divine nature of loving, playing and creating, they were willing to participate in this new idea.

Each of the 12 tones, imbued with the tone 13, moved out from the supporting curve of life energy and formed a great spiraling swirl. This swirl moved through the void, knowing exactly where it was going. As it moved, it took on a beautiful color of coral pink with large silver particles that moved and tumbled within the energy mass. It hummed the song of anticipation.

When the site of our solar system was reached, the energy came to a gradual stop and began to change its configuration. The 13 tones of energy now hummed the song of creation, a deep, echoing tone, as they formed all that we know of as our world and universe. Each of the 13 tones had a specific contribution and was charged with the guardianship of a particular function of creation.

After our world was set in place, the 13 great creative energies of Father/Mother/God returned to the supporting curve of life, leaving us with an energy link so that we wouldn't be forgotten. This link was needed to sustain the new creation. It provided for the flow of vital energy from the Source to the creation. All 13 tones of creation energy could ride down this link.

Since the creation of our world, these energies have been busy creating other worlds that we can't even imagine. They have never forgotten about us because the energy link is always there, but at certain points in time their attention was more focused on a new creation.

It was during one of these lapses in full attention that Lucifer made his entry into our world and altered the original energy frequency in our atoms. At that time he was a powerful and beautiful being, and a frequency master, meaning he could manipulate reality on a grand scale. Being one of the first born of God, he was originally called an archangel. He was always allowed to try new things so that God could have the enjoyment of seeing things change in unexpected ways.

Lucifer's idea was to experiment with us. He wanted to see what would happen in our world if he lowered our electrical frequency just to the point where we would forget that we were children of God and divine in nature. He thought it would be interesting to watch us figure out how to survive if our full telepathic connection with the creative energies was reduced. His intent wasn't to hurt us. He was just playing a game.

This game started a long time ago. It was so long ago that none of us can remember it very clearly, even in our dreams. It happened during the time when the inhabitants on planet Earth were always happy.

Since the first lowering of our frequencies, and the great forgetting of our Divine heritage, the quality of life on planet Earth has gotten worse and worse. In spite of technical marvels, the planet has been very heavy with problems. The troubled energy of these problems has made its way into the consciousness of every living thing on Earth. There has been a great sadness accumulating over the past several eons.

You may be aware that Jesus came to assist the planet at a certain point in time. If it hadn't been for his coming, we wouldn't be here today. He succeeded in raising the planetary frequency for us. He gave us the example of a higher energy, a higher love, and he carried an amazing inner light called, *Christ energy*. He channeled it through his own body. He helped people remember that they are children of God, that they are greatly loved, and that they should be good to one another.

When Jesus left, we were supposed to love ourselves and one another in order to recover our clear, telepathic connection with the thirteen energies of creation. Well, that proved to be impossible. Lucifer's game had spawned a powerful group of adversaries of the light, and they weren't willing to let go of us and go somewhere else.

In spite of the fact that there have been many holy people on the planet since Jesus' time, who remembered our heritage and our birthright, and who held the high frequencies in their own bodies, the resistance to love and light was sometimes overwhelming. Many of the holy people were killed or despised by the ones they were trying to help.

But there was a promise. And there were cycles to be taken into consideration. When a creation is put into place, there is a certain latitude given so that it can evolve in its own unique way. In our case, the original lowering of the frequency by Lucifer, and the great forgetting of who we are was allowed. But eventually it was seen that this lowering of frequency was leading to the extinction of the planet. That is because the lower vibrations started feeding on themselves and becoming lower and lower.

Every creation needs a minimum level of frequency or vibration in order to exist. Atoms must vibrate at a certain minimum rate in order to hold dense matter in form. The frequency on planet Earth was moving toward lowering itself out of existence.

The great sadness that we all sometimes feel is our intuitive awareness of this cosmic predicament. If our planet goes, the solar system and worlds beyond worlds will go with it because we are all connected on an energy level as one creation. Everyone on this planet knows that our existence is threatened and feels a certain dread about the future.

Other worlds have lowered their frequencies out of existence. It has happened before. But it is not going to happen here. This planet is going to survive.

Even Lucifer has had enough of the game and is not interested in watching our annihilation. Boring. But some of his lieutenants, who aren't very bright, have been unaware of the potential for our total destruction, and they continue to challenge the light. This is about to end. Their game is over.

The great cycle of darkness and ignorance is coming to a close. A new cycle of peace and happiness is on the horizon. It is coming no matter what we think or do, because the energy that sustains darkness and ignorance is being gradually withdrawn. Lucifer has ended his game.

Now, the restoration of the higher frequency on this planet has to be done gradually. A drastic change in frequency would kill everybody. We are all enmeshed in the lower vibrations and have to move ourselves gently out of the many subtle traps of modern human existence, and gradually into the higher frequency. It has already started to happen. Many of us are doing it already!

The new information that is becoming available concerning the symbols of the Mayan Calendar is being given to help us through this gradual raising of our planetary frequency. **The Mayan Calendar is a repository of frequency. It holds all the vibrations of the creative energies!**

The 13 tones of the Mayan Calendar represent the 13 streams of energy that issued forth from the supporting curve of life to create our world. The 20 solar glyphs are energy templates, derived from the 13 tones. They are like energy formulas that deal with a specific area of wisdom that the soul needs to incorporate in order to raise the frequency in the body. The 13 tones and the 20 solar glyph symbols remember and hold the frequency for us. We can tap into this frequency in order to raise our own vibrations. We can do this telepathically and it is very easy. It just takes some quiet time and an intention to evolve.

Meditating with the solar glyphs and tones can attune our bodies and spirits to the higher frequency that once governed our world. Once we learn these symbols and know how to hold the higher vibration in our bodies, we will begin to influence everything around us. The energy is available now to support and protect us, and more of us are able to hold the higher frequencies than ever before. We will be helping one another and helping the planet shift to the higher frequencies of the original creation, and then even higher.

What that means to us on a practical level is that life is starting to be fun. We are learning that nothing bad can exist in our world when we own the higher frequencies. We can just look around us, decide what we would most like to do, and then do it for the sheer joy of life. Once we learn to use the creative energies in our daily lives, things go very smoothly. This is a state of being that most Earth people can hardly grasp, being so conditioned and addicted to hardships and problems.

Well, the change is already underway, and each one of us has great reason for optimism and joy.

HOW TO USE THE CHARTS IN THIS BOOK

The *Mayan Calendar Birthday Book* is an easy handbook for finding and understanding your birthday solar glyph and tone. Once you have the day, month and year of your birthday you can look through the following charts to find the year. Three different years are listed at the top of each page. The Mayan birthdays repeat every 52 years, so the same birthday on each of these three years will have the same solar glyph and tone.

Always read the charts from left to right, starting with the column that is labeled *BIRTHDAY*. The birthday column shows the days and months. Find the day and month you are looking for, and in the next column you will see the solar glyph that was on the calendar for that birthday. In the following column you will find the tone that goes with that birthday.

EXAMPLE

January 22, 1952

Look at the top of the pages until you find 1900, 1952, 2004. The birthdays for these three years will have the same solar glyph and tone.

In the first column labeled *BIRTHDAY* you will find 1/22 which is January 22. Read along into the next two columns and you will see *Ix* and *9*. This means that your solar glyph is *Ix* and your tone is *9*.

Now you can refer to the explanations at the beginning of the book to see what it means to be an *Ix/9*. You can then **refer to the section on the planets to see which planet correlates** with *Ix*.

EXAMPLE

February 15, 1982

Find the pages that are labeled 1930, 1982, 2034 at the top.

Look in the *BIRTHDAY* column for 2/15. Read the next two columns to the right and you will see *Lamat* and *11*. You are a *Lamat/11*.

EXAMPLE

March 18, 1884

Oops. That date isn't at the top of any of the pages because the charts start with the year 1900. Since the Mayan birthdays repeat every 52 years, we just add 52 to the year 1884. That gives us 1936.

Now we look at the top of the pages until we find 1936. We follow the normal procedure for March 18, or 3/18. The solar glyph and tone are *Muluc/9*.

If the birthday you want is more than 52 years before 1900, just keep adding 52 to the birthday until you are into the charts. It is easy.

EXAMPLE

April 10, 2075

The last year on these charts is 2055. If you want to go out past that year just subtract 52 years from the date. If the date you want is more than 52 years from the charts just keep subtracting another 52 until you are into the charts.

The year 2075 is the same as 2023, which is in the charts. April 10, or 4/10 is *Manik/2*.

SAMPLE			BIRTHDAY		SOLAR GLYPH	TONE	BIRTHDAY		SOLAR GLYPH	TONE
			1/1	9/18	Ben	1	2/22	11/9	Chicchan	1
BIRTHDAY	SOLAR GLYPH	TONE	1/2	9/19	Ix	2	2/23	11/10	Cimi	2
			1/3	9/20	Men	3	2/24	11/11	Manik	3
ALWAYS READ CHART FROM			1/4	9/21	Cib	4	2/25	11/12	Lamat	4
LEFT TO RIGHT			1/5	9/22	Caban	5	2/26	11/13	Muluc	5
STARTING WITH BIRTHDAY			1/6	9/23	Etznab	6	2/27	11/14	Oc	6
			1/7	9/24	Cauac	7	2/28	11/15	Chuen	7
DOUBLE LINES			1/8	9/25	Ahau	8	3/1	11/16	Eb	8
SEPARATE SECTIONS			1/9	9/26	Imix	9	3/2	11/17	Ben	9
			1/10	9/27	Ik	10	3/3	11/18	Ix	10
USE SPACE BELOW			1/11	9/28	Akbal	11	3/4	11/19	Men	11
FOR RECORDING BIRTHDAYS			1/12	9/29	Kan	12	3/5	11/20	Cib	12
			1/13	9/30	Chicchan	13	3/6	11/21	Caban	13
			1/14	10/1	Cimi	1	3/7	11/22	Etznab	1
			1/15	10/2	Manik	2	3/8	11/23	Cauac	2
			1/16	10/3	Lamat	3	3/9	11/24	Ahau	3
			1/17	10/4	Muluc	4	3/10	11/25	Imix	4
			1/18	10/5	Oc	5	3/11	11/26	Ik	5
			1/19	10/6	Chuen	6	3/12	11/27	Akbal	6
			1/20	10/7	Eb	7	3/13	11/28	Kan	7
			1/21	10/8	Ben	8	3/14	11/29	Chicchan	8
			1/22	10/9	Ix	9	3/15	11/30	Cimi	9
			1/23	10/10	Men	10	3/16	12/1	Manik	10
			1/24	10/11	Cib	11	3/17	12/2	Lamat	11
			1/25	10/12	Caban	12	3/18	12/3	Muluc	12
			1/26	10/13	Etznab	13	3/19	12/4	Oc	13
			1/27	10/14	Cauac	1	3/20	12/5	Chuen	1
			1/28	10/15	Ahau	2	3/21	12/6	Eb	2
			1/29	10/16	Imix	3	3/22	12/7	Ben	3
			1/30	10/17	Ik	4	3/23	12/8	Ix	4
			1/31	10/18	Akbal	5	3/24	12/9	Men	5
			2/1	10/19	Kan	6	3/25	12/10	Cib	6
			2/2	10/20	Chicchan	7	3/26	12/11	Caban	7
			2/3	10/21	Cimi	8	3/27	12/12	Etznab	8
			2/4	10/22	Manik	9	3/28	12/13	Cauac	9
			2/5	10/23	Lamat	10	3/29	12/14	Ahau	10
			2/6	10/24	Muluc	11	3/30	12/15	Imix	11
			2/7	10/25	Oc	12	3/31	12/16	Ik	12
			2/8	10/26	Chuen	13	4/1	12/17	Akbal	13
			2/9	10/27	Eb	1	4/2	12/18	Kan	1
			2/10	10/28	Ben	2	4/3	12/19	Chicchan	2
			2/11	10/29	Ix	3	4/4	12/20	Cimi	3
			2/12	10/30	Men	4	4/5	12/21	Manik	4
			2/13	10/31	Cib	5	4/6	12/22	Lamat	5
			2/14	11/1	Caban	6	4/7	12/23	Muluc	6
			2/15	11/2	Etznab	7	4/8	12/24	Oc	7
			2/16	11/3	Cauac	8	4/9	12/25	Chuen	8
			2/17	11/4	Ahau	9	4/10	12/26	Eb	9
			2/18	11/5	Imix	10	4/11	12/27	Ben	10
			2/19	11/6	Ik	11	4/12	12/28	Ix	11
			2/20	11/7	Akbal	12	4/13	12/29	Men	12
			2/21	11/8	Kan	13	4/14	12/30	Cib	13

BIRTHDAY		SOLAR GLYPH	TONE	BIRTHDAY	SOLAR GLYPH	TONE	BIRTHDAY	SOLAR GLYPH	TONE
4/15	12/31	Caban	1	6/6	Muluc	1	7/28	Imix	1
4/16		Etznab	2	6/7	Oc	2	7/29	Ik	2
4/17		Cauac	3	6/8	Chuen	3	7/30	Akbal	3
4/18		Ahau	4	6/9	Eb	4	7/31	Kan	4
4/19		Imix	5	6/10	Ben	5	8/1	Chicchan	5
4/20		Ik	6	6/11	Ix	6	8/2	Cimi	6
4/21		Akbal	7	6/12	Men	7	8/3	Manik	7
4/22		Kan	8	6/13	Cib	8	8/4	Lamat	8
4/23		Chiccan	9	6/14	Caban	9	8/5	Muluc	9
4/24		Cimi	10	6/15	Etznab	10	8/6	Oc	10
4/25		Manik	11	6/16	Cauac	11	8/7	Chuen	11
4/26		Lamat	12	6/17	Ahau	12	8/8	Eb	12
4/27		Muluc	13	6/18	Imix	13	8/9	Ben	13
4/28		Oc	1	6/19	Ik	1	8/10	Ix	1
4/29		Chuen	2	6/20	Akbal	2	8/11	Men	2
4/30		Eb	3	6/21	Kan	3	8/12	Cib	3
5/1		Ben	4	6/22	Chicchan	4	8/13	Caban	4
5/2		Ix	5	6/23	Cimi	5	8/14	Etznab	5
5/3		Men	6	6/24	Manik	6	8/15	Cauac	6
5/4		Cib	7	6/25	Lamat	7	8/16	Ahau	7
5/5		Caban	8	6/26	Muluc	8	8/17	Imix	8
5/6		Etznab	9	6/27	Oc	9	8/18	Ik	9
5/7		Cauac	10	6/28	Chuen	10	8/19	Akbal	10
5/8		Ahau	11	6/29	Eb	11	8/20	Kan	11
5/9		Imix	12	6/30	Ben	12	8/21	Chicchan	12
5/10		Ik	13	7/1	Ix	13	8/22	Cimi	13
5/11		Akbal	1	7/2	Men	1	8/23	Manik	1
5/12		Kan	2	7/3	Cib	2	8/24	Lamat	2
5/13		Chicchan	3	7/4	Caban	3	8/25	Muluc	3
5/14		Cimi	4	7/5	Etznab	4	8/26	Oc	4
5/15		Manik	5	7/6	Cauac	5	8/27	Chuen	5
5/16		Lamat	6	7/7	Ahau	6	8/28	Eb	6
5/17		Muluc	7	7/8	Imix	7	8/29	Ben	7
5/18		Oc	8	7/9	Ik	8	8/30	Ix	8
5/19		Chuen	9	7/10	Akbal	9	8/31	Men	9
5/20		Eb	10	7/11	Kan	10	9/1	Cib	10
5/21		Ben	11	7/12	Chicchan	11	9/2	Caban	11
5/22		Ix	12	7/13	Cimi	12	9/3	Etznab	12
5/23		Men	13	7/14	Manik	13	9/4	Cauac	13
5/24		Cib	1	7/15	Lamat	1	9/5	Ahau	1
5/25		Caban	2	7/16	Muluc	2	9/6	Imix	2
5/26		Etznab	3	7/17	Oc	3	9/7	Ik	3
5/27		Cauac	4	7/18	Chuen	4	9/8	Akbal	4
5/28		Ahau	5	7/19	Eb	5	9/9	Kan	5
5/29		Imix	6	7/20	Ben	6	9/10	Chicchan	6
5/30		Ik	7	7/21	Ix	7	9/11	Cimi	7
5/31		Akbal	8	7/22	Men	8	9/12	Manik	8
6/1		Kan	9	7/23	Cib	9	9/13	Lamat	9
6/2		Chicchan	10	7/24	Caban	10	9/14	Muluc	10
6/3		Cimi	11	7/25	Etznab	11	9/15	Oc	11
6/4		Manik	12	7/26	Cauac	12	9/16	Chuen	12
6/5		Lamat	13	7/27	Ahau	13	9/17	Eb	13

SAMPLE			BIRTHDAY	SOLAR GLYPH	TONE	BIRTHDAY	SOLAR GLYPH	TONE
				9/17	Caban	1	2/21	11/8	Muluc	1
BIRTHDAY	SOLAR GLYPH	TONE	1/1	9/18	Etznab	2	2/22	11/9	Oc	2
			1/2	9/19	Cauac	3	2/23	11/10	Chuen	3
ALWAYS READ CHART FROM			1/3	9/20	Ahau	4	2/24	11/11	Eb	4
LEFT TO RIGHT			1/4	9/21	Imix	5	2/25	11/12	Ben	5
STARTING WITH BIRTHDAY			1/5	9/22	Ik	6	2/26	11/13	Ix	6
			1/6	9/23	Akbal	7	2/27	11/14	Men	7
DOUBLE LINES			1/7	9/24	Kan	8	2/28	11/15	Cib	8
SEPARATE SECTIONS			1/8	9/25	Chiccan	9	3/1	11/16	Caban	9
			1/9	9/26	Cimi	10	3/2	11/17	Etznab	10
USE SPACE BELOW			1/10	9/27	Manik	11	3/3	11/18	Cauac	11
FOR RECORDING BIRTHDAYS			1/11	9/28	Lamat	12	3/4	11/19	Ahau	12
			1/12	9/29	Muluc	13	3/5	11/20	Imix	13
			1/13	9/30	Oc	1	3/6	11/21	Ik	1
			1/14	10/1	Chuen	2	3/7	11/22	Akbal	2
			1/15	10/2	Eb	3	3/8	11/23	Kan	3
			1/16	10/3	Ben	4	3/9	11/24	Chicchan	4
			1/17	10/4	Ix	5	3/10	11/25	Cimi	5
			1/18	10/5	Men	6	3/11	11/26	Manik	6
			1/19	10/6	Cib	7	3/12	11/27	Lamat	7
			1/20	10/7	Caban	8	3/13	11/28	Muluc	8
			1/21	10/8	Etznab	9	3/14	11/29	Oc	9
			1/22	10/9	Cauac	10	3/15	11/30	Chuen	10
			1/23	10/10	Ahau	11	3/16	12/1	Eb	11
			1/24	10/11	Imix	12	3/17	12/2	Ben	12
			1/25	10/12	Ik	13	3/18	12/3	Ix	13
			1/26	10/13	Akbal	1	3/19	12/4	Men	1
			1/27	10/14	Kan	2	3/20	12/5	Cib	2
			1/28	10/15	Chicchan	3	3/21	12/6	Caban	3
			1/29	10/16	Cimi	4	3/22	12/7	Etznab	4
			1/30	10/17	Manik	5	3/23	12/8	Cauac	5
			1/31	10/18	Lamat	6	3/24	12/9	Ahau	6
			2/1	10/19	Muluc	7	3/25	12/10	Imix	7
			2/2	10/20	Oc	8	3/26	12/11	Ik	8
			2/3	10/21	Chuen	9	3/27	12/12	Akbal	9
			2/4	10/22	Eb	10	3/28	12/13	Kan	10
			2/5	10/23	Ben	11	3/29	12/14	Chicchan	11
			2/6	10/24	Ix	12	3/30	12/15	Cimi	12
			2/7	10/25	Men	13	3/31	12/16	Manik	13
			2/8	10/26	Cib	1	4/1	12/17	Lamat	1
			2/9	10/27	Caban	2	4/2	12/18	Muluc	2
			2/10	10/28	Etznab	3	4/3	12/19	Oc	3
			2/11	10/29	Cauac	4	4/4	12/20	Chuen	4
			2/12	10/30	Ahau	5	4/5	12/21	Eb	5
			2/13	10/31	Imix	6	4/6	12/22	Ben	6
			2/14	11/1	Ik	7	4/7	12/23	Ix	7
			2/15	11/2	Akbal	8	4/8	12/24	Men	8
			2/16	11/3	Kan	9	4/9	12/25	Cib	9
			2/17	11/4	Chicchan	10	4/10	12/26	Caban	10
			2/18	11/5	Cimi	11	4/11	12/27	Etznab	11
			2/19	11/6	Manik	12	4/12	12/28	Cauac	12
			2/20	11/7	Lamat	13	4/13	12/29	Ahau	13

BIRTHDAY		SOLAR GLYPH	TONE	BIRTHDAY	SOLAR GLYPH	TONE	BIRTHDAY	SOLAR GLYPH	TONE
4/14	12/30	Imix	1	6/5	Ben	1	7/27	Chicchan	1
4/15	12/31	Ik	2	6/6	Ix	2	7/28	Cimi	2
4/16		Akbal	3	6/7	Men	3	7/29	Manik	3
4/17		Kan	4	6/8	Cib	4	7/30	Lamat	4
4/18		Chicchan	5	6/9	Caban	5	7/31	Muluc	5
4/19		Cimi	6	6/10	Etznab	6	8/1	Oc	6
4/20		Manik	7	6/11	Cauac	7	8/2	Chuen	7
4/21		Lamat	8	6/12	Ahau	8	8/3	Eb	8
4/22		Muluc	9	6/13	Imix	9	8/4	Ben	9
4/23		Oc	10	6/14	Ik	10	8/5	Ix	10
4/24		Chuen	11	6/15	Akbal	11	8/6	Men	11
4/25		Eb	12	6/16	Kan	12	8/7	Cib	12
4/26		Ben	13	6/17	Chicchan	13	8/8	Caban	13
4/27		Ix	1	6/18	Cimi	1	8/9	Etznab	1
4/28		Men	2	6/19	Manik	2	8/10	Cauac	2
4/29		Cib	3	6/20	Lamat	3	8/11	Ahau	3
4/30		Caban	4	6/21	Muluc	4	8/12	Imix	4
5/1		Etznab	5	6/22	Oc	5	8/13	Ik	5
5/2		Cauac	6	6/23	Chuen	6	8/14	Akbal	6
5/3		Ahau	7	6/24	Eb	7	8/15	Kan	7
5/4		Imix	8	6/25	Ben	8	8/16	Chicchan	8
5/5		Ik	9	6/26	Ix	9	8/17	Cimi	9
5/6		Akbal	10	6/27	Men	10	8/18	Manik	10
5/7		Kan	11	6/28	Cib	11	8/19	Lamat	11
5/8		Chicchan	12	6/29	Caban	12	8/20	Muluc	12
5/9		Cimi	13	6/30	Etznab	13	8/21	Oc	13
5/10		Manik	1	7/1	Cauac	1	8/22	Chuen	1
5/11		Lamat	2	7/2	Ahau	2	8/23	Eb	2
5/12		Muluc	3	7/3	Imix	3	8/24	Ben	3
5/13		Oc	4	7/4	Ik	4	8/25	Ix	4
5/14		Chuen	5	7/5	Akbal	5	8/26	Men	5
5/15		Eb	6	7/6	Kan	6	8/27	Cib	6
5/16		Ben	7	7/7	Chicchan	7	8/28	Caban	7
5/17		Ix	8	7/8	Cimi	8	8/29	Etznab	8
5/18		Men	9	7/9	Manik	9	8/30	Cauac	9
5/19		Cib	10	7/10	Lamat	10	8/31	Ahau	10
5/20		Caban	11	7/11	Muluc	11	9/1	Imix	11
5/21		Etznab	12	7/12	Oc	12	9/2	Ik	12
5/22		Cauac	13	7/13	Chuen	13	9/3	Akbal	13
5/23		Ahau	1	7/14	Eb	1	9/4	Kan	1
5/24		Imix	2	7/15	Ben	2	9/5	Chicchan	2
5/25		Ik	3	7/16	Ix	3	9/6	Cimi	3
5/26		Akbal	4	7/17	Men	4	9/7	Manik	4
5/27		Kan	5	7/18	Cib	5	9/8	Lamat	5
5/28		Chicchan	6	7/19	Caban	6	9/9	Muluc	6
5/29		Cimi	7	7/20	Etznab	7	9/10	Oc	7
5/30		Manik	8	7/21	Cauac	8	9/11	Chuen	8
5/31		Lamat	9	7/22	Ahau	9	9/12	Eb	9
6/1		Muluc	10	7/23	Imix	10	9/13	Ben	10
6/2		Oc	11	7/24	Ik	11	9/14	Ix	11
6/3		Chuen	12	7/25	Akbal	12	9/15	Men	12
6/4		Eb	13	7/26	Kan	13	9/16	Cib	13

SAMPLE			BIRTHDAY		SOLAR GLYPH	TONE	BIRTHDAY		SOLAR GLYPH	TONE
				9/16	Imix	1	2/20	11/7	Ben	1
BIRTHDAY	SOLAR GLYPH	TONE		9/17	Ik	2	2/21	11/8	Ix	2
			1/1	9/18	Akbal	3	2/22	11/9	Men	3
ALWAYS READ CHART FROM			1/2	9/19	Kan	4	2/23	11/10	Cib	4
LEFT TO RIGHT			1/3	9/20	Chicchan	5	2/24	11/11	Caban	5
STARTING WITH BIRTHDAY			1/4	9/21	Cimi	6	2/25	11/12	Etznab	6
			1/5	9/22	Manik	7	2/26	11/13	Cauac	7
DOUBLE LINES			1/6	9/23	Lamat	8	2/27	11/14	Ahau	8
SEPARATE SECTIONS			1/7	9/24	Muluc	9	2/28	11/15	Imix	9
			1/8	9/25	Oc	10	3/1	11/16	Ik	10
USE SPACE BELOW			1/9	9/26	Chuen	11	3/2	11/17	Akbal	11
FOR RECORDING BIRTHDAYS			1/10	9/27	Eb	12	3/3	11/18	Kan	12
			1/11	9/28	Ben	13	3/4	11/19	Chicchan	13
			1/12	9/29	Ix	1	3/5	11/20	Cimi	1
			1/13	9/30	Men	2	3/6	11/21	Manik	2
			1/14	10/1	Cib	3	3/7	11/22	Lamat	3
			1/15	10/2	Caban	4	3/8	11/23	Muluc	4
			1/16	10/3	Etznab	5	3/9	11/24	Oc	5
			1/17	10/4	Cauac	6	3/10	11/25	Chuen	6
			1/18	10/5	Ahau	7	3/11	11/26	Eb	7
			1/19	10/6	Imix	8	3/12	11/27	Ben	8
			1/20	10/7	Ik	9	3/13	11/28	Ix	9
			1/21	10/8	Akbal	10	3/14	11/29	Men	10
			1/22	10/9	Kan	11	3/15	11/30	Cib	11
			1/23	10/10	Chicchan	12	3/16	12/1	Caban	12
			1/24	10/11	Cimi	13	3/17	12/2	Etznab	13
			1/25	10/12	Manik	1	3/18	12/3	Cauac	1
			1/26	10/13	Lamat	2	3/19	12/4	Ahau	2
			1/27	10/14	Muluc	3	3/20	12/5	Imix	3
			1/28	10/15	Oc	4	3/21	12/6	Ik	4
			1/29	10/16	Chuen	5	3/22	12/7	Akbal	5
			1/30	10/17	Eb	6	3/23	12/8	Kan	6
			1/31	10/18	Ben	7	3/24	12/9	Chicchan	7
			2/1	10/19	Ix	8	3/25	12/10	Cimi	8
			2/2	10/20	Men	9	3/26	12/11	Manik	9
			2/3	10/21	Cib	10	3/27	12/12	Lamat	10
			2/4	10/22	Caban	11	3/28	12/13	Muluc	11
			2/5	10/23	Etznab	12	3/29	12/14	Oc	12
			2/6	10/24	Cauac	13	3/30	12/15	Chuen	13
			2/7	10/25	Ahau	1	3/31	12/16	Eb	1
			2/8	10/26	Imix	2	4/1	12/17	Ben	2
			2/9	10/27	Ik	3	4/2	12/18	Ix	3
			2/10	10/28	Akbal	4	4/3	12/19	Men	4
			2/11	10/29	Kan	5	4/4	12/20	Cib	5
			2/12	10/30	Chicchan	6	4/5	12/21	Caban	6
			2/13	10/31	Cimi	7	4/6	12/22	Etznab	7
			2/14	11/1	Manik	8	4/7	12/23	Cauac	8
			2/15	11/2	Lamat	9	4/8	12/24	Ahau	9
			2/16	11/3	Muluc	10	4/9	12/25	Imix	10
			2/17	11/4	Oc	11	4/10	12/26	Ik	11
			2/18	11/5	Chuen	12	4/11	12/27	Akbal	12
			2/19	11/6	Eb	13	4/12	12/28	Kan	13

BIRTHDAY		SOLAR GLYPH	TONE	BIRTHDAY	SOLAR GLYPH	TONE	BIRTHDAY	SOLAR GLYPH	TONE
4/13	12/29	Chicchan	1	6/4	Caban	1	7/26	Muluc	1
4/14	12/30	Cimi	2	6/5	Etznab	2	7/27	Oc	2
4/15	12/31	Manik	3	6/6	Cauac	3	7/28	Chuen	3
4/16		Lamat	4	6/7	Ahau	4	7/29	Eb	4
4/17		Muluc	5	6/8	Imix	5	7/30	Ben	5
4/18		Oc	6	6/9	Ik	6	7/31	Ix	6
4/19		Chuen	7	6/10	Akbal	7	8/1	Men	7
4/20		Eb	8	6/11	Kan	8	8/2	Cib	8
4/21		Ben	9	6/12	Chiccan	9	8/3	Caban	9
4/22		Ix	10	6/13	Cimi	10	8/4	Etznab	10
4/23		Men	11	6/14	Manik	11	8/5	Cauac	11
4/24		Cib	12	6/15	Lamat	12	8/6	Ahau	12
4/25		Caban	13	6/16	Muluc	13	8/7	Imix	13
4/26		Etznab	1	6/17	Oc	1	8/8	Ik	1
4/27		Cauac	2	6/18	Chuen	2	8/9	Akbal	2
4/28		Ahau	3	6/19	Eb	3	8/10	Kan	3
4/29		Imix	4	6/20	Ben	4	8/11	Chicchan	4
4/30		Ik	5	6/21	Ix	5	8/12	Cimi	5
5/1		Akbal	6	6/22	Men	6	8/13	Manik	6
5/2		Kan	7	6/23	Cib	7	8/14	Lamat	7
5/3		Chicchan	8	6/24	Caban	8	8/15	Muluc	8
5/4		Cimi	9	6/25	Etznab	9	8/16	Oc	9
5/5		Manik	10	6/26	Cauac	10	8/17	Chuen	10
5/6		Lamat	11	6/27	Ahau	11	8/18	Eb	11
5/7		Muluc	12	6/28	Imix	12	8/19	Ben	12
5/8		Oc	13	6/29	Ik	13	8/20	Ix	13
5/9		Chuen	1	6/30	Akbal	1	8/21	Men	1
5/10		Eb	2	7/1	Kan	2	8/22	Cib	2
5/11		Ben	3	7/2	Chicchan	3	8/23	Caban	3
5/12		Ix	4	7/3	Cimi	4	8/24	Etznab	4
5/13		Men	5	7/4	Manik	5	8/25	Cauac	5
5/14		Cib	6	7/5	Lamat	6	8/26	Ahau	6
5/15		Caban	7	7/6	Muluc	7	8/27	Imix	7
5/16		Etznab	8	7/7	Oc	8	8/28	Ik	8
5/17		Cauac	9	7/8	Chuen	9	8/29	Akbal	9
5/18		Ahau	10	7/9	Eb	10	8/30	Kan	10
5/19		Imix	11	7/10	Ben	11	8/31	Chicchan	11
5/20		Ik	12	7/11	Ix	12	9/1	Cimi	12
5/21		Akbal	13	7/12	Men	13	9/2	Manik	13
5/22		Kan	1	7/13	Cib	1	9/3	Lamat	1
5/23		Chicchan	2	7/14	Caban	2	9/4	Muluc	2
5/24		Cimi	3	7/15	Etznab	3	9/5	Oc	3
5/25		Manik	4	7/16	Cauac	4	9/6	Chuen	4
5/26		Lamat	5	7/17	Ahau	5	9/7	Eb	5
5/27		Muluc	6	7/18	Imix	6	9/8	Ben	6
5/28		Oc	7	7/19	Ik	7	9/9	Ix	7
5/29		Chuen	8	7/20	Akbal	8	9/10	Men	8
5/30		Eb	9	7/21	Kan	9	9/11	Cib	9
5/31		Ben	10	7/22	Chicchan	10	9/12	Caban	10
6/1		Ix	11	7/23	Cimi	11	9/13	Etznab	11
6/2		Men	12	7/24	Manik	12	9/14	Cauac	12
6/3		Cib	13	7/25	Lamat	13	9/15	Ahau	13

SAMPLE			BIRTHDAY		SOLAR GLYPH	TONE	BIRTHDAY		SOLAR GLYPH	TONE
				9/15	Chicchan	1	2/19	11/6	Caban	1
BIRTHDAY	SOLAR GLYPH	TONE		9/16	Cimi	2	2/20	11/7	Etznab	2
				9/17	Manik	3	2/21	11/8	Cauac	3
ALWAYS READ CHART FROM			1/1	9/18	Lamat	4	2/22	11/9	Ahau	4
LEFT TO RIGHT			1/2	9/19	Muluc	5	2/23	11/10	Imix	5
STARTING WITH BIRTHDAY			1/3	9/20	Oc	6	2/24	11/11	Ik	6
			1/4	9/21	Chuen	7	2/25	11/12	Akbal	7
DOUBLE LINES			1/5	9/22	Eb	8	2/26	11/13	Kan	8
SEPARATE SECTIONS			1/6	9/23	Ben	9	2/27	11/14	Chiccan	9
			1/7	9/24	Ix	10	2/28	11/15	Cimi	10
USE SPACE BELOW			1/8	9/25	Men	11	3/1	11/16	Manik	11
FOR RECORDING BIRTHDAYS			1/9	9/26	Cib	12	3/2	11/17	Lamat	12
			1/10	9/27	Caban	13	3/3	11/18	Muluc	13
			1/11	9/28	Etznab	1	3/4	11/19	Oc	1
			1/12	9/29	Cauac	2	3/5	11/20	Chuen	2
			1/13	9/30	Ahau	3	3/6	11/21	Eb	3
			1/14	10/1	Imix	4	3/7	11/22	Ben	4
			1/15	10/2	Ik	5	3/8	11/23	Ix	5
			1/16	10/3	Akbal	6	3/9	11/24	Men	6
			1/17	10/4	Kan	7	3/10	11/25	Cib	7
			1/18	10/5	Chicchan	8	3/11	11/26	Caban	8
			1/19	10/6	Cimi	9	3/12	11/27	Etznab	9
			1/20	10/7	Manik	10	3/13	11/28	Cauac	10
			1/21	10/8	Lamat	11	3/14	11/29	Ahau	11
			1/22	10/9	Muluc	12	3/15	11/30	Imix	12
			1/23	10/10	Oc	13	3/16	12/1	Ik	13
			1/24	10/11	Chuen	1	3/17	12/2	Akbal	1
			1/25	10/12	Eb	2	3/18	12/3	Kan	2
			1/26	10/13	Ben	3	3/19	12/4	Chicchan	3
			1/27	10/14	Ix	4	3/20	12/5	Cimi	4
			1/28	10/15	Men	5	3/21	12/6	Manik	5
			1/29	10/16	Cib	6	3/22	12/7	Lamat	6
			1/30	10/17	Caban	7	3/23	12/8	Muluc	7
			1/31	10/18	Etznab	8	3/24	12/9	Oc	8
			2/1	10/19	Cauac	9	3/25	12/10	Chuen	9
			2/2	10/20	Ahau	10	3/26	12/11	Eb	10
			2/3	10/21	Imix	11	3/27	12/12	Ben	11
			2/4	10/22	Ik	12	3/28	12/13	Ix	12
			2/5	10/23	Akbal	13	3/29	12/14	Men	13
			2/6	10/24	Kan	1	3/30	12/15	Cib	1
			2/7	10/25	Chicchan	2	3/31	12/16	Caban	2
			2/8	10/26	Cimi	3	4/1	12/17	Etznab	3
			2/9	10/27	Manik	4	4/2	12/18	Cauac	4
			2/10	10/28	Lamat	5	4/3	12/19	Ahau	5
			2/11	10/29	Muluc	6	4/4	12/20	Imix	6
			2/12	10/30	Oc	7	4/5	12/21	Ik	7
			2/13	10/31	Chuen	8	4/6	12/22	Akbal	8
			2/14	11/1	Eb	9	4/7	12/23	Kan	9
			2/15	11/2	Ben	10	4/8	12/24	Chicchan	10
			2/16	11/3	Ix	11	4/9	12/25	Cimi	11
			2/17	11/4	Men	12	4/10	12/26	Manik	12
			2/18	11/5	Cib	13	4/11	12/27	Lamat	13

BIRTHDAY		SOLAR GLYPH	TONE	BIRTHDAY	SOLAR GLYPH	TONE	BIRTHDAY	SOLAR GLYPH	TONE
4/12	12/28	Muluc	1	6/3	Imix	1	7/25	Ben	1
4/13	12/29	Oc	2	6/4	Ik	2	7/26	Ix	2
4/14	12/30	Chuen	3	6/5	Akbal	3	7/27	Men	3
4/15	12/31	Eb	4	6/6	Kan	4	7/28	Cib	4
4/16		Ben	5	6/7	Chicchan	5	7/29	Caban	5
4/17		Ix	6	6/8	Cimi	6	7/30	Etznab	6
4/18		Men	7	6/9	Manik	7	7/31	Cauac	7
4/19		Cib	8	6/10	Lamat	8	8/1	Ahau	8
4/20		Caban	9	6/11	Muluc	9	8/2	Imix	9
4/21		Etznab	10	6/12	Oc	10	8/3	Ik	10
4/22		Cauac	11	6/13	Chuen	11	8/4	Akbal	11
4/23		Ahau	12	6/14	Eb	12	8/5	Kan	12
4/24		Imix	13	6/15	Ben	13	8/6	Chicchan	13
4/25		Ik	1	6/16	Ix	1	8/7	Cimi	1
4/26		Akbal	2	6/17	Men	2	8/8	Manik	2
4/27		Kan	3	6/18	Cib	3	8/9	Lamat	3
4/28		Chicchan	4	6/19	Caban	4	8/10	Muluc	4
4/29		Cimi	5	6/20	Etznab	5	8/11	Oc	5
4/30		Manik	6	6/21	Cauac	6	8/12	Chuen	6
5/1		Lamat	7	6/22	Ahau	7	8/13	Eb	7
5/2		Muluc	8	6/23	Imix	8	8/14	Ben	8
5/3		Oc	9	6/24	Ik	9	8/15	Ix	9
5/4		Chuen	10	6/25	Akbal	10	8/16	Men	10
5/5		Eb	11	6/26	Kan	11	8/17	Cib	11
5/6		Ben	12	6/27	Chicchan	12	8/18	Caban	12
5/7		Ix	13	6/28	Cimi	13	8/19	Etznab	13
5/8		Men	1	6/29	Manik	1	8/20	Cauac	1
5/9		Cib	2	6/30	Lamat	2	8/21	Ahau	2
5/10		Caban	3	7/1	Muluc	3	8/22	Imix	3
5/11		Etznab	4	7/2	Oc	4	8/23	Ik	4
5/12		Cauac	5	7/3	Chuen	5	8/24	Akbal	5
5/13		Ahau	6	7/4	Eb	6	8/25	Kan	6
5/14		Imix	7	7/5	Ben	7	8/26	Chicchan	7
5/15		Ik	8	7/6	Ix	8	8/27	Cimi	8
5/16		Akbal	9	7/7	Men	9	8/28	Manik	9
5/17		Kan	10	7/8	Cib	10	8/29	Lamat	10
5/18		Chicchan	11	7/9	Caban	11	8/30	Muluc	11
5/19		Cimi	12	7/10	Etznab	12	8/31	Oc	12
5/20		Manik	13	7/11	Cauac	13	9/1	Chuen	13
5/21		Lamat	1	7/12	Ahau	1	9/2	Eb	1
5/22		Muluc	2	7/13	Imix	2	9/3	Ben	2
5/23		Oc	3	7/14	Ik	3	9/4	Ix	3
5/24		Chuen	4	7/15	Akbal	4	9/5	Men	4
5/25		Eb	5	7/16	Kan	5	9/6	Cib	5
5/26		Ben	6	7/17	Chicchan	6	9/7	Caban	6
5/27		Ix	7	7/18	Cimi	7	9/8	Etznab	7
5/28		Men	8	7/19	Manik	8	9/9	Cauac	8
5/29		Cib	9	7/20	Lamat	9	9/10	Ahau	9
5/30		Caban	10	7/21	Muluc	10	9/11	Imix	10
5/31		Etznab	11	7/22	Oc	11	9/12	Ik	11
6/1		Cauac	12	7/23	Chuen	12	9/13	Akbal	12
6/2		Ahau	13	7/24	Eb	13	9/14	Kan	13

SAMPLE				BIRTHDAY	SOLAR GLYPH	TONE	BIRTHDAY		SOLAR GLYPH	TONE
				9/14	Muluc	1	2/18	11/5	Imix	1
BIRTHDAY	SOLAR GLYPH	TONE		9/15	Oc	2	2/19	11/6	Ik	2
				9/16	Chuen	3	2/20	11/7	Akbal	3
ALWAYS READ CHART FROM				9/17	Eb	4	2/21	11/8	Kan	4
LEFT TO RIGHT			1/1	9/18	Ben	5	2/22	11/9	Chicchan	5
STARTING WITH BIRTHDAY			1/2	9/19	Ix	6	2/23	11/10	Cimi	6
			1/3	9/20	Men	7	2/24	11/11	Manik	7
DOUBLE LINES			1/4	9/21	Cib	8	2/25	11/12	Lamat	8
SEPARATE SECTIONS			1/5	9/22	Caban	9	2/26	11/13	Muluc	9
			1/6	9/23	Etznab	10	2/27	11/14	Oc	10
USE SPACE BELOW			1/7	9/24	Cauac	11	2/28	11/15	Chuen	11
FOR RECORDING BIRTHDAYS			1/8	9/25	Ahau	12	3/1	11/16	Eb	12
			1/9	9/26	Imix	13	3/2	11/17	Ben	13
			1/10	9/27	Ik	1	3/3	11/18	Ix	1
			1/11	9/28	Akbal	2	3/4	11/19	Men	2
			1/12	9/29	Kan	3	3/5	11/20	Cib	3
			1/13	9/30	Chicchan	4	3/6	11/21	Caban	4
			1/14	10/1	Cimi	5	3/7	11/22	Etznab	5
			1/15	10/2	Manik	6	3/8	11/23	Cauac	6
			1/16	10/3	Lamat	7	3/9	11/24	Ahau	7
			1/17	10/4	Muluc	8	3/10	11/25	Imix	8
			1/18	10/5	Oc	9	3/11	11/26	Ik	9
			1/19	10/6	Chuen	10	3/12	11/27	Akbal	10
			1/20	10/7	Eb	11	3/13	11/28	Kan	11
			1/21	10/8	Ben	12	3/14	11/29	Chicchan	12
			1/22	10/9	Ix	13	3/15	11/30	Cimi	13
			1/23	10/10	Men	1	3/16	12/1	Manik	1
			1/24	10/11	Cib	2	3/17	12/2	Lamat	2
			1/25	10/12	Caban	3	3/18	12/3	Muluc	3
			1/26	10/13	Etznab	4	3/19	12/4	Oc	4
			1/27	10/14	Cauac	5	3/20	12/5	Chuen	5
			1/28	10/15	Ahau	6	3/21	12/6	Eb	6
			1/29	10/16	Imix	7	3/22	12/7	Ben	7
			1/30	10/17	Ik	8	3/23	12/8	Ix	8
			1/31	10/18	Akbal	9	3/24	12/9	Men	9
			2/1	10/19	Kan	10	3/25	12/10	Cib	10
			2/2	10/20	Chicchan	11	3/26	12/11	Caban	11
			2/3	10/21	Cimi	12	3/27	12/12	Etznab	12
			2/4	10/22	Manik	13	3/28	12/13	Cauac	13
			2/5	10/23	Lamat	1	3/29	12/14	Ahau	1
			2/6	10/24	Muluc	2	3/30	12/15	Imix	2
			2/7	10/25	Oc	3	3/31	12/16	Ik	3
			2/8	10/26	Chuen	4	4/1	12/17	Akbal	4
			2/9	10/27	Eb	5	4/2	12/18	Kan	5
			2/10	10/28	Ben	6	4/3	12/19	Chicchan	6
			2/11	10/29	Ix	7	4/4	12/20	Cimi	7
			2/12	10/30	Men	8	4/5	12/21	Manik	8
			2/13	10/31	Cib	9	4/6	12/22	Lamat	9
			2/14	11/1	Caban	10	4/7	12/23	Muluc	10
			2/15	11/2	Etznab	11	4/8	12/24	Oc	11
			2/16	11/3	Cauac	12	4/9	12/25	Chuen	12
			2/17	11/4	Ahau	13	4/10	12/26	Eb	13

BIRTHDAY		SOLAR GLYPH	TONE	BIRTHDAY	SOLAR GLYPH	TONE	BIRTHDAY	SOLAR GLYPH	TONE
4/11	12/27	Ben	1	6/2	Chicchan	1	7/24	Caban	1
4/12	12/28	Ix	2	6/3	Cimi	2	7/25	Etznab	2
4/13	12/29	Men	3	6/4	Manik	3	7/26	Cauac	3
4/14	12/30	Cib	4	6/5	Lamat	4	7/27	Ahau	4
4/15	12/31	Caban	5	6/6	Muluc	5	7/28	Imix	5
4/16		Etznab	6	6/7	Oc	6	7/29	Ik	6
4/17		Cauac	7	6/8	Chuen	7	7/30	Akbal	7
4/18		Ahau	8	6/9	Eb	8	7/31	Kan	8
4/19		Imix	9	6/10	Ben	9	8/1	Chiccan	9
4/20		Ik	10	6/11	Ix	10	8/2	Cimi	10
4/21		Akbal	11	6/12	Men	11	8/3	Manik	11
4/22		Kan	12	6/13	Cib	12	8/4	Lamat	12
4/23		Chicchan	13	6/14	Caban	13	8/5	Muluc	13
4/24		Cimi	1	6/15	Etznab	1	8/6	Oc	1
4/25		Manik	2	6/16	Cauac	2	8/7	Chuen	2
4/26		Lamat	3	6/17	Ahau	3	8/8	Eb	3
4/27		Muluc	4	6/18	Imix	4	8/9	Ben	4
4/28		Oc	5	6/19	Ik	5	8/10	Ix	5
4/29		Chuen	6	6/20	Akbal	6	8/11	Men	6
4/30		Eb	7	6/21	Kan	7	8/12	Cib	7
5/1		Ben	8	6/22	Chicchan	8	8/13	Caban	8
5/2		Ix	9	6/23	Cimi	9	8/14	Etznab	9
5/3		Men	10	6/24	Manik	10	8/15	Cauac	10
5/4		Cib	11	6/25	Lamat	11	8/16	Ahau	11
5/5		Caban	12	6/26	Muluc	12	8/17	Imix	12
5/6		Etznab	13	6/27	Oc	13	8/18	Ik	13
5/7		Cauac	1	6/28	Chuen	1	8/19	Akbal	1
5/8		Ahau	2	6/29	Eb	2	8/20	Kan	2
5/9		Imix	3	6/30	Ben	3	8/21	Chicchan	3
5/10		Ik	4	7/1	Ix	4	8/22	Cimi	4
5/11		Akbal	5	7/2	Men	5	8/23	Manik	5
5/12		Kan	6	7/3	Cib	6	8/24	Lamat	6
5/13		Chicchan	7	7/4	Caban	7	8/25	Muluc	7
5/14		Cimi	8	7/5	Etznab	8	8/26	Oc	8
5/15		Manik	9	7/6	Cauac	9	8/27	Chuen	9
5/16		Lamat	10	7/7	Ahau	10	8/28	Eb	10
5/17		Muluc	11	7/8	Imix	11	8/29	Ben	11
5/18		Oc	12	7/9	Ik	12	8/30	Ix	12
5/19		Chuen	13	7/10	Akbal	13	8/31	Men	13
5/20		Eb	1	7/11	Kan	1	9/1	Cib	1
5/21		Ben	2	7/12	Chicchan	2	9/2	Caban	2
5/22		Ix	3	7/13	Cimi	3	9/3	Etznab	3
5/23		Men	4	7/14	Manik	4	9/4	Cauac	4
5/24		Cib	5	7/15	Lamat	5	9/5	Ahau	5
5/25		Caban	6	7/16	Muluc	6	9/6	Imix	6
5/26		Etznab	7	7/17	Oc	7	9/7	Ik	7
5/27		Cauac	8	7/18	Chuen	8	9/8	Akbal	8
5/28		Ahau	9	7/19	Eb	9	9/9	Kan	9
5/29		Imix	10	7/20	Ben	10	9/10	Chicchan	10
5/30		Ik	11	7/21	Ix	11	9/11	Cimi	11
5/31		Akbal	12	7/22	Men	12	9/12	Manik	12
6/1		Kan	13	7/23	Cib	13	9/13	Lamat	13

SAMPLE

BIRTHDAY	SOLAR GLYPH	TONE

ALWAYS READ CHART FROM
LEFT TO RIGHT
STARTING WITH BIRTHDAY

DOUBLE LINES
SEPARATE SECTIONS

USE SPACE BELOW
FOR RECORDING BIRTHDAYS

BIRTHDAY	BIRTHDAY	SOLAR GLYPH	TONE	BIRTHDAY	BIRTHDAY	SOLAR GLYPH	TONE
	9/13	Ben	1	2/17	11/4	Chicchan	1
	9/14	Ix	2	2/18	11/5	Cimi	2
	9/15	Men	3	2/19	11/6	Manik	3
	9/16	Cib	4	2/20	11/7	Lamat	4
	9/17	Caban	5	2/21	11/8	Muluc	5
1/1	9/18	Etznab	6	2/22	11/9	Oc	6
1/2	9/19	Cauac	7	2/23	11/10	Chuen	7
1/3	9/20	Ahau	8	2/24	11/11	Eb	8
1/4	9/21	Imix	9	2/25	11/12	Ben	9
1/5	9/22	Ik	10	2/26	11/13	Ix	10
1/6	9/23	Akbal	11	2/27	11/14	Men	11
1/7	9/24	Kan	12	2/28	11/15	Cib	12
1/8	9/25	Chicchan	13	3/1	11/16	Caban	13
1/9	9/26	Cimi	1	3/2	11/17	Etznab	1
1/10	9/27	Manik	2	3/3	11/18	Cauac	2
1/11	9/28	Lamat	3	3/4	11/19	Ahau	3
1/12	9/29	Muluc	4	3/5	11/20	Imix	4
1/13	9/30	Oc	5	3/6	11/21	Ik	5
1/14	10/1	Chuen	6	3/7	11/22	Akbal	6
1/15	10/2	Eb	7	3/8	11/23	Kan	7
1/16	10/3	Ben	8	3/9	11/24	Chicchan	8
1/17	10/4	Ix	9	3/10	11/25	Cimi	9
1/18	10/5	Men	10	3/11	11/26	Manik	10
1/19	10/6	Cib	11	3/12	11/27	Lamat	11
1/20	10/7	Caban	12	3/13	11/28	Muluc	12
1/21	10/8	Etznab	13	3/14	11/29	Oc	13
1/22	10/9	Cauac	1	3/15	11/30	Chuen	1
1/23	10/10	Ahau	2	3/16	12/1	Eb	2
1/24	10/11	Imix	3	3/17	12/2	Ben	3
1/25	10/12	Ik	4	3/18	12/3	Ix	4
1/26	10/13	Akbal	5	3/19	12/4	Men	5
1/27	10/14	Kan	6	3/20	12/5	Cib	6
1/28	10/15	Chicchan	7	3/21	12/6	Caban	7
1/29	10/16	Cimi	8	3/22	12/7	Etznab	8
1/30	10/17	Manik	9	3/23	12/8	Cauac	9
1/31	10/18	Lamat	10	3/24	12/9	Ahau	10
2/1	10/19	Muluc	11	3/25	12/10	Imix	11
2/2	10/20	Oc	12	3/26	12/11	Ik	12
2/3	10/21	Chuen	13	3/27	12/12	Akbal	13
2/4	10/22	Eb	1	3/28	12/13	Kan	1
2/5	10/23	Ben	2	3/29	12/14	Chicchan	2
2/6	10/24	Ix	3	3/30	12/15	Cimi	3
2/7	10/25	Men	4	3/31	12/16	Manik	4
2/8	10/26	Cib	5	4/1	12/17	Lamat	5
2/9	10/27	Caban	6	4/2	12/18	Muluc	6
2/10	10/28	Etznab	7	4/3	12/19	Oc	7
2/11	10/29	Cauac	8	4/4	12/20	Chuen	8
2/12	10/30	Ahau	9	4/5	12/21	Eb	9
2/13	10/31	Imix	10	4/6	12/22	Ben	10
2/14	11/1	Ik	11	4/7	12/23	Ix	11
2/15	11/2	Akbal	12	4/8	12/24	Men	12
2/16	11/3	Kan	13	4/9	12/25	Cib	13

BIRTHDAY		SOLAR GLYPH	TONE	BIRTHDAY	SOLAR GLYPH	TONE	BIRTHDAY	SOLAR GLYPH	TONE
4/10	12/26	Caban	1	6/1	Muluc	1	7/23	Imix	1
4/11	12/27	Etznab	2	6/2	Oc	2	7/24	Ik	2
4/12	12/28	Cauac	3	6/3	Chuen	3	7/25	Akbal	3
4/13	12/29	Ahau	4	6/4	Eb	4	7/26	Kan	4
4/14	12/30	Imix	5	6/5	Ben	5	7/27	Chicchan	5
4/15	12/31	Ik	6	6/6	Ix	6	7/28	Cimi	6
4/16		Akbal	7	6/7	Men	7	7/29	Manik	7
4/17		Kan	8	6/8	Cib	8	7/30	Lamat	8
4/18		Chiccan	9	6/9	Caban	9	7/31	Muluc	9
4/19		Cimi	10	6/10	Etznab	10	8/1	Oc	10
4/20		Manik	11	6/11	Cauac	11	8/2	Chuen	11
4/21		Lamat	12	6/12	Ahau	12	8/3	Eb	12
4/22		Muluc	13	6/13	Imix	13	8/4	Ben	13
4/23		Oc	1	6/14	Ik	1	8/5	Ix	1
4/24		Chuen	2	6/15	Akbal	2	8/6	Men	2
4/25		Eb	3	6/16	Kan	3	8/7	Cib	3
4/26		Ben	4	6/17	Chicchan	4	8/8	Caban	4
4/27		Ix	5	6/18	Cimi	5	8/9	Etznab	5
4/28		Men	6	6/19	Manik	6	8/10	Cauac	6
4/29		Cib	7	6/20	Lamat	7	8/11	Ahau	7
4/30		Caban	8	6/21	Muluc	8	8/12	Imix	8
5/1		Etznab	9	6/22	Oc	9	8/13	Ik	9
5/2		Cauac	10	6/23	Chuen	10	8/14	Akbal	10
5/3		Ahau	11	6/24	Eb	11	8/15	Kan	11
5/4		Imix	12	6/25	Ben	12	8/16	Chicchan	12
5/5		Ik	13	6/26	Ix	13	8/17	Cimi	13
5/6		Akbal	1	6/27	Men	1	8/18	Manik	1
5/7		Kan	2	6/28	Cib	2	8/19	Lamat	2
5/8		Chicchan	3	6/29	Caban	3	8/20	Muluc	3
5/9		Cimi	4	6/30	Etznab	4	8/21	Oc	4
5/10		Manik	5	7/1	Cauac	5	8/22	Chuen	5
5/11		Lamat	6	7/2	Ahau	6	8/23	Eb	6
5/12		Muluc	7	7/3	Imix	7	8/24	Ben	7
5/13		Oc	8	7/4	Ik	8	8/25	Ix	8
5/14		Chuen	9	7/5	Akbal	9	8/26	Men	9
5/15		Eb	10	7/6	Kan	10	8/27	Cib	10
5/16		Ben	11	7/7	Chicchan	11	8/28	Caban	11
5/17		Ix	12	7/8	Cimi	12	8/29	Etznab	12
5/18		Men	13	7/9	Manik	13	8/30	Cauac	13
5/19		Cib	1	7/10	Lamat	1	8/31	Ahau	1
5/20		Caban	2	7/11	Muluc	2	9/1	Imix	2
5/21		Etznab	3	7/12	Oc	3	9/2	Ik	3
5/22		Cauac	4	7/13	Chuen	4	9/3	Akbal	4
5/23		Ahau	5	7/14	Eb	5	9/4	Kan	5
5/24		Imix	6	7/15	Ben	6	9/5	Chicchan	6
5/25		Ik	7	7/16	Ix	7	9/6	Cimi	7
5/26		Akbal	8	7/17	Men	8	9/7	Manik	8
5/27		Kan	9	7/18	Cib	9	9/8	Lamat	9
5/28		Chiccan	10	7/19	Caban	10	9/9	Muluc	10
5/29		Cimi	11	7/20	Etznab	11	9/10	Oc	11
5/30		Manik	12	7/21	Cauac	12	9/11	Chuen	12
5/31		Lamat	13	7/22	Ahau	13	9/12	Eb	13

SAMPLE			BIRTHDAY	SOLAR GLYPH	TONE	BIRTHDAY		SOLAR GLYPH	TONE
			9/12	Caban	1	2/16	11/3	Muluc	1
BIRTHDAY	SOLAR GLYPH	TONE	9/13	Etznab	2	2/17	11/4	Oc	2
			9/14	Cauac	3	2/18	11/5	Chuen	3
ALWAYS READ CHART FROM			9/15	Ahau	4	2/19	11/6	Eb	4
LEFT TO RIGHT			9/16	Imix	5	2/20	11/7	Ben	5
STARTING WITH BIRTHDAY			9/17	Ik	6	2/21	11/8	Ix	6
			1/1	9/18	Akbal	7	2/22	11/9	Men	7
DOUBLE LINES			1/2	9/19	Kan	8	2/23	11/10	Cib	8
SEPARATE SECTIONS			1/3	9/20	Chiccan	9	2/24	11/11	Caban	9
			1/4	9/21	Cimi	10	2/25	11/12	Etznab	10
USE SPACE BELOW			1/5	9/22	Manik	11	2/26	11/13	Cauac	11
FOR RECORDING BIRTHDAYS			1/6	9/23	Lamat	12	2/27	11/14	Ahau	12
			1/7	9/24	Muluc	13	2/28	11/15	Imix	13
			1/8	9/25	Oc	1	3/1	11/16	Ik	1
			1/9	9/26	Chuen	2	3/2	11/17	Akbal	2
			1/10	9/27	Eb	3	3/3	11/18	Kan	3
			1/11	9/28	Ben	4	3/4	11/19	Chiccan	4
			1/12	9/29	Ix	5	3/5	11/20	Cimi	5
			1/13	9/30	Men	6	3/6	11/21	Manik	6
			1/14	10/1	Cib	7	3/7	11/22	Lamat	7
			1/15	10/2	Caban	8	3/8	11/23	Muluc	8
			1/16	10/3	Etznab	9	3/9	11/24	Oc	9
			1/17	10/4	Cauac	10	3/10	11/25	Chuen	10
			1/18	10/5	Ahau	11	3/11	11/26	Eb	11
			1/19	10/6	Imix	12	3/12	11/27	Ben	12
			1/20	10/7	Ik	13	3/13	11/28	Ix	13
			1/21	10/8	Akbal	1	3/14	11/29	Men	1
			1/22	10/9	Kan	2	3/15	11/30	Cib	2
			1/23	10/10	Chiccan	3	3/16	12/1	Caban	3
			1/24	10/11	Cimi	4	3/17	12/2	Etznab	4
			1/25	10/12	Manik	5	3/18	12/3	Cauac	5
			1/26	10/13	Lamat	6	3/19	12/4	Ahau	6
			1/27	10/14	Muluc	7	3/20	12/5	Imix	7
			1/28	10/15	Oc	8	3/21	12/6	Ik	8
			1/29	10/16	Chuen	9	3/22	12/7	Akbal	9
			1/30	10/17	Eb	10	3/23	12/8	Kan	10
			1/31	10/18	Ben	11	3/24	12/9	Chiccan	11
			2/1	10/19	Ix	12	3/25	12/10	Cimi	12
			2/2	10/20	Men	13	3/26	12/11	Manik	13
			2/3	10/21	Cib	1	3/27	12/12	Lamat	1
			2/4	10/22	Caban	2	3/28	12/13	Muluc	2
			2/5	10/23	Etznab	3	3/29	12/14	Oc	3
			2/6	10/24	Cauac	4	3/30	12/15	Chuen	4
			2/7	10/25	Ahau	5	3/31	12/16	Eb	5
			2/8	10/26	Imix	6	4/1	12/17	Ben	6
			2/9	10/27	Ik	7	4/2	12/18	Ix	7
			2/10	10/28	Akbal	8	4/3	12/19	Men	8
			2/11	10/29	Kan	9	4/4	12/20	Cib	9
			2/12	10/30	Chiccan	10	4/5	12/21	Caban	10
			2/13	10/31	Cimi	11	4/6	12/22	Etznab	11
			2/14	11/1	Manik	12	4/7	12/23	Cauac	12
			2/15	11/2	Lamat	13	4/8	12/24	Ahau	13

BIRTHDAY		SOLAR GLYPH	TONE	BIRTHDAY	SOLAR GLYPH	TONE	BIRTHDAY	SOLAR GLYPH	TONE
4/9	12/25	Imix	1	5/31	Ben	1	7/22	Chicchan	1
4/10	12/26	Ik	2	6/1	Ix	2	7/23	Cimi	2
4/11	12/27	Akbal	3	6/2	Men	3	7/24	Manik	3
4/12	12/28	Kan	4	6/3	Cib	4	7/25	Lamat	4
4/13	12/29	Chicchan	5	6/4	Caban	5	7/26	Muluc	5
4/14	12/30	Cimi	6	6/5	Etznab	6	7/27	Oc	6
4/15	12/31	Manik	7	6/6	Cauac	7	7/28	Chuen	7
4/16		Lamat	8	6/7	Ahau	8	7/29	Eb	8
4/17		Muluc	9	6/8	Imix	9	7/30	Ben	9
4/18		Oc	10	6/9	Ik	10	7/31	Ix	10
4/19		Chuen	11	6/10	Akbal	11	8/1	Men	11
4/20		Eb	12	6/11	Kan	12	8/2	Cib	12
4/21		Ben	13	6/12	Chicchan	13	8/3	Caban	13
4/22		Ix	1	6/13	Cimi	1	8/4	Etznab	1
4/23		Men	2	6/14	Manik	2	8/5	Cauac	2
4/24		Cib	3	6/15	Lamat	3	8/6	Ahau	3
4/25		Caban	4	6/16	Muluc	4	8/7	Imix	4
4/26		Etznab	5	6/17	Oc	5	8/8	Ik	5
4/27		Cauac	6	6/18	Chuen	6	8/9	Akbal	6
4/28		Ahau	7	6/19	Eb	7	8/10	Kan	7
4/29		Imix	8	6/20	Ben	8	8/11	Chicchan	8
4/30		Ik	9	6/21	Ix	9	8/12	Cimi	9
5/1		Akbal	10	6/22	Men	10	8/13	Manik	10
5/2		Kan	11	6/23	Cib	11	8/14	Lamat	11
5/3		Chicchan	12	6/24	Caban	12	8/15	Muluc	12
5/4		Cimi	13	6/25	Etznab	13	8/16	Oc	13
5/5		Manik	1	6/26	Cauac	1	8/17	Chuen	1
5/6		Lamat	2	6/27	Ahau	2	8/18	Eb	2
5/7		Muluc	3	6/28	Imix	3	8/19	Ben	3
5/8		Oc	4	6/29	Ik	4	8/20	Ix	4
5/9		Chuen	5	6/30	Akbal	5	8/21	Men	5
5/10		Eb	6	7/1	Kan	6	8/22	Cib	6
5/11		Ben	7	7/2	Chicchan	7	8/23	Caban	7
5/12		Ix	8	7/3	Cimi	8	8/24	Etznab	8
5/13		Men	9	7/4	Manik	9	8/25	Cauac	9
5/14		Cib	10	7/5	Lamat	10	8/26	Ahau	10
5/15		Caban	11	7/6	Muluc	11	8/27	Imix	11
5/16		Etznab	12	7/7	Oc	12	8/28	Ik	12
5/17		Cauac	13	7/8	Chuen	13	8/29	Akbal	13
5/18		Ahau	1	7/9	Eb	1	8/30	Kan	1
5/19		Imix	2	7/10	Ben	2	8/31	Chicchan	2
5/20		Ik	3	7/11	Ix	3	9/1	Cimi	3
5/21		Akbal	4	7/12	Men	4	9/2	Manik	4
5/22		Kan	5	7/13	Cib	5	9/3	Lamat	5
5/23		Chicchan	6	7/14	Caban	6	9/4	Muluc	6
5/24		Cimi	7	7/15	Etznab	7	9/5	Oc	7
5/25		Manik	8	7/16	Cauac	8	9/6	Chuen	8
5/26		Lamat	9	7/17	Ahau	9	9/7	Eb	9
5/27		Muluc	10	7/18	Imix	10	9/8	Ben	10
5/28		Oc	11	7/19	Ik	11	9/9	Ix	11
5/29		Chuen	12	7/20	Akbal	12	9/10	Men	12
5/30		Eb	13	7/21	Kan	13	9/11	Cib	13

1907, 1959, 2011

SAMPLE			BIRTHDAY	SOLAR GLYPH	TONE	BIRTHDAY	SOLAR GLYPH	TONE
			9/11	Imix	1	2/15 · 11/2	Ben	1
BIRTHDAY	SOLAR GLYPH	TONE	9/12	Ik	2	2/16 · 11/3	Ix	2
			9/13	Akbal	3	2/17 · 11/4	Men	3
ALWAYS READ CHART FROM			9/14	Kan	4	2/18 · 11/5	Cib	4
LEFT TO RIGHT			9/15	Chicchan	5	2/19 · 11/6	Caban	5
STARTING WITH BIRTHDAY			9/16	Cimi	6	2/20 · 11/7	Etznab	6
			9/17	Manik	7	2/21 · 11/8	Cauac	7
DOUBLE LINES			1/1 · 9/18	Lamat	8	2/22 · 11/9	Ahau	8
SEPARATE SECTIONS			1/2 · 9/19	Muluc	9	2/23 · 11/10	Imix	9
			1/3 · 9/20	Oc	10	2/24 · 11/11	Ik	10
USE SPACE BELOW			1/4 · 9/21	Chuen	11	2/25 · 11/12	Akbal	11
FOR RECORDING BIRTHDAYS			1/5 · 9/22	Eb	12	2/26 · 11/13	Kan	12
			1/6 · 9/23	Ben	13	2/27 · 11/14	Chicchan	13
			1/7 · 9/24	Ix	1	2/28 · 11/15	Cimi	1
			1/8 · 9/25	Men	2	3/1 · 11/16	Manik	2
			1/9 · 9/26	Cib	3	3/2 · 11/17	Lamat	3
			1/10 · 9/27	Caban	4	3/3 · 11/18	Muluc	4
			1/11 · 9/28	Etznab	5	3/4 · 11/19	Oc	5
			1/12 · 9/29	Cauac	6	3/5 · 11/20	Chuen	6
			1/13 · 9/30	Ahau	7	3/6 · 11/21	Eb	7
			1/14 · 10/1	Imix	8	3/7 · 11/22	Ben	8
			1/15 · 10/2	Ik	9	3/8 · 11/23	Ix	9
			1/16 · 10/3	Akbal	10	3/9 · 11/24	Men	10
			1/17 · 10/4	Kan	11	3/10 · 11/25	Cib	11
			1/18 · 10/5	Chicchan	12	3/11 · 11/26	Caban	12
			1/19 · 10/6	Cimi	13	3/12 · 11/27	Etznab	13
			1/20 · 10/7	Manik	1	3/13 · 11/28	Cauac	1
			1/21 · 10/8	Lamat	2	3/14 · 11/29	Ahau	2
			1/22 · 10/9	Muluc	3	3/15 · 11/30	Imix	3
			1/23 · 10/10	Oc	4	3/16 · 12/1	Ik	4
			1/24 · 10/11	Chuen	5	3/17 · 12/2	Akbal	5
			1/25 · 10/12	Eb	6	3/18 · 12/3	Kan	6
			1/26 · 10/13	Ben	7	3/19 · 12/4	Chicchan	7
			1/27 · 10/14	Ix	8	3/20 · 12/5	Cimi	8
			1/28 · 10/15	Men	9	3/21 · 12/6	Manik	9
			1/29 · 10/16	Cib	10	3/22 · 12/7	Lamat	10
			1/30 · 10/17	Caban	11	3/23 · 12/8	Muluc	11
			1/31 · 10/18	Etznab	12	3/24 · 12/9	Oc	12
			2/1 · 10/19	Cauac	13	3/25 · 12/10	Chuen	13
			2/2 · 10/20	Ahau	1	3/26 · 12/11	Eb	1
			2/3 · 10/21	Imix	2	3/27 · 12/12	Ben	2
			2/4 · 10/22	Ik	3	3/28 · 12/13	Ix	3
			2/5 · 10/23	Akbal	4	3/29 · 12/14	Men	4
			2/6 · 10/24	Kan	5	3/30 · 12/15	Cib	5
			2/7 · 10/25	Chicchan	6	3/31 · 12/16	Caban	6
			2/8 · 10/26	Cimi	7	4/1 · 12/17	Etznab	7
			2/9 · 10/27	Manik	8	4/2 · 12/18	Cauac	8
			2/10 · 10/28	Lamat	9	4/3 · 12/19	Ahau	9
			2/11 · 10/29	Muluc	10	4/4 · 12/20	Imix	10
			2/12 · 10/30	Oc	11	4/5 · 12/21	Ik	11
			2/13 · 10/31	Chuen	12	4/6 · 12/22	Akbal	12
			2/14 · 11/1	Eb	13	4/7 · 12/23	Kan	13

BIRTHDAY		SOLAR GLYPH	TONE	BIRTHDAY	SOLAR GLYPH	TONE	BIRTHDAY	SOLAR GLYPH	TONE
4/8	12/24	Chicchan	1	5/30	Caban	1	7/21	Muluc	1
4/9	12/25	Cimi	2	5/31	Etznab	2	7/22	Oc	2
4/10	12/26	Manik	3	6/1	Cauac	3	7/23	Chuen	3
4/11	12/27	Lamat	4	6/2	Ahau	4	7/24	Eb	4
4/12	12/28	Muluc	5	6/3	Imix	5	7/25	Ben	5
4/13	12/29	Oc	6	6/4	Ik	6	7/26	Ix	6
4/14	12/30	Chuen	7	6/5	Akbal	7	7/27	Men	7
4/15	12/31	Eb	8	6/6	Kan	8	7/28	Cib	8
4/16		Ben	9	6/7	Chiccan	9	7/29	Caban	9
4/17		Ix	10	6/8	Cimi	10	7/30	Etznab	10
4/18		Men	11	6/9	Manik	11	7/31	Cauac	11
4/19		Cib	12	6/10	Lamat	12	8/1	Ahau	12
4/20		Caban	13	6/11	Muluc	13	8/2	Imix	13
4/21		Etznab	1	6/12	Oc	1	8/3	Ik	1
4/22		Cauac	2	6/13	Chuen	2	8/4	Akbal	2
4/23		Ahau	3	6/14	Eb	3	8/5	Kan	3
4/24		Imix	4	6/15	Ben	4	8/6	Chicchan	4
4/25		Ik	5	6/16	Ix	5	8/7	Cimi	5
4/26		Akbal	6	6/17	Men	6	8/8	Manik	6
4/27		Kan	7	6/18	Cib	7	8/9	Lamat	7
4/28		Chicchan	8	6/19	Caban	8	8/10	Muluc	8
4/29		Cimi	9	6/20	Etznab	9	8/11	Oc	9
4/30		Manik	10	6/21	Cauac	10	8/12	Chuen	10
5/1		Lamat	11	6/22	Ahau	11	8/13	Eb	11
5/2		Muluc	12	6/23	Imix	12	8/14	Ben	12
5/3		Oc	13	6/24	Ik	13	8/15	Ix	13
5/4		Chuen	1	6/25	Akbal	1	8/16	Men	1
5/5		Eb	2	6/26	Kan	2	8/17	Cib	2
5/6		Ben	3	6/27	Chicchan	3	8/18	Caban	3
5/7		Ix	4	6/28	Cimi	4	8/19	Etznab	4
5/8		Men	5	6/29	Manik	5	8/20	Cauac	5
5/9		Cib	6	6/30	Lamat	6	8/21	Ahau	6
5/10		Caban	7	7/1	Muluc	7	8/22	Imix	7
5/11		Etznab	8	7/2	Oc	8	8/23	Ik	8
5/12		Cauac	9	7/3	Chuen	9	8/24	Akbal	9
5/13		Ahau	10	7/4	Eb	10	8/25	Kan	10
5/14		Imix	11	7/5	Ben	11	8/26	Chicchan	11
5/15		Ik	12	7/6	Ix	12	8/27	Cimi	12
5/16		Akbal	13	7/7	Men	13	8/28	Manik	13
5/17		Kan	1	7/8	Cib	1	8/29	Lamat	1
5/18		Chicchan	2	7/9	Caban	2	8/30	Muluc	2
5/19		Cimi	3	7/10	Etznab	3	8/31	Oc	3
5/20		Manik	4	7/11	Cauac	4	9/1	Chuen	4
5/21		Lamat	5	7/12	Ahau	5	9/2	Eb	5
5/22		Muluc	6	7/13	Imix	6	9/3	Ben	6
5/23		Oc	7	7/14	Ik	7	9/4	Ix	7
5/24		Chuen	8	7/15	Akbal	8	9/5	Men	8
5/25		Eb	9	7/16	Kan	9	9/6	Cib	9
5/26		Ben	10	7/17	Chicchan	10	9/7	Caban	10
5/27		Ix	11	7/18	Cimi	11	9/8	Etznab	11
5/28		Men	12	7/19	Manik	12	9/9	Cauac	12
5/29		Cib	13	7/20	Lamat	13	9/10	Ahau	13

SAMPLE

BIRTHDAY	SOLAR GLYPH	TONE

ALWAYS READ CHART FROM
LEFT TO RIGHT
STARTING WITH BIRTHDAY

DOUBLE LINES
SEPARATE SECTIONS

USE SPACE BELOW
FOR RECORDING BIRTHDAYS

BIRTHDAY	BIRTHDAY	SOLAR GLYPH	TONE	BIRTHDAY	BIRTHDAY	SOLAR GLYPH	TONE
	9/10	Chicchan	1	2/14	11/1	Caban	1
	9/11	Cimi	2	2/15	11/2	Etznab	2
	9/12	Manik	3	2/16	11/3	Cauac	3
	9/13	Lamat	4	2/17	11/4	Ahau	4
	9/14	Muluc	5	2/18	11/5	Imix	5
	9/15	Oc	6	2/19	11/6	Ik	6
	9/16	Chuen	7	2/20	11/7	Akbal	7
	9/17	Eb	8	2/21	11/8	Kan	8
1/1	9/18	Ben	9	2/22	11/9	Chiccan	9
1/2	9/19	Ix	10	2/23	11/10	Cimi	10
1/3	9/20	Men	11	2/24	11/11	Manik	11
1/4	9/21	Cib	12	2/25	11/12	Lamat	12
1/5	9/22	Caban	13	2/26	11/13	Muluc	13
1/6	9/23	Etznab	1	2/27	11/14	Oc	1
1/7	9/24	Cauac	2	2/28	11/15	Chuen	2
1/8	9/25	Ahau	3	3/1	11/16	Eb	3
1/9	9/26	Imix	4	3/2	11/17	Ben	4
1/10	9/27	Ik	5	3/3	11/18	Ix	5
1/11	9/28	Akbal	6	3/4	11/19	Men	6
1/12	9/29	Kan	7	3/5	11/20	Cib	7
1/13	9/30	Chicchan	8	3/6	11/21	Caban	8
1/14	10/1	Cimi	9	3/7	11/22	Etznab	9
1/15	10/2	Manik	10	3/8	11/23	Cauac	10
1/16	10/3	Lamat	11	3/9	11/24	Ahau	11
1/17	10/4	Muluc	12	3/10	11/25	Imix	12
1/18	10/5	Oc	13	3/11	11/26	Ik	13
1/19	10/6	Chuen	1	3/12	11/27	Akbal	1
1/20	10/7	Eb	2	3/13	11/28	Kan	2
1/21	10/8	Ben	3	3/14	11/29	Chicchan	3
1/22	10/9	Ix	4	3/15	11/30	Cimi	4
1/23	10/10	Men	5	3/16	12/1	Manik	5
1/24	10/11	Cib	6	3/17	12/2	Lamat	6
1/25	10/12	Caban	7	3/18	12/3	Muluc	7
1/26	10/13	Etznab	8	3/19	12/4	Oc	8
1/27	10/14	Cauac	9	3/20	12/5	Chuen	9
1/28	10/15	Ahau	10	3/21	12/6	Eb	10
1/29	10/16	Imix	11	3/22	12/7	Ben	11
1/30	10/17	Ik	12	3/23	12/8	Ix	12
1/31	10/18	Akbal	13	3/24	12/9	Men	13
2/1	10/19	Kan	1	3/25	12/10	Cib	1
2/2	10/20	Chicchan	2	3/26	12/11	Caban	2
2/3	10/21	Cimi	3	3/27	12/12	Etznab	3
2/4	10/22	Manik	4	3/28	12/13	Cauac	4
2/5	10/23	Lamat	5	3/29	12/14	Ahau	5
2/6	10/24	Muluc	6	3/30	12/15	Imix	6
2/7	10/25	Oc	7	3/31	12/16	Ik	7
2/8	10/26	Chuen	8	4/1	12/17	Akbal	8
2/9	10/27	Eb	9	4/2	12/18	Kan	9
2/10	10/28	Ben	10	4/3	12/19	Chicchan	10
2/11	10/29	Ix	11	4/4	12/20	Cimi	11
2/12	10/30	Men	12	4/5	12/21	Manik	12
2/13	10/31	Cib	13	4/6	12/22	Lamat	13

BIRTHDAY		SOLAR GLYPH	TONE	BIRTHDAY	SOLAR GLYPH	TONE	BIRTHDAY	SOLAR GLYPH	TONE
4/7	12/23	Muluc	1	5/29	Imix	1	7/20	Ben	1
4/8	12/24	Oc	2	5/30	Ik	2	7/21	Ix	2
4/9	12/25	Chuen	3	5/31	Akbal	3	7/22	Men	3
4/10	12/26	Eb	4	6/1	Kan	4	7/23	Cib	4
4/11	12/27	Ben	5	6/2	Chicchan	5	7/24	Caban	5
4/12	12/28	Ix	6	6/3	Cimi	6	7/25	Etznab	6
4/13	12/29	Men	7	6/4	Manik	7	7/26	Cauac	7
4/14	12/30	Cib	8	6/5	Lamat	8	7/27	Ahau	8
4/15	12/31	Caban	9	6/6	Muluc	9	7/28	Imix	9
4/16		Etznab	10	6/7	Oc	10	7/29	Ik	10
4/17		Cauac	11	6/8	Chuen	11	7/30	Akbal	11
4/18		Ahau	12	6/9	Eb	12	7/31	Kan	12
4/19		Imix	13	6/10	Ben	13	8/1	Chicchan	13
4/20		Ik	1	6/11	Ix	1	8/2	Cimi	1
4/21		Akbal	2	6/12	Men	2	8/3	Manik	2
4/22		Kan	3	6/13	Cib	3	8/4	Lamat	3
4/23		Chicchan	4	6/14	Caban	4	8/5	Muluc	4
4/24		Cimi	5	6/15	Etznab	5	8/6	Oc	5
4/25		Manik	6	6/16	Cauac	6	8/7	Chuen	6
4/26		Lamat	7	6/17	Ahau	7	8/8	Eb	7
4/27		Muluc	8	6/18	Imix	8	8/9	Ben	8
4/28		Oc	9	6/19	Ik	9	8/10	Ix	9
4/29		Chuen	10	6/20	Akbal	10	8/11	Men	10
4/30		Eb	11	6/21	Kan	11	8/12	Cib	11
5/1		Ben	12	6/22	Chicchan	12	8/13	Caban	12
5/2		Ix	13	6/23	Cimi	13	8/14	Etznab	13
5/3		Men	1	6/24	Manik	1	8/15	Cauac	1
5/4		Cib	2	6/25	Lamat	2	8/16	Ahau	2
5/5		Caban	3	6/26	Muluc	3	8/17	Imix	3
5/6		Etznab	4	6/27	Oc	4	8/18	Ik	4
5/7		Cauac	5	6/28	Chuen	5	8/19	Akbal	5
5/8		Ahau	6	6/29	Eb	6	8/20	Kan	6
5/9		Imix	7	6/30	Ben	7	8/21	Chicchan	7
5/10		Ik	8	7/1	Ix	8	8/22	Cimi	8
5/11		Akbal	9	7/2	Men	9	8/23	Manik	9
5/12		Kan	10	7/3	Cib	10	8/24	Lamat	10
5/13		Chicchan	11	7/4	Caban	11	8/25	Muluc	11
5/14		Cimi	12	7/5	Etznab	12	8/26	Oc	12
5/15		Manik	13	7/6	Cauac	13	8/27	Chuen	13
5/16		Lamat	1	7/7	Ahau	1	8/28	Eb	1
5/17		Muluc	2	7/8	Imix	2	8/29	Ben	2
5/18		Oc	3	7/9	Ik	3	8/30	Ix	3
5/19		Chuen	4	7/10	Akbal	4	8/31	Men	4
5/20		Eb	5	7/11	Kan	5	9/1	Cib	5
5/21		Ben	6	7/12	Chicchan	6	9/2	Caban	6
5/22		Ix	7	7/13	Cimi	7	9/3	Etznab	7
5/23		Men	8	7/14	Manik	8	9/4	Cauac	8
5/24		Cib	9	7/15	Lamat	9	9/5	Ahau	9
5/25		Caban	10	7/16	Muluc	10	9/6	Imix	10
5/26		Etznab	11	7/17	Oc	11	9/7	Ik	11
5/27		Cauac	12	7/18	Chuen	12	9/8	Akbal	12
5/28		Ahau	13	7/19	Eb	13	9/9	Kan	13

SAMPLE			BIRTHDAY	SOLAR GLYPH	TONE	BIRTHDAY		SOLAR GLYPH	TONE
			9/9	Muluc	1	2/13	10/31	Imix	1
BIRTHDAY	SOLAR GLYPH	TONE	9/10	Oc	2	2/14	11/1	Ik	2
			9/11	Chuen	3	2/15	11/2	Akbal	3
ALWAYS READ CHART FROM			9/12	Eb	4	2/16	11/3	Kan	4
LEFT TO RIGHT			9/13	Ben	5	2/17	11/4	Chicchan	5
STARTING WITH BIRTHDAY			9/14	Ix	6	2/18	11/5	Cimi	6
			9/15	Men	7	2/19	11/6	Manik	7
DOUBLE LINES			9/16	Cib	8	2/20	11/7	Lamat	8
SEPARATE SECTIONS			9/17	Caban	9	2/21	11/8	Muluc	9
			1/1	9/18	Etznab	10	2/22	11/9	Oc	10
USE SPACE BELOW			1/2	9/19	Cauac	11	2/23	11/10	Chuen	11
FOR RECORDING BIRTHDAYS			1/3	9/20	Ahau	12	2/24	11/11	Eb	12
			1/4	9/21	Imix	13	2/25	11/12	Ben	13
			1/5	9/22	Ik	1	2/26	11/13	Ix	1
			1/6	9/23	Akbal	2	2/27	11/14	Men	2
			1/7	9/24	Kan	3	2/28	11/15	Cib	3
			1/8	9/25	Chicchan	4	3/1	11/16	Caban	4
			1/9	9/26	Cimi	5	3/2	11/17	Etznab	5
			1/10	9/27	Manik	6	3/3	11/18	Cauac	6
			1/11	9/28	Lamat	7	3/4	11/19	Ahau	7
			1/12	9/29	Muluc	8	3/5	11/20	Imix	8
			1/13	9/30	Oc	9	3/6	11/21	Ik	9
			1/14	10/1	Chuen	10	3/7	11/22	Akbal	10
			1/15	10/2	Eb	11	3/8	11/23	Kan	11
			1/16	10/3	Ben	12	3/9	11/24	Chicchan	12
			1/17	10/4	Ix	13	3/10	11/25	Cimi	13
			1/18	10/5	Men	1	3/11	11/26	Manik	1
			1/19	10/6	Cib	2	3/12	11/27	Lamat	2
			1/20	10/7	Caban	3	3/13	11/28	Muluc	3
			1/21	10/8	Etznab	4	3/14	11/29	Oc	4
			1/22	10/9	Cauac	5	3/15	11/30	Chuen	5
			1/23	10/10	Ahau	6	3/16	12/1	Eb	6
			1/24	10/11	Imix	7	3/17	12/2	Ben	7
			1/25	10/12	Ik	8	3/18	12/3	Ix	8
			1/26	10/13	Akbal	9	3/19	12/4	Men	9
			1/27	10/14	Kan	10	3/20	12/5	Cib	10
			1/28	10/15	Chicchan	11	3/21	12/6	Caban	11
			1/29	10/16	Cimi	12	3/22	12/7	Etznab	12
			1/30	10/17	Manik	13	3/23	12/8	Cauac	13
			1/31	10/18	Lamat	1	3/24	12/9	Ahau	1
			2/1	10/19	Muluc	2	3/25	12/10	Imix	2
			2/2	10/20	Oc	3	3/26	12/11	Ik	3
			2/3	10/21	Chuen	4	3/27	12/12	Akbal	4
			2/4	10/22	Eb	5	3/28	12/13	Kan	5
			2/5	10/23	Ben	6	3/29	12/14	Chicchan	6
			2/6	10/24	Ix	7	3/30	12/15	Cimi	7
			2/7	10/25	Men	8	3/31	12/16	Manik	8
			2/8	10/26	Cib	9	4/1	12/17	Lamat	9
			2/9	10/27	Caban	10	4/2	12/18	Muluc	10
			2/10	10/28	Etznab	11	4/3	12/19	Oc	11
			2/11	10/29	Cauac	12	4/4	12/20	Chuen	12
			2/12	10/30	Ahau	13	4/5	12/21	Eb	13

BIRTHDAY		SOLAR GLYPH	TONE	BIRTHDAY	SOLAR GLYPH	TONE	BIRTHDAY	SOLAR GLYPH	TONE
4/6	12/22	Ben	1	5/28	Chicchan	1	7/19	Caban	1
4/7	12/23	Ix	2	5/29	Cimi	2	7/20	Etznab	2
4/8	12/24	Men	3	5/30	Manik	3	7/21	Cauac	3
4/9	12/25	Cib	4	5/31	Lamat	4	7/22	Ahau	4
4/10	12/26	Caban	5	6/1	Muluc	5	7/23	Imix	5
4/11	12/27	Etznab	6	6/2	Oc	6	7/24	Ik	6
4/12	12/28	Cauac	7	6/3	Chuen	7	7/25	Akbal	7
4/13	12/29	Ahau	8	6/4	Eb	8	7/26	Kan	8
4/14	12/30	Imix	9	6/5	Ben	9	7/27	Chiccan	9
4/15	12/31	Ik	10	6/6	Ix	10	7/28	Cimi	10
4/16		Akbal	11	6/7	Men	11	7/29	Manik	11
4/17		Kan	12	6/8	Cib	12	7/30	Lamat	12
4/18		Chicchan	13	6/9	Caban	13	7/31	Muluc	13
4/19		Cimi	1	6/10	Etznab	1	8/1	Oc	1
4/20		Manik	2	6/11	Cauac	2	8/2	Chuen	2
4/21		Lamat	3	6/12	Ahau	3	8/3	Eb	3
4/22		Muluc	4	6/13	Imix	4	8/4	Ben	4
4/23		Oc	5	6/14	Ik	5	8/5	Ix	5
4/24		Chuen	6	6/15	Akbal	6	8/6	Men	6
4/25		Eb	7	6/16	Kan	7	8/7	Cib	7
4/26		Ben	8	6/17	Chicchan	8	8/8	Caban	8
4/27		Ix	9	6/18	Cimi	9	8/9	Etznab	9
4/28		Men	10	6/19	Manik	10	8/10	Cauac	10
4/29		Cib	11	6/20	Lamat	11	8/11	Ahau	11
4/30		Caban	12	6/21	Muluc	12	8/12	Imix	12
5/1		Etznab	13	6/22	Oc	13	8/13	Ik	13
5/2		Cauac	1	6/23	Chuen	1	8/14	Akbal	1
5/3		Ahau	2	6/24	Eb	2	8/15	Kan	2
5/4		Imix	3	6/25	Ben	3	8/16	Chicchan	3
5/5		Ik	4	6/26	Ix	4	8/17	Cimi	4
5/6		Akbal	5	6/27	Men	5	8/18	Manik	5
5/7		Kan	6	6/28	Cib	6	8/19	Lamat	6
5/8		Chicchan	7	6/29	Caban	7	8/20	Muluc	7
5/9		Cimi	8	6/30	Etznab	8	8/21	Oc	8
5/10		Manik	9	7/1	Cauac	9	8/22	Chuen	9
5/11		Lamat	10	7/2	Ahau	10	8/23	Eb	10
5/12		Muluc	11	7/3	Imix	11	8/24	Ben	11
5/13		Oc	12	7/4	Ik	12	8/25	Ix	12
5/14		Chuen	13	7/5	Akbal	13	8/26	Men	13
5/15		Eb	1	7/6	Kan	1	8/27	Cib	1
5/16		Ben	2	7/7	Chicchan	2	8/28	Caban	2
5/17		Ix	3	7/8	Cimi	3	8/29	Etznab	3
5/18		Men	4	7/9	Manik	4	8/30	Cauac	4
5/19		Cib	5	7/10	Lamat	5	8/31	Ahau	5
5/20		Caban	6	7/11	Muluc	6	9/1	Imix	6
5/21		Etznab	7	7/12	Oc	7	9/2	Ik	7
5/22		Cauac	8	7/13	Chuen	8	9/3	Akbal	8
5/23		Ahau	9	7/14	Eb	9	9/4	Kan	9
5/24		Imix	10	7/15	Ben	10	9/5	Chicchan	10
5/25		Ik	11	7/16	Ix	11	9/6	Cimi	11
5/26		Akbal	12	7/17	Men	12	9/7	Manik	12
5/27		Kan	13	7/18	Cib	13	9/8	Lamat	13

SAMPLE

BIRTHDAY	SOLAR GLYPH	TONE

ALWAYS READ CHART FROM
LEFT TO RIGHT
STARTING WITH BIRTHDAY

DOUBLE LINES
SEPARATE SECTIONS

USE SPACE BELOW
FOR RECORDING BIRTHDAYS

Record	BIRTHDAY	SOLAR GLYPH	TONE	BIRTHDAY		SOLAR GLYPH	TONE
	9/8	Ben	1	2/12	10/30	Chicchan	1
	9/9	Ix	2	2/13	10/31	Cimi	2
	9/10	Men	3	2/14	11/1	Manik	3
	9/11	Cib	4	2/15	11/2	Lamat	4
	9/12	Caban	5	2/16	11/3	Muluc	5
	9/13	Etznab	6	2/17	11/4	Oc	6
	9/14	Cauac	7	2/18	11/5	Chuen	7
	9/15	Ahau	8	2/19	11/6	Eb	8
	9/16	Imix	9	2/20	11/7	Ben	9
	9/17	Ik	10	2/21	11/8	Ix	10
1/1	9/18	Akbal	11	2/22	11/9	Men	11
1/2	9/19	Kan	12	2/23	11/10	Cib	12
1/3	9/20	Chicchan	13	2/24	11/11	Caban	13
1/4	9/21	Cimi	1	2/25	11/12	Etznab	1
1/5	9/22	Manik	2	2/26	11/13	Cauac	2
1/6	9/23	Lamat	3	2/27	11/14	Ahau	3
1/7	9/24	Muluc	4	2/28	11/15	Imix	4
1/8	9/25	Oc	5	3/1	11/16	Ik	5
1/9	9/26	Chuen	6	3/2	11/17	Akbal	6
1/10	9/27	Eb	7	3/3	11/18	Kan	7
1/11	9/28	Ben	8	3/4	11/19	Chicchan	8
1/12	9/29	Ix	9	3/5	11/20	Cimi	9
1/13	9/30	Men	10	3/6	11/21	Manik	10
1/14	10/1	Cib	11	3/7	11/22	Lamat	11
1/15	10/2	Caban	12	3/8	11/23	Muluc	12
1/16	10/3	Etznab	13	3/9	11/24	Oc	13
1/17	10/4	Cauac	1	3/10	11/25	Chuen	1
1/18	10/5	Ahau	2	3/11	11/26	Eb	2
1/19	10/6	Imix	3	3/12	11/27	Ben	3
1/20	10/7	Ik	4	3/13	11/28	Ix	4
1/21	10/8	Akbal	5	3/14	11/29	Men	5
1/22	10/9	Kan	6	3/15	11/30	Cib	6
1/23	10/10	Chicchan	7	3/16	12/1	Caban	7
1/24	10/11	Cimi	8	3/17	12/2	Etznab	8
1/25	10/12	Manik	9	3/18	12/3	Cauac	9
1/26	10/13	Lamat	10	3/19	12/4	Ahau	10
1/27	10/14	Muluc	11	3/20	12/5	Imix	11
1/28	10/15	Oc	12	3/21	12/6	Ik	12
1/29	10/16	Chuen	13	3/22	12/7	Akbal	13
1/30	10/17	Eb	1	3/23	12/8	Kan	1
1/31	10/18	Ben	2	3/24	12/9	Chicchan	2
2/1	10/19	Ix	3	3/25	12/10	Cimi	3
2/2	10/20	Men	4	3/26	12/11	Manik	4
2/3	10/21	Cib	5	3/27	12/12	Lamat	5
2/4	10/22	Caban	6	3/28	12/13	Muluc	6
2/5	10/23	Etznab	7	3/29	12/14	Oc	7
2/6	10/24	Cauac	8	3/30	12/15	Chuen	8
2/7	10/25	Ahau	9	3/31	12/16	Eb	9
2/8	10/26	Imix	10	4/1	12/17	Ben	10
2/9	10/27	Ik	11	4/2	12/18	Ix	11
2/10	10/28	Akbal	12	4/3	12/19	Men	12
2/11	10/29	Kan	13	4/4	12/20	Cib	13

BIRTHDAY		SOLAR GLYPH	TONE	BIRTHDAY	SOLAR GLYPH	TONE	BIRTHDAY	SOLAR GLYPH	TONE
4/5	12/21	Caban	1	5/27	Muluc	1	7/18	Imix	1
4/6	12/22	Etznab	2	5/28	Oc	2	7/19	Ik	2
4/7	12/23	Cauac	3	5/29	Chuen	3	7/20	Akbal	3
4/8	12/24	Ahau	4	5/30	Eb	4	7/21	Kan	4
4/9	12/25	Imix	5	5/31	Ben	5	7/22	Chicchan	5
4/10	12/26	Ik	6	6/1	Ix	6	7/23	Cimi	6
4/11	12/27	Akbal	7	6/2	Men	7	7/24	Manik	7
4/12	12/28	Kan	8	6/3	Cib	8	7/25	Lamat	8
4/13	12/29	Chiccan	9	6/4	Caban	9	7/26	Muluc	9
4/14	12/30	Cimi	10	6/5	Etznab	10	7/27	Oc	10
4/15	12/31	Manik	11	6/6	Cauac	11	7/28	Chuen	11
4/16		Lamat	12	6/7	Ahau	12	7/29	Eb	12
4/17		Muluc	13	6/8	Imix	13	7/30	Ben	13
4/18		Oc	1	6/9	Ik	1	7/31	Ix	1
4/19		Chuen	2	6/10	Akbal	2	8/1	Men	2
4/20		Eb	3	6/11	Kan	3	8/2	Cib	3
4/21		Ben	4	6/12	Chicchan	4	8/3	Caban	4
4/22		Ix	5	6/13	Cimi	5	8/4	Etznab	5
4/23		Men	6	6/14	Manik	6	8/5	Cauac	6
4/24		Cib	7	6/15	Lamat	7	8/6	Ahau	7
4/25		Caban	8	6/16	Muluc	8	8/7	Imix	8
4/26		Etznab	9	6/17	Oc	9	8/8	Ik	9
4/27		Cauac	10	6/18	Chuen	10	8/9	Akbal	10
4/28		Ahau	11	6/19	Eb	11	8/10	Kan	11
4/29		Imix	12	6/20	Ben	12	8/11	Chicchan	12
4/30		Ik	13	6/21	Ix	13	8/12	Cimi	13
5/1		Akbal	1	6/22	Men	1	8/13	Manik	1
5/2		Kan	2	6/23	Cib	2	8/14	Lamat	2
5/3		Chicchan	3	6/24	Caban	3	8/15	Muluc	3
5/4		Cimi	4	6/25	Etznab	4	8/16	Oc	4
5/5		Manik	5	6/26	Cauac	5	8/17	Chuen	5
5/6		Lamat	6	6/27	Ahau	6	8/18	Eb	6
5/7		Muluc	7	6/28	Imix	7	8/19	Ben	7
5/8		Oc	8	6/29	Ik	8	8/20	Ix	8
5/9		Chuen	9	6/30	Akbal	9	8/21	Men	9
5/10		Eb	10	7/1	Kan	10	8/22	Cib	10
5/11		Ben	11	7/2	Chicchan	11	8/23	Caban	11
5/12		Ix	12	7/3	Cimi	12	8/24	Etznab	12
5/13		Men	13	7/4	Manik	13	8/25	Cauac	13
5/14		Cib	1	7/5	Lamat	1	8/26	Ahau	1
5/15		Caban	2	7/6	Muluc	2	8/27	Imix	2
5/16		Etznab	3	7/7	Oc	3	8/28	Ik	3
5/17		Cauac	4	7/8	Chuen	4	8/29	Akbal	4
5/18		Ahau	5	7/9	Eb	5	8/30	Kan	5
5/19		Imix	6	7/10	Ben	6	8/31	Chicchan	6
5/20		Ik	7	7/11	Ix	7	9/1	Cimi	7
5/21		Akbal	8	7/12	Men	8	9/2	Manik	8
5/22		Kan	9	7/13	Cib	9	9/3	Lamat	9
5/23		Chicchan	10	7/14	Caban	10	9/4	Muluc	10
5/24		Cimi	11	7/15	Etznab	11	9/5	Oc	11
5/25		Manik	12	7/16	Cauac	12	9/6	Chuen	12
5/26		Lamat	13	7/17	Ahau	13	9/7	Eb	13

SAMPLE			BIRTHDAY	SOLAR GLYPH	TONE	BIRTHDAY		SOLAR GLYPH	TONE
			9/7	Caban	1	2/11	10/29	Muluc	1
BIRTHDAY	SOLAR GLYPH	TONE	9/8	Etznab	2	2/12	10/30	Oc	2
			9/9	Cauac	3	2/13	10/31	Chuen	3
ALWAYS READ CHART FROM			9/10	Ahau	4	2/14	11/1	Eb	4
LEFT TO RIGHT			9/11	Imix	5	2/15	11/2	Ben	5
STARTING WITH BIRTHDAY			9/12	Ik	6	2/16	11/3	Ix	6
			9/13	Akbal	7	2/17	11/4	Men	7
DOUBLE LINES			9/14	Kan	8	2/18	11/5	Cib	8
SEPARATE SECTIONS			9/15	Chiccan	9	2/19	11/6	Caban	9
			9/16	Cimi	10	2/20	11/7	Etznab	10
USE SPACE BELOW			9/17	Manik	11	2/21	11/8	Cauac	11
FOR RECORDING BIRTHDAYS			9/18	Lamat	12	2/22	11/9	Ahau	12
			1/1	9/19	Muluc	13	2/23	11/10	Imix	13
			1/2	9/20	Oc	1	2/24	11/11	Ik	1
			1/3	9/21	Chuen	2	2/25	11/12	Akbal	2
			1/4	9/22	Eb	3	2/26	11/13	Kan	3
			1/5	9/23	Ben	4	2/27	11/14	Chiccan	4
			1/6	9/24	Ix	5	2/28	11/15	Cimi	5
			1/7	9/25	Men	6	3/1	11/16	Manik	6
			1/8	9/26	Cib	7	3/2	11/17	Lamat	7
			1/9	9/27	Caban	8	3/3	11/18	Muluc	8
			1/10	9/28	Etznab	9	3/4	11/19	Oc	9
			1/11	9/29	Cauac	10	3/5	11/20	Chuen	10
			1/12	9/30	Ahau	11	3/6	11/21	Eb	11
			1/13	10/1	Imix	12	3/7	11/22	Ben	12
			1/14	10/2	Ik	13	3/8	11/23	Ix	13
			1/15	10/3	Akbal	1	3/9	11/24	Men	1
			1/16	10/4	Kan	2	3/10	11/25	Cib	2
			1/17	10/5	Chicchan	3	3/11	11/26	Caban	3
			1/18	10/6	Cimi	4	3/12	11/27	Etznab	4
			1/19	10/7	Manik	5	3/13	11/28	Cauac	5
			1/20	10/8	Lamat	6	3/14	11/29	Ahau	6
			1/21	10/9	Muluc	7	3/15	11/30	Imix	7
			1/22	10/10	Oc	8	3/16	12/1	Ik	8
			1/23	10/11	Chuen	9	3/17	12/2	Akbal	9
			1/24	10/12	Eb	10	3/18	12/3	Kan	10
			1/25	10/13	Ben	11	3/19	12/4	Chicchan	11
			1/26	10/14	Ix	12	3/20	12/5	Cimi	12
			1/27	10/15	Men	13	3/21	12/6	Manik	13
			1/28	10/16	Cib	1	3/22	12/7	Lamat	1
			1/29	10/17	Caban	2	3/23	12/8	Muluc	2
			1/30	10/18	Etznab	3	3/24	12/9	Oc	3
			1/31	10/19	Cauac	4	3/25	12/10	Chuen	4
			2/1	10/20	Ahau	5	3/26	12/11	Eb	5
			2/2	10/21	Imix	6	3/27	12/12	Ben	6
			2/3	10/22	Ik	7	3/28	12/13	Ix	7
			2/4	10/23	Akbal	8	3/29	12/14	Men	8
			2/5	10/24	Kan	9	3/30	12/15	Cib	9
			2/6	10/25	Chicchan	10	3/31	12/16	Caban	10
			2/7	10/26	Cimi	11	4/1	12/17	Etznab	11
			2/8	10/27	Manik	12	4/2	12/18	Cauac	12
			2/9	10/28	Lamat	13	4/3	12/19	Ahau	13
			2/10							

BIRTHDAY		SOLAR GLYPH	TONE	BIRTHDAY	SOLAR GLYPH	TONE	BIRTHDAY	SOLAR GLYPH	TONE
4/4	12/20	Imix	1	5/26	Ben	1	7/17	Chicchan	1
4/5	12/21	Ik	2	5/27	Ix	2	7/18	Cimi	2
4/6	12/22	Akbal	3	5/28	Men	3	7/19	Manik	3
4/7	12/23	Kan	4	5/29	Cib	4	7/20	Lamat	4
4/8	12/24	Chicchan	5	5/30	Caban	5	7/21	Muluc	5
4/9	12/25	Cimi	6	5/31	Etznab	6	7/22	Oc	6
4/10	12/26	Manik	7	6/1	Cauac	7	7/23	Chuen	7
4/11	12/27	Lamat	8	6/2	Ahau	8	7/24	Eb	8
4/12	12/28	Muluc	9	6/3	Imix	9	7/25	Ben	9
4/13	12/29	Oc	10	6/4	Ik	10	7/26	Ix	10
4/14	12/30	Chuen	11	6/5	Akbal	11	7/27	Men	11
4/15	12/31	Eb	12	6/6	Kan	12	7/28	Cib	12
4/16		Ben	13	6/7	Chicchan	13	7/29	Caban	13
4/17		Ix	1	6/8	Cimi	1	7/30	Etznab	1
4/18		Men	2	6/9	Manik	2	7/31	Cauac	2
4/19		Cib	3	6/10	Lamat	3	8/1	Ahau	3
4/20		Caban	4	6/11	Muluc	4	8/2	Imix	4
4/21		Etznab	5	6/12	Oc	5	8/3	Ik	5
4/22		Cauac	6	6/13	Chuen	6	8/4	Akbal	6
4/23		Ahau	7	6/14	Eb	7	8/5	Kan	7
4/24		Imix	8	6/15	Ben	8	8/6	Chicchan	8
4/25		Ik	9	6/16	Ix	9	8/7	Cimi	9
4/26		Akbal	10	6/17	Men	10	8/8	Manik	10
4/27		Kan	11	6/18	Cib	11	8/9	Lamat	11
4/28		Chicchan	12	6/19	Caban	12	8/10	Muluc	12
4/29		Cimi	13	6/20	Etznab	13	8/11	Oc	13
4/30		Manik	1	6/21	Cauac	1	8/12	Chuen	1
5/1		Lamat	2	6/22	Ahau	2	8/13	Eb	2
5/2		Muluc	3	6/23	Imix	3	8/14	Ben	3
5/3		Oc	4	6/24	Ik	4	8/15	Ix	4
5/4		Chuen	5	6/25	Akbal	5	8/16	Men	5
5/5		Eb	6	6/26	Kan	6	8/17	Cib	6
5/6		Ben	7	6/27	Chicchan	7	8/18	Caban	7
5/7		Ix	8	6/28	Cimi	8	8/19	Etznab	8
5/8		Men	9	6/29	Manik	9	8/20	Cauac	9
5/9		Cib	10	6/30	Lamat	10	8/21	Ahau	10
5/10		Caban	11	7/1	Muluc	11	8/22	Imix	11
5/11		Etznab	12	7/2	Oc	12	8/23	Ik	12
5/12		Cauac	13	7/3	Chuen	13	8/24	Akbal	13
5/13		Ahau	1	7/4	Eb	1	8/25	Kan	1
5/14		Imix	2	7/5	Ben	2	8/26	Chicchan	2
5/15		Ik	3	7/6	Ix	3	8/27	Cimi	3
5/16		Akbal	4	7/7	Men	4	8/28	Manik	4
5/17		Kan	5	7/8	Cib	5	8/29	Lamat	5
5/18		Chicchan	6	7/9	Caban	6	8/30	Muluc	6
5/19		Cimi	7	7/10	Etznab	7	8/31	Oc	7
5/20		Manik	8	7/11	Cauac	8	9/1	Chuen	8
5/21		Lamat	9	7/12	Ahau	9	9/2	Eb	9
5/22		Muluc	10	7/13	Imix	10	9/3	Ben	10
5/23		Oc	11	7/14	Ik	11	9/4	Ix	11
5/24		Chuen	12	7/15	Akbal	12	9/5	Men	12
5/25		Eb	13	7/16	Kan	13	9/6	Cib	13

SAMPLE			BIRTHDAY	SOLAR GLYPH	TONE	BIRTHDAY		SOLAR GLYPH	TONE
			9/6	Imix	1	2/10	10/28	Ben	1
BIRTHDAY	SOLAR GLYPH	TONE	9/7	Ik	2	2/11	10/29	Ix	2
			9/8	Akbal	3	2/12	10/30	Men	3
ALWAYS READ CHART FROM			9/9	Kan	4	2/13	10/31	Cib	4
LEFT TO RIGHT			9/10	Chicchan	5	2/14	11/1	Caban	5
STARTING WITH BIRTHDAY			9/11	Cimi	6	2/15	11/2	Etznab	6
			9/12	Manik	7	2/16	11/3	Cauac	7
DOUBLE LINES			9/13	Lamat	8	2/17	11/4	Ahau	8
SEPARATE SECTIONS			9/14	Muluc	9	2/18	11/5	Imix	9
			9/15	Oc	10	2/19	11/6	Ik	10
USE SPACE BELOW			9/16	Chuen	11	2/20	11/7	Akbal	11
FOR RECORDING BIRTHDAYS			9/17	Eb	12	2/21	11/8	Kan	12
			1/1	9/18	Ben	13	2/22	11/9	Chicchan	13
			1/2	9/19	Ix	1	2/23	11/10	Cimi	1
			1/3	9/20	Men	2	2/24	11/11	Manik	2
			1/4	9/21	Cib	3	2/25	11/12	Lamat	3
			1/5	9/22	Caban	4	2/26	11/13	Muluc	4
			1/6	9/23	Etznab	5	2/27	11/14	Oc	5
			1/7	9/24	Cauac	6	2/28	11/15	Chuen	6
			1/8	9/25	Ahau	7	3/1	11/16	Eb	7
			1/9	9/26	Imix	8	3/2	11/17	Ben	8
			1/10	9/27	Ik	9	3/3	11/18	Ix	9
			1/11	9/28	Akbal	10	3/4	11/19	Men	10
			1/12	9/29	Kan	11	3/5	11/20	Cib	11
			1/13	9/30	Chicchan	12	3/6	11/21	Caban	12
			1/14	10/1	Cimi	13	3/7	11/22	Etznab	13
			1/15	10/2	Manik	1	3/8	11/23	Cauac	1
			1/16	10/3	Lamat	2	3/9	11/24	Ahau	2
			1/17	10/4	Muluc	3	3/10	11/25	Imix	3
			1/18	10/5	Oc	4	3/11	11/26	Ik	4
			1/19	10/6	Chuen	5	3/12	11/27	Akbal	5
			1/20	10/7	Eb	6	3/13	11/28	Kan	6
			1/21	10/8	Ben	7	3/14	11/29	Chicchan	7
			1/22	10/9	Ix	8	3/15	11/30	Cimi	8
			1/23	10/10	Men	9	3/16	12/1	Manik	9
			1/24	10/11	Cib	10	3/17	12/2	Lamat	10
			1/25	10/12	Caban	11	3/18	12/3	Muluc	11
			1/26	10/13	Etznab	12	3/19	12/4	Oc	12
			1/27	10/14	Cauac	13	3/20	12/5	Chuen	13
			1/28	10/15	Ahau	1	3/21	12/6	Eb	1
			1/29	10/16	Imix	2	3/22	12/7	Ben	2
			1/30	10/17	Ik	3	3/23	12/8	Ix	3
			1/31	10/18	Akbal	4	3/24	12/9	Men	4
			2/1	10/19	Kan	5	3/25	12/10	Cib	5
			2/2	10/20	Chicchan	6	3/26	12/11	Caban	6
			2/3	10/21	Cimi	7	3/27	12/12	Etznab	7
			2/4	10/22	Manik	8	3/28	12/13	Cauac	8
			2/5	10/23	Lamat	9	3/29	12/14	Ahau	9
			2/6	10/24	Muluc	10	3/30	12/15	Imix	10
			2/7	10/25	Oc	11	3/31	12/16	Ik	11
			2/8	10/26	Chuen	12	4/1	12/17	Akbal	12
			2/9	10/27	Eb	13	4/2	12/18	Kan	13

BIRTHDAY		SOLAR GLYPH	TONE	BIRTHDAY	SOLAR GLYPH	TONE	BIRTHDAY	SOLAR GLYPH	TONE
4/3	12/19	Chicchan	1	5/25	Caban	1	7/16	Muluc	1
4/4	12/20	Cimi	2	5/26	Etznab	2	7/17	Oc	2
4/5	12/21	Manik	3	5/27	Cauac	3	7/18	Chuen	3
4/6	12/22	Lamat	4	5/28	Ahau	4	7/19	Eb	4
4/7	12/23	Muluc	5	5/29	Imix	5	7/20	Ben	5
4/8	12/24	Oc	6	5/30	Ik	6	7/21	Ix	6
4/9	12/25	Chuen	7	5/31	Akbal	7	7/22	Men	7
4/10	12/26	Eb	8	6/1	Kan	8	7/23	Cib	8
4/11	12/27	Ben	9	6/2	Chiccan	9	7/24	Caban	9
4/12	12/28	Ix	10	6/3	Cimi	10	7/25	Etznab	10
4/13	12/29	Men	11	6/4	Manik	11	7/26	Cauac	11
4/14	12/30	Cib	12	6/5	Lamat	12	7/27	Ahau	12
4/15	12/31	Caban	13	6/6	Muluc	13	7/28	Imix	13
4/16		Etznab	1	6/7	Oc	1	7/29	Ik	1
4/17		Cauac	2	6/8	Chuen	2	7/30	Akbal	2
4/18		Ahau	3	6/9	Eb	3	7/31	Kan	3
4/19		Imix	4	6/10	Ben	4	8/1	Chicchan	4
4/20		Ik	5	6/11	Ix	5	8/2	Cimi	5
4/21		Akbal	6	6/12	Men	6	8/3	Manik	6
4/22		Kan	7	6/13	Cib	7	8/4	Lamat	7
4/23		Chicchan	8	6/14	Caban	8	8/5	Muluc	8
4/24		Cimi	9	6/15	Etznab	9	8/6	Oc	9
4/25		Manik	10	6/16	Cauac	10	8/7	Chuen	10
4/26		Lamat	11	6/17	Ahau	11	8/8	Eb	11
4/27		Muluc	12	6/18	Imix	12	8/9	Ben	12
4/28		Oc	13	6/19	Ik	13	8/10	Ix	13
4/29		Chuen	1	6/20	Akbal	1	8/11	Men	1
4/30		Eb	2	6/21	Kan	2	8/12	Cib	2
5/1		Ben	3	6/22	Chicchan	3	8/13	Caban	3
5/2		Ix	4	6/23	Cimi	4	8/14	Etznab	4
5/3		Men	5	6/24	Manik	5	8/15	Cauac	5
5/4		Cib	6	6/25	Lamat	6	8/16	Ahau	6
5/5		Caban	7	6/26	Muluc	7	8/17	Imix	7
5/6		Etznab	8	6/27	Oc	8	8/18	Ik	8
5/7		Cauac	9	6/28	Chuen	9	8/19	Akbal	9
5/8		Ahau	10	6/29	Eb	10	8/20	Kan	10
5/9		Imix	11	6/30	Ben	11	8/21	Chicchan	11
5/10		Ik	12	7/1	Ix	12	8/22	Cimi	12
5/11		Akbal	13	7/2	Men	13	8/23	Manik	13
5/12		Kan	1	7/3	Cib	1	8/24	Lamat	1
5/13		Chicchan	2	7/4	Caban	2	8/25	Muluc	2
5/14		Cimi	3	7/5	Etznab	3	8/26	Oc	3
5/15		Manik	4	7/6	Cauac	4	8/27	Chuen	4
5/16		Lamat	5	7/7	Ahau	5	8/28	Eb	5
5/17		Muluc	6	7/8	Imix	6	8/29	Ben	6
5/18		Oc	7	7/9	Ik	7	8/30	Ix	7
5/19		Chuen	8	7/10	Akbal	8	8/31	Men	8
5/20		Eb	9	7/11	Kan	9	9/1	Cib	9
5/21		Ben	10	7/12	Chicchan	10	9/2	Caban	10
5/22		Ix	11	7/13	Cimi	11	9/3	Etznab	11
5/23		Men	12	7/14	Manik	12	9/4	Cauac	12
5/24		Cib	13	7/15	Lamat	13	9/5	Ahau	13

SAMPLE			BIRTHDAY	SOLAR GLYPH	TONE	BIRTHDAY		SOLAR GLYPH	TONE
			9/5	Chicchan	1	2/9	10/27	Caban	1
BIRTHDAY	SOLAR GLYPH	TONE	9/6	Cimi	2	2/10	10/28	Etznab	2
			9/7	Manik	3	2/11	10/29	Cauac	3
ALWAYS READ CHART FROM			9/8	Lamat	4	2/12	10/30	Ahau	4
LEFT TO RIGHT			9/9	Muluc	5	2/13	10/31	Imix	5
STARTING WITH BIRTHDAY			9/10	Oc	6	2/14	11/1	Ik	6
			9/11	Chuen	7	2/15	11/2	Akbal	7
DOUBLE LINES			9/12	Eb	8	2/16	11/3	Kan	8
SEPARATE SECTIONS			9/13	Ben	9	2/17	11/4	Chiccan	9
			9/14	Ix	10	2/18	11/5	Cimi	10
USE SPACE BELOW			9/15	Men	11	2/19	11/6	Manik	11
FOR RECORDING BIRTHDAYS			9/16	Cib	12	2/20	11/7	Lamat	12
			9/17	Caban	13	2/21	11/8	Muluc	13
		1/1	9/18	Etznab	1	2/22	11/9	Oc	1
		1/2	9/19	Cauac	2	2/23	11/10	Chuen	2
		1/3	9/20	Ahau	3	2/24	11/11	Eb	3
		1/4	9/21	Imix	4	2/25	11/12	Ben	4
		1/5	9/22	Ik	5	2/26	11/13	Ix	5
		1/6	9/23	Akbal	6	2/27	11/14	Men	6
		1/7	9/24	Kan	7	2/28	11/15	Cib	7
		1/8	9/25	Chicchan	8	3/1	11/16	Caban	8
		1/9	9/26	Cimi	9	3/2	11/17	Etznab	9
		1/10	9/27	Manik	10	3/3	11/18	Cauac	10
		1/11	9/28	Lamat	11	3/4	11/19	Ahau	11
		1/12	9/29	Muluc	12	3/5	11/20	Imix	12
		1/13	9/30	Oc	13	3/6	11/21	Ik	13
		1/14	10/1	Chuen	1	3/7	11/22	Akbal	1
		1/15	10/2	Eb	2	3/8	11/23	Kan	2
		1/16	10/3	Ben	3	3/9	11/24	Chicchan	3
		1/17	10/4	Ix	4	3/10	11/25	Cimi	4
		1/18	10/5	Men	5	3/11	11/26	Manik	5
		1/19	10/6	Cib	6	3/12	11/27	Lamat	6
		1/20	10/7	Caban	7	3/13	11/28	Muluc	7
		1/21	10/8	Etznab	8	3/14	11/29	Oc	8
		1/22	10/9	Cauac	9	3/15	11/30	Chuen	9
		1/23	10/10	Ahau	10	3/16	12/1	Eb	10
		1/24	10/11	Imix	11	3/17	12/2	Ben	11
		1/25	10/12	Ik	12	3/18	12/3	Ix	12
		1/26	10/13	Akbal	13	3/19	12/4	Men	13
		1/27	10/14	Kan	1	3/20	12/5	Cib	1
		1/28	10/15	Chicchan	2	3/21	12/6	Caban	2
		1/29	10/16	Cimi	3	3/22	12/7	Etznab	3
		1/30	10/17	Manik	4	3/23	12/8	Cauac	4
		1/31	10/18	Lamat	5	3/24	12/9	Ahau	5
		2/1	10/19	Muluc	6	3/25	12/10	Imix	6
		2/2	10/20	Oc	7	3/26	12/11	Ik	7
		2/3	10/21	Chuen	8	3/27	12/12	Akbal	8
		2/4	10/22	Eb	9	3/28	12/13	Kan	9
		2/5	10/23	Ben	10	3/29	12/14	Chicchan	10
		2/6	10/24	Ix	11	3/30	12/15	Cimi	11
		2/7	10/25	Men	12	3/31	12/16	Manik	12
		2/8	10/26	Cib	13	4/1	12/17	Lamat	13

BIRTHDAY		SOLAR GLYPH	TONE	BIRTHDAY	SOLAR GLYPH	TONE	BIRTHDAY	SOLAR GLYPH	TONE
4/2	12/18	Muluc	1	5/24	Imix	1	7/15	Ben	1
4/3	12/19	Oc	2	5/25	Ik	2	7/16	Ix	2
4/4	12/20	Chuen	3	5/26	Akbal	3	7/17	Men	3
4/5	12/21	Eb	4	5/27	Kan	4	7/18	Cib	4
4/6	12/22	Ben	5	5/28	Chicchan	5	7/19	Caban	5
4/7	12/23	Ix	6	5/29	Cimi	6	7/20	Etznab	6
4/8	12/24	Men	7	5/30	Manik	7	7/21	Cauac	7
4/9	12/25	Cib	8	5/31	Lamat	8	7/22	Ahau	8
4/10	12/26	Caban	9	6/1	Muluc	9	7/23	Imix	9
4/11	12/27	Etznab	10	6/2	Oc	10	7/24	Ik	10
4/12	12/28	Cauac	11	6/3	Chuen	11	7/25	Akbal	11
4/13	12/29	Ahau	12	6/4	Eb	12	7/26	Kan	12
4/14	12/30	Imix	13	6/5	Ben	13	7/27	Chicchan	13
4/15	12/31	Ik	1	6/6	Ix	1	7/28	Cimi	1
4/16		Akbal	2	6/7	Men	2	7/29	Manik	2
4/17		Kan	3	6/8	Cib	3	7/30	Lamat	3
4/18		Chicchan	4	6/9	Caban	4	7/31	Muluc	4
4/19		Cimi	5	6/10	Etznab	5	8/1	Oc	5
4/20		Manik	6	6/11	Cauac	6	8/2	Chuen	6
4/21		Lamat	7	6/12	Ahau	7	8/3	Eb	7
4/22		Muluc	8	6/13	Imix	8	8/4	Ben	8
4/23		Oc	9	6/14	Ik	9	8/5	Ix	9
4/24		Chuen	10	6/15	Akbal	10	8/6	Men	10
4/25		Eb	11	6/16	Kan	11	8/7	Cib	11
4/26		Ben	12	6/17	Chicchan	12	8/8	Caban	12
4/27		Ix	13	.6/18	Cimi	13	8/9	Etznab	13
4/28		Men	1	6/19	Manik	1	8/10	Cauac	1
4/29		Cib	2	6/20	Lamat	2	8/11	Ahau	2
4/30		Caban	3	6/21	Muluc	3	8/12	Imix	3
5/1		Etznab	4	6/22	Oc	4	8/13	Ik	4
5/2		Cauac	5	6/23	Chuen	5	8/14	Akbal	5
5/3		Ahau	6	6/24	Eb	6	8/15	Kan	6
5/4		Imix	7	6/25	Ben	7	8/16	Chicchan	7
5/5		Ik	8	6/26	Ix	8	8/17	Cimi	8
5/6		Akbal	9	6/27	Men	9	8/18	Manik	9
5/7		Kan	10	6/28	Cib	10	8/19	Lamat	10
5/8		Chicchan	11	6/29	Caban	11	8/20	Muluc	11
5/9		Cimi	12	6/30	Etznab	12	8/21	Oc	12
5/10		Manik	13	7/1	Cauac	13	8/22	Chuen	13
5/11		Lamat	1	7/2	Ahau	1	8/23	Eb	1
5/12		Muluc	2	7/3	Imix	2	8/24	Ben	2
5/13		Oc	3	7/4	Ik	3	8/25	Ix	3
5/14		Chuen	4	7/5	Akbal	4	8/26	Men	4
5/15		Eb	5	7/6	Kan	5	8/27	Cib	5
5/16		Ben	6	7/7	Chicchan	6	8/28	Caban	6
5/17		Ix	7	7/8	Cimi	7	8/29	Etznab	7
5/18		Men	8	7/9	Manik	8	8/30	Cauac	8
5/19		Cib	9	7/10	Lamat	9	8/31	Ahau	9
5/20		Caban	10	7/11	Muluc	10	9/1	Imix	10
5/21		Etznab	11	7/12	Oc	11	9/2	Ik	11
5/22		Cauac	12	7/13	Chuen	12	9/3	Akbal	12
5/23		Ahau	13	7/14	Eb	13	9/4	Kan	13

SAMPLE

BIRTHDAY	SOLAR GLYPH	TONE

ALWAYS READ CHART FROM
LEFT TO RIGHT
STARTING WITH BIRTHDAY

DOUBLE LINES
SEPARATE SECTIONS

USE SPACE BELOW
FOR RECORDING BIRTHDAYS

BIRTHDAY	BIRTHDAY	SOLAR GLYPH	TONE	BIRTHDAY	BIRTHDAY	SOLAR GLYPH	TONE
	9/4	Muluc	1	2/8	10/26	Imix	1
	9/5	Oc	2	2/9	10/27	Ik	2
	9/6	Chuen	3	2/10	10/28	Akbal	3
	9/7	Eb	4	2/11	10/29	Kan	4
	9/8	Ben	5	2/12	10/30	Chicchan	5
	9/9	Ix	6	2/13	10/31	Cimi	6
	9/10	Men	7	2/14	11/1	Manik	7
	9/11	Cib	8	2/15	11/2	Lamat	8
	9/12	Caban	9	2/16	11/3	Muluc	9
	9/13	Etznab	10	2/17	11/4	Oc	10
	9/14	Cauac	11	2/18	11/5	Chuen	11
	9/15	Ahau	12	2/19	11/6	Eb	12
	9/16	Imix	13	2/20	11/7	Ben	13
	9/17	Ik	1	2/21	11/8	Ix	1
1/1	9/18	Akbal	2	2/22	11/9	Men	2
1/2	9/19	Kan	3	2/23	11/10	Cib	3
1/3	9/20	Chicchan	4	2/24	11/11	Caban	4
1/4	9/21	Cimi	5	2/25	11/12	Etznab	5
1/5	9/22	Manik	6	2/26	11/13	Cauac	6
1/6	9/23	Lamat	7	2/27	11/14	Ahau	7
1/7	9/24	Muluc	8	2/28	11/15	Imix	8
1/8	9/25	Oc	9	3/1	11/16	Ik	9
1/9	9/26	Chuen	10	3/2	11/17	Akbal	10
1/10	9/27	Eb	11	3/3	11/18	Kan	11
1/11	9/28	Ben	12	3/4	11/19	Chicchan	12
1/12	9/29	Ix	13	3/5	11/20	Cimi	13
1/13	9/30	Men	1	3/6	11/21	Manik	1
1/14	10/1	Cib	2	3/7	11/22	Lamat	2
1/15	10/2	Caban	3	3/8	11/23	Muluc	3
1/16	10/3	Etznab	4	3/9	11/24	Oc	4
1/17	10/4	Cauac	5	3/10	11/25	Chuen	5
1/18	10/5	Ahau	6	3/11	11/26	Eb	6
1/19	10/6	Imix	7	3/12	11/27	Ben	7
1/20	10/7	Ik	8	3/13	11/28	Ix	8
1/21	10/8	Akbal	9	3/14	11/29	Men	9
1/22	10/9	Kan	10	3/15	11/30	Cib	10
1/23	10/10	Chicchan	11	3/16	12/1	Caban	11
1/24	10/11	Cimi	12	3/17	12/2	Etznab	12
1/25	10/12	Manik	13	3/18	12/3	Cauac	13
1/26	10/13	Lamat	1	3/19	12/4	Ahau	1
1/27	10/14	Muluc	2	3/20	12/5	Imix	2
1/28	10/15	Oc	3	3/21	12/6	Ik	3
1/29	10/16	Chuen	4	3/22	12/7	Akbal	4
1/30	10/17	Eb	5	3/23	12/8	Kan	5
1/31	10/18	Ben	6	3/24	12/9	Chicchan	6
2/1	10/19	Ix	7	3/25	12/10	Cimi	7
2/2	10/20	Men	8	3/26	12/11	Manik	8
2/3	10/21	Cib	9	3/27	12/12	Lamat	9
2/4	10/22	Caban	10	3/28	12/13	Muluc	10
2/5	10/23	Etznab	11	3/29	12/14	Oc	11
2/6	10/24	Cauac	12	3/30	12/15	Chuen	12
2/7	10/25	Ahau	13	3/31	12/16	Eb	13

BIRTHDAY		SOLAR GLYPH	TONE	BIRTHDAY	SOLAR GLYPH	TONE	BIRTHDAY	SOLAR GLYPH	TONE
4/1	12/17	Ben	1	5/23	Chicchan	1	7/14	Caban	1
4/2	12/18	Ix	2	5/24	Cimi	2	7/15	Etznab	2
4/3	12/19	Men	3	5/25	Manik	3	7/16	Cauac	3
4/4	12/20	Cib	4	5/26	Lamat	4	7/17	Ahau	4
4/5	12/21	Caban	5	5/27	Muluc	5	7/18	Imix	5
4/6	12/22	Etznab	6	5/28	Oc	6	7/19	Ik	6
4/7	12/23	Cauac	7	5/29	Chuen	7	7/20	Akbal	7
4/8	12/24	Ahau	8	5/30	Eb	8	7/21	Kan	8
4/9	12/25	Imix	9	5/31	Ben	9	7/22	Chiccan	9
4/10	12/26	Ik	10	6/1	Ix	10	7/23	Cimi	10
4/11	12/27	Akbal	11	6/2	Men	11	7/24	Manik	11
4/12	12/28	Kan	12	6/3	Cib	12	7/25	Lamat	12
4/13	12/29	Chicchan	13	6/4	Caban	13	7/26	Muluc	13
4/14	12/30	Cimi	1	6/5	Etznab	1	7/27	Oc	1
4/15	12/31	Manik	2	6/6	Cauac	2	7/28	Chuen	2
4/16		Lamat	3	6/7	Ahau	3	7/29	Eb	3
4/17		Muluc	4	6/8	Imix	4	7/30	Ben	4
4/18		Oc	5	6/9	Ik	5	7/31	Ix	5
4/19		Chuen	6	6/10	Akbal	6	8/1	Men	6
4/20		Eb	7	6/11	Kan	7	8/2	Cib	7
4/21		Ben	8	6/12	Chicchan	8	8/3	Caban	8
4/22		Ix	9	6/13	Cimi	9	8/4	Etznab	9
4/23		Men	10	6/14	Manik	10	8/5	Cauac	10
4/24		Cib	11	6/15	Lamat	11	8/6	Ahau	11
4/25		Caban	12	6/16	Muluc	12	8/7	Imix	12
4/26		Etznab	13	6/17	Oc	13	8/8	Ik	13
4/27		Cauac	1	6/18	Chuen	1	8/9	Akbal	1
4/28		Ahau	2	6/19	Eb	2	8/10	Kan	2
4/29		Imix	3	6/20	Ben	3	8/11	Chicchan	3
4/30		Ik	4	6/21	Ix	4	8/12	Cimi	4
5/1		Akbal	5	6/22	Men	5	8/13	Manik	5
5/2		Kan	6	6/23	Cib	6	8/14	Lamat	6
5/3		Chicchan	7	6/24	Caban	7	8/15	Muluc	7
5/4		Cimi	8	6/25	Etznab	8	8/16	Oc	8
5/5		Manik	9	6/26	Cauac	9	8/17	Chuen	9
5/6		Lamat	10	6/27	Ahau	10	8/18	Eb	10
5/7		Muluc	11	6/28	Imix	11	8/19	Ben	11
5/8		Oc	12	6/29	Ik	12	8/20	Ix	12
5/9		Chuen	13	6/30	Akbal	13	8/21	Men	13
5/10		Eb	1	7/1	Kan	1	8/22	Cib	1
5/11		Ben	2	7/2	Chicchan	2	8/23	Caban	2
5/12		Ix	3	7/3	Cimi	3	8/24	Etznab	3
5/13		Men	4	7/4	Manik	4	8/25	Cauac	4
5/14		Cib	5	7/5	Lamat	5	8/26	Ahau	5
5/15		Caban	6	7/6	Muluc	6	8/27	Imix	6
5/16		Etznab	7	7/7	Oc	7	8/28	Ik	7
5/17		Cauac	8	7/8	Chuen	8	8/29	Akbal	8
5/18		Ahau	9	7/9	Eb	9	8/30	Kan	9
5/19		Imix	10	7/10	Ben	10	8/31	Chicchan	10
5/20		Ik	11	7/11	Ix	11	9/1	Cimi	11
5/21		Akbal	12	7/12	Men	12	9/2	Manik	12
5/22		Kan	13	7/13	Cib	13	9/3	Lamat	13

1915, 1967, 2019

SAMPLE			BIRTHDAY		SOLAR GLYPH	TONE	BIRTHDAY		SOLAR GLYPH	TONE
BIRTHDAY	SOLAR GLYPH	TONE		9/3	Ben	1	2/7	10/25	Chicchan	1
				9/4	Ix	2	2/8	10/26	Cimi	2
ALWAYS READ CHART FROM				9/5	Men	3	2/9	10/27	Manik	3
LEFT TO RIGHT				9/6	Cib	4	2/10	10/28	Lamat	4
STARTING WITH BIRTHDAY				9/7	Caban	5	2/11	10/29	Muluc	5
				9/8	Etznab	6	2/12	10/30	Oc	6
				9/9	Cauac	7	2/13	10/31	Chuen	7
DOUBLE LINES				9/10	Ahau	8	2/14	11/1	Eb	8
SEPARATE SECTIONS				9/11	Imix	9	2/15	11/2	Ben	9
				9/12	Ik	10	2/16	11/3	Ix	10
USE SPACE BELOW				9/13	Akbal	11	2/17	11/4	Men	11
FOR RECORDING BIRTHDAYS				9/14	Kan	12	2/18	11/5	Cib	12
				9/15	Chicchan	13	2/19	11/6	Caban	13
				9/16	Cimi	1	2/20	11/7	Etznab	1
				9/17	Manik	2	2/21	11/8	Cauac	2
			1/1	9/18	Lamat	3	2/22	11/9	Ahau	3
			1/2	9/19	Muluc	4	2/23	11/10	Imix	4
			1/3	9/20	Oc	5	2/24	11/11	Ik	5
			1/4	9/21	Chuen	6	2/25	11/12	Akbal	6
			1/5	9/22	Eb	7	2/26	11/13	Kan	7
			1/6	9/23	Ben	8	2/27	11/14	Chicchan	8
			1/7	9/24	Ix	9	2/28	11/15	Cimi	9
			1/8	9/25	Men	10	3/1	11/16	Manik	10
			1/9	9/26	Cib	11	3/2	11/17	Lamat	11
			1/10	9/27	Caban	12	3/3	11/18	Muluc	12
			1/11	9/28	Etznab	13	3/4	11/19	Oc	13
			1/12	9/29	Cauac	1	3/5	11/20	Chuen	1
			1/13	9/30	Ahau	2	3/6	11/21	Eb	2
			1/14	10/1	Imix	3	3/7	11/22	Ben	3
			1/15	10/2	Ik	4	3/8	11/23	Ix	4
			1/16	10/3	Akbal	5	3/9	11/24	Men	5
			1/17	10/4	Kan	6	3/10	11/25	Cib	6
			1/18	10/5	Chicchan	7	3/11	11/26	Caban	7
			1/19	10/6	Cimi	8	3/12	11/27	Etznab	8
			1/20	10/7	Manik	9	3/13	11/28	Cauac	9
			1/21	10/8	Lamat	10	3/14	11/29	Ahau	10
			1/22	10/9	Muluc	11	3/15	11/30	Imix	11
			1/23	10/10	Oc	12	3/16	12/1	Ik	12
			1/24	10/11	Chuen	13	3/17	12/2	Akbal	13
			1/25	10/12	Eb	1	3/18	12/3	Kan	1
			1/26	10/13	Ben	2	3/19	12/4	Chicchan	2
			1/27	10/14	Ix	3	3/20	12/5	Cimi	3
			1/28	10/15	Men	4	3/21	12/6	Manik	4
			1/29	10/16	Cib	5	3/22	12/7	Lamat	5
			1/30	10/17	Caban	6	3/23	12/8	Muluc	6
			1/31	10/18	Etznab	7	3/24	12/9	Oc	7
			2/1	10/19	Cauac	8	3/25	12/10	Chuen	8
			2/2	10/20	Ahau	9	3/26	12/11	Eb	9
			2/3	10/21	Imix	10	3/27	12/12	Ben	10
			2/4	10/22	Ik	11	3/28	12/13	Ix	11
			2/5	10/23	Akbal	12	3/29	12/14	Men	12
			2/6	10/24	Kan	13	3/30	12/15	Cib	13

BIRTHDAY		SOLAR GLYPH	TONE
3/31	12/16	Caban	1
4/1	12/17	Etznab	2
4/2	12/18	Cauac	3
4/3	12/19	Ahau	4
4/4	12/20	Imix	5
4/5	12/21	Ik	6
4/6	12/22	Akbal	7
4/7	12/23	Kan	8
4/8	12/24	Chiccan	9
4/9	12/25	Cimi	10
4/10	12/26	Manik	11
4/11	12/27	Lamat	12
4/12	12/28	Muluc	13
4/13	12/29	Oc	1
4/14	12/30	Chuen	2
4/15	12/31	Eb	3
4/16		Ben	4
4/17		Ix	5
4/18		Men	6
4/19		Cib	7
4/20		Caban	8
4/21		Etznab	9
4/22		Cauac	10
4/23		Ahau	11
4/24		Imix	12
4/25		Ik	13
4/26		Akbal	1
4/27		Kan	2
4/28		Chicchan	3
4/29		Cimi	4
4/30		Manik	5
5/1		Lamat	6
5/2		Muluc	7
5/3		Oc	8
5/4		Chuen	9
5/5		Eb	10
5/6		Ben	11
5/7		Ix	12
5/8		Men	13
5/9		Cib	1
5/10		Caban	2
5/11		Etznab	3
5/12		Cauac	4
5/13		Ahau	5
5/14		Imix	6
5/15		Ik	7
5/16		Akbal	8
5/17		Kan	9
5/18		Chicchan	10
5/19		Cimi	11
5/20		Manik	12
5/21		Lamat	13

BIRTHDAY	SOLAR GLYPH	TONE
5/22	Muluc	1
5/23	Oc	2
5/24	Chuen	3
5/25	Eb	4
5/26	Ben	5
5/27	Ix	6
5/28	Men	7
5/29	Cib	8
5/30	Caban	9
5/31	Etznab	10
6/1	Cauac	11
6/2	Ahau	12
6/3	Imix	13
6/4	Ik	1
6/5	Akbal	2
6/6	Kan	3
6/7	Chicchan	4
6/8	Cimi	5
6/9	Manik	6
6/10	Lamat	7
6/11	Muluc	8
6/12	Oc	9
6/13	Chuen	10
6/14	Eb	11
6/15	Ben	12
6/16	Ix	13
6/17	Men	1
6/18	Cib	2
6/19	Caban	3
6/20	Etznab	4
6/21	Cauac	5
6/22	Ahau	6
6/23	Imix	7
6/24	Ik	8
6/25	Akbal	9
6/26	Kan	10
6/27	Chicchan	11
6/28	Cimi	12
6/29	Manik	13
6/30	Lamat	1
7/1	Muluc	2
7/2	Oc	3
7/3	Chuen	4
7/4	Eb	5
7/5	Ben	6
7/6	Ix	7
7/7	Men	8
7/8	Cib	9
7/9	Caban	10
7/10	Etznab	11
7/11	Cauac	12
7/12	Ahau	13

BIRTHDAY	SOLAR GLYPH	TONE
7/13	Imix	1
7/14	Ik	2
7/15	Akbal	3
7/16	Kan	4
7/17	Chicchan	5
7/18	Cimi	6
7/19	Manik	7
7/20	Lamat	8
7/21	Muluc	9
7/22	Oc	10
7/23	Chuen	11
7/24	Eb	12
7/25	Ben	13
7/26	Ix	1
7/27	Men	2
7/28	Cib	3
7/29	Caban	4
7/30	Etznab	5
7/31	Cauac	6
8/1	Ahau	7
8/2	Imix	8
8/3	Ik	9
8/4	Akbal	10
8/5	Kan	11
8/6	Chicchan	12
8/7	Cimi	13
8/8	Manik	1
8/9	Lamat	2
8/10	Muluc	3
8/11	Oc	4
8/12	Chuen	5
8/13	Eb	6
8/14	Ben	7
8/15	Ix	8
8/16	Men	9
8/17	Cib	10
8/18	Caban	11
8/19	Etznab	12
8/20	Cauac	13
8/21	Ahau	1
8/22	Imix	2
8/23	Ik	3
8/24	Akbal	4
8/25	Kan	5
8/26	Chicchan	6
8/27	Cimi	7
8/28	Manik	8
8/29	Lamat	9
8/30	Muluc	10
8/31	Oc	11
9/1	Chuen	12
9/2	Eb	13

1916, 1968, 2020

SAMPLE			BIRTHDAY	SOLAR GLYPH	TONE	BIRTHDAY		SOLAR GLYPH	TONE
BIRTHDAY	SOLAR GLYPH	TONE	9/2	Caban	1	2/6	10/24	Muluc	1
			9/3	Etznab	2	2/7	10/25	Oc	2
ALWAYS READ CHART FROM			9/4	Cauac	3	2/8	10/26	Chuen	3
LEFT TO RIGHT			9/5	Ahau	4	2/9	10/27	Eb	4
STARTING WITH BIRTHDAY			9/6	Imix	5	2/10	10/28	Ben	5
			9/7	Ik	6	2/11	10/29	Ix	6
			9/8	Akbal	7	2/12	10/30	Men	7
DOUBLE LINES			9/9	Kan	8	2/13	10/31	Cib	8
SEPARATE SECTIONS			9/10	Chiccan	9	2/14	11/1	Caban	9
			9/11	Cimi	10	2/15	11/2	Etznab	10
USE SPACE BELOW			9/12	Manik	11	2/16	11/3	Cauac	11
FOR RECORDING BIRTHDAYS			9/13	Lamat	12	2/17	11/4	Ahau	12
			9/14	Muluc	13	2/18	11/5	Imix	13
			9/15	Oc	1	2/19	11/6	Ik	1
			9/16	Chuen	2	2/20	11/7	Akbal	2
			9/17	Eb	3	2/21	11/8	Kan	3
		1/1	9/18	Ben	4	2/22	11/9	Chicchan	4
		1/2	9/19	Ix	5	2/23	11/10	Cimi	5
		1/3	9/20	Men	6	2/24	11/11	Manik	6
		1/4	9/21	Cib	7	2/25	11/12	Lamat	7
		1/5	9/22	Caban	8	2/26	11/13	Muluc	8
		1/6	9/23	Etznab	9	2/27	11/14	Oc	9
		1/7	9/24	Cauac	10	2/28	11/15	Chuen	10
		1/8	9/25	Ahau	11	3/1	11/16	Eb	11
		1/9	9/26	Imix	12	3/2	11/17	Ben	12
		1/10	9/27	Ik	13	3/3	11/18	Ix	13
		1/11	9/28	Akbal	1	3/4	11/19	Men	1
		1/12	9/29	Kan	2	3/5	11/20	Cib	2
		1/13	9/30	Chicchan	3	3/6	11/21	Caban	3
		1/14	10/1	Cimi	4	3/7	11/22	Etznab	4
		1/15	10/2	Manik	5	3/8	11/23	Cauac	5
		1/16	10/3	Lamat	6	3/9	11/24	Ahau	6
		1/17	10/4	Muluc	7	3/10	11/25	Imix	7
		1/18	10/5	Oc	8	3/11	11/26	Ik	8
		1/19	10/6	Chuen	9	3/12	11/27	Akbal	9
		1/20	10/7	Eb	10	3/13	11/28	Kan	10
		1/21	10/8	Ben	11	3/14	11/29	Chicchan	11
		1/22	10/9	Ix	12	3/15	11/30	Cimi	12
		1/23	10/10	Men	13	3/16	12/1	Manik	13
		1/24	10/11	Cib	1	3/17	12/2	Lamat	1
		1/25	10/12	Caban	2	3/18	12/3	Muluc	2
		1/26	10/13	Etznab	3	3/19	12/4	Oc	3
		1/27	10/14	Cauac	4	3/20	12/5	Chuen	4
		1/28	10/15	Ahau	5	3/21	12/6	Eb	5
		1/29	10/16	Imix	6	3/22	12/7	Ben	6
		1/30	10/17	Ik	7	3/23	12/8	Ix	7
		1/31	10/18	Akbal	8	3/24	12/9	Men	8
		2/1	10/19	Kan	9	3/25	12/10	Cib	9
		2/2	10/20	Chiccan	10	3/26	12/11	Caban	10
		2/3	10/21	Cimi	11	3/27	12/12	Etznab	11
		2/4	10/22	Manik	12	3/28	12/13	Cauac	12
		2/5	10/23	Lamat	13	3/29	12/14	Ahau	13

BIRTHDAY		SOLAR GLYPH	TONE	BIRTHDAY	SOLAR GLYPH	TONE	BIRTHDAY	SOLAR GLYPH	TONE
3/30	12/15	Imix	1	5/21	Ben	1	7/12	Chicchan	1
3/31	12/16	Ik	2	5/22	Ix	2	7/13	Cimi	2
4/1	12/17	Akbal	3	5/23	Men	3	7/14	Manik	3
4/2	12/18	Kan	4	5/24	Cib	4	7/15	Lamat	4
4/3	12/19	Chicchan	5	5/25	Caban	5	7/16	Muluc	5
4/4	12/20	Cimi	6	5/26	Etznab	6	7/17	Oc	6
4/5	12/21	Manik	7	5/27	Cauac	7	7/18	Chuen	7
4/6	12/22	Lamat	8	5/28	Ahau	8	7/19	Eb	8
4/7	12/23	Muluc	9	5/29	Imix	9	7/20	Ben	9
4/8	12/24	Oc	10	5/30	Ik	10	7/21	Ix	10
4/9	12/25	Chuen	11	5/31	Akbal	11	7/22	Men	11
4/10	12/26	Eb	12	6/1	Kan	12	7/23	Cib	12
4/11	12/27	Ben	13	6/2	Chicchan	13	7/24	Caban	13
4/12	12/28	Ix	1	6/3	Cimi	1	7/25	Etznab	1
4/13	12/29	Men	2	6/4	Manik	2	7/26	Cauac	2
4/14	12/30	Cib	3	6/5	Lamat	3	7/27	Ahau	3
4/15	12/31	Caban	4	6/6	Muluc	4	7/28	Imix	4
4/16		Etznab	5	6/7	Oc	5	7/29	Ik	5
4/17		Cauac	6	6/8	Chuen	6	7/30	Akbal	6
4/18		Ahau	7	6/9	Eb	7	7/31	Kan	7
4/19		Imix	8	6/10	Ben	8	8/1	Chicchan	8
4/20		Ik	9	6/11	Ix	9	8/2	Cimi	9
4/21		Akbal	10	6/12	Men	10	8/3	Manik	10
4/22		Kan	11	6/13	Cib	11	8/4	Lamat	11
4/23		Chicchan	12	6/14	Caban	12	8/5	Muluc	12
4/24		Cimi	13	6/15	Etznab	13	8/6	Oc	13
4/25		Manik	1	6/16	Cauac	1	8/7	Chuen	1
4/26		Lamat	2	6/17	Ahau	2	8/8	Eb	2
4/27		Muluc	3	6/18	Imix	3	8/9	Ben	3
4/28		Oc	4	6/19	Ik	4	8/10	Ix	4
4/29		Chuen	5	6/20	Akbal	5	8/11	Men	5
4/30		Eb	6	6/21	Kan	6	8/12	Cib	6
5/1		Ben	7	6/22	Chicchan	7	8/13	Caban	7
5/2		Ix	8	6/23	Cimi	8	8/14	Etznab	8
5/3		Men	9	6/24	Manik	9	8/15	Cauac	9
5/4		Cib	10	6/25	Lamat	10	8/16	Ahau	10
5/5		Caban	11	6/26	Muluc	11	8/17	Imix	11
5/6		Etznab	12	6/27	Oc	12	8/18	Ik	12
5/7		Cauac	13	6/28	Chuen	13	8/19	Akbal	13
5/8		Ahau	1	6/29	Eb	1	8/20	Kan	1
5/9		Imix	2	6/30	Ben	2	8/21	Chicchan	2
5/10		Ik	3	7/1	Ix	3	8/22	Cimi	3
5/11		Akbal	4	7/2	Men	4	8/23	Manik	4
5/12		Kan	5	7/3	Cib	5	8/24	Lamat	5
5/13		Chicchan	6	7/4	Caban	6	8/25	Muluc	6
5/14		Cimi	7	7/5	Etznab	7	8/26	Oc	7
5/15		Manik	8	7/6	Cauac	8	8/27	Chuen	8
5/16		Lamat	9	7/7	Ahau	9	8/28	Eb	9
5/17		Muluc	10	7/8	Imix	10	8/29	Ben	10
5/18		Oc	11	7/9	Ik	11	8/30	Ix	11
5/19		Chuen	12	7/10	Akbal	12	8/31	Men	12
5/20		Eb	13	7/11	Kan	13	9/1	Cib	13

SAMPLE			BIRTHDAY	SOLAR GLYPH	TONE	BIRTHDAY		SOLAR GLYPH	TONE
BIRTHDAY	SOLAR GLYPH	TONE	9/1	Imix	1	2/5	10/23	Ben	1
			9/2	Ik	2	2/6	10/24	Ix	2
			9/3	Akbal	3	2/7	10/25	Men	3
ALWAYS READ CHART FROM			9/4	Kan	4	2/8	10/26	Cib	4
LEFT TO RIGHT			9/5	Chicchan	5	2/9	10/27	Caban	5
STARTING WITH BIRTHDAY			9/6	Cimi	6	2/10	10/28	Etznab	6
			9/7	Manik	7	2/11	10/29	Cauac	7
DOUBLE LINES			9/8	Lamat	8	2/12	10/30	Ahau	8
SEPARATE SECTIONS			9/9	Muluc	9	2/13	10/31	Imix	9
			9/10	Oc	10	2/14	11/1	Ik	10
USE SPACE BELOW			9/11	Chuen	11	2/15	11/2	Akbal	11
FOR RECORDING BIRTHDAYS			9/12	Eb	12	2/16	11/3	Kan	12
			9/13	Ben	13	2/17	11/4	Chicchan	13
			9/14	Ix	1	2/18	11/5	Cimi	1
			9/15	Men	2	2/19	11/6	Manik	2
			9/16	Cib	3	2/20	11/7	Lamat	3
			9/17	Caban	4	2/21	11/8	Muluc	4
		1/1	9/18	Etznab	5	2/22	11/9	Oc	5
		1/2	9/19	Cauac	6	2/23	11/10	Chuen	6
		1/3	9/20	Ahau	7	2/24	11/11	Eb	7
		1/4	9/21	Imix	8	2/25	11/12	Ben	8
		1/5	9/22	Ik	9	2/26	11/13	Ix	9
		1/6	9/23	Akbal	10	2/27	11/14	Men	10
		1/7	9/24	Kan	11	2/28	11/15	Cib	11
		1/8	9/25	Chicchan	12	3/1	11/16	Caban	12
		1/9	9/26	Cimi	13	3/2	11/17	Etznab	13
		1/10	9/27	Manik	1	3/3	11/18	Cauac	1
		1/11	9/28	Lamat	2	3/4	11/19	Ahau	2
		1/12	9/29	Muluc	3	3/5	11/20	Imix	3
		1/13	9/30	Oc	4	3/6	11/21	Ik	4
		1/14	10/1	Chuen	5	3/7	11/22	Akbal	5
		1/15	10/2	Eb	6	3/8	11/23	Kan	6
		1/16	10/3	Ben	7	3/9	11/24	Chicchan	7
		1/17	10/4	Ix	8	3/10	11/25	Cimi	8
		1/18	10/5	Men	9	3/11	11/26	Manik	9
		1/19	10/6	Cib	10	3/12	11/27	Lamat	10
		1/20	10/7	Caban	11	3/13	11/28	Muluc	11
		1/21	10/8	Etznab	12	3/14	11/29	Oc	12
		1/22	10/9	Cauac	13	3/15	11/30	Chuen	13
		1/23	10/10	Ahau	1	3/16	12/1	Eb	1
		1/24	10/11	Imix	2	3/17	12/2	Ben	2
		1/25	10/12	Ik	3	3/18	12/3	Ix	3
		1/26	10/13	Akbal	4	3/19	12/4	Men	4
		1/27	10/14	Kan	5	3/20	12/5	Cib	5
		1/28	10/15	Chicchan	6	3/21	12/6	Caban	6
		1/29	10/16	Cimi	7	3/22	12/7	Etznab	7
		1/30	10/17	Manik	8	3/23	12/8	Cauac	8
		1/31	10/18	Lamat	9	3/24	12/9	Ahau	9
		2/1	10/19	Muluc	10	3/25	12/10	Imix	10
		2/2	10/20	Oc	11	3/26	12/11	Ik	11
		2/3	10/21	Chuen	12	3/27	12/12	Akbal	12
		2/4	10/22	Eb	13	3/28	12/13	Kan	13

BIRTHDAY		SOLAR GLYPH	TONE	BIRTHDAY	SOLAR GLYPH	TONE	BIRTHDAY	SOLAR GLYPH	TONE
3/29	12/14	Chicchan	1	5/20	Caban	1	7/11	Muluc	1
3/30	12/15	Cimi	2	5/21	Etznab	2	7/12	Oc	2
3/31	12/16	Manik	3	5/22	Cauac	3	7/13	Chuen	3
4/1	12/17	Lamat	4	5/23	Ahau	4	7/14	Eb	4
4/2	12/18	Muluc	5	5/24	Imix	5	7/15	Ben	5
4/3	12/19	Oc	6	5/25	Ik	6	7/16	Ix	6
4/4	12/20	Chuen	7	5/26	Akbal	7	7/17	Men	7
4/5	12/21	Eb	8	5/27	Kan	8	7/18	Cib	8
4/6	12/22	Ben	9	5/28	Chiccan	9	7/19	Caban	9
4/7	12/23	Ix	10	5/29	Cimi	10	7/20	Etznab	10
4/8	12/24	Men	11	5/30	Manik	11	7/21	Cauac	11
4/9	12/25	Cib	12	5/31	Lamat	12	7/22	Ahau	12
4/10	12/26	Caban	13	6/1	Muluc	13	7/23	Imix	13
4/11	12/27	Etznab	1	6/2	Oc	1	7/24	Ik	1
4/12	12/28	Cauac	2	6/3	Chuen	2	7/25	Akbal	2
4/13	12/29	Ahau	3	6/4	Eb	3	7/26	Kan	3
4/14	12/30	Imix	4	6/5	Ben	4	7/27	Chicchan	4
4/15	12/31	Ik	5	6/6	Ix	5	7/28	Cimi	5
4/16		Akbal	6	6/7	Men	6	7/29	Manik	6
4/17		Kan	7	6/8	Cib	7	7/30	Lamat	7
4/18		Chicchan	8	6/9	Caban	8	7/31	Muluc	8
4/19		Cimi	9	6/10	Etznab	9	8/1	Oc	9
4/20		Manik	10	6/11	Cauac	10	8/2	Chuen	10
4/21		Lamat	11	6/12	Ahau	11	8/3	Eb	11
4/22		Muluc	12	6/13	Imix	12	8/4	Ben	12
4/23		Oc	13	6/14	Ik	13	8/5	Ix	13
4/24		Chuen	1	6/15	Akbal	1	8/6	Men	1
4/25		Eb	2	6/16	Kan	2	8/7	Cib	2
4/26		Ben	3	6/17	Chicchan	3	8/8	Caban	3
4/27		Ix	4	6/18	Cimi	4	8/9	Etznab	4
4/28		Men	5	6/19	Manik	5	8/10	Cauac	5
4/29		Cib	6	6/20	Lamat	6	8/11	Ahau	6
4/30		Caban	7	6/21	Muluc	7	8/12	Imix	7
5/1		Etznab	8	6/22	Oc	8	8/13	Ik	8
5/2		Cauac	9	6/23	Chuen	9	8/14	Akbal	9
5/3		Ahau	10	6/24	Eb	10	8/15	Kan	10
5/4		Imix	11	6/25	Ben	11	8/16	Chicchan	11
5/5		Ik	12	6/26	Ix	12	8/17	Cimi	12
5/6		Akbal	13	6/27	Men	13	8/18	Manik	13
5/7		Kan	1	6/28	Cib	1	8/19	Lamat	1
5/8		Chicchan	2	6/29	Caban	2	8/20	Muluc	2
5/9		Cimi	3	6/30	Etznab	3	8/21	Oc	3
5/10		Manik	4	7/1	Cauac	4	8/22	Chuen	4
5/11		Lamat	5	7/2	Ahau	5	8/23	Eb	5
5/12		Muluc	6	7/3	Imix	6	8/24	Ben	6
5/13		Oc	7	7/4	Ik	7	8/25	Ix	7
5/14		Chuen	8	7/5	Akbal	8	8/26	Men	8
5/15		Eb	9	7/6	Kan	9	8/27	Cib	9
5/16		Ben	10	7/7	Chicchan	10	8/28	Caban	10
5/17		Ix	11	7/8	Cimi	11	8/29	Etznab	11
5/18		Men	12	7/9	Manik	12	8/30	Cauac	12
5/19		Cib	13	7/10	Lamat	13	8/31	Ahau	13

SAMPLE			BIRTHDAY	SOLAR GLYPH	TONE	BIRTHDAY		SOLAR GLYPH	TONE
			8/31	Chicchan	1	2/4	10/22	Caban	1
BIRTHDAY	SOLAR GLYPH	TONE	9/1	Cimi	2	2/5	10/23	Etznab	2
			9/2	Manik	3	2/6	10/24	Cauac	3
ALWAYS READ CHART FROM			9/3	Lamat	4	2/7	10/25	Ahau	4
LEFT TO RIGHT			9/4	Muluc	5	2/8	10/26	Imix	5
STARTING WITH BIRTHDAY			9/5	Oc	6	2/9	10/27	Ik	6
			9/6	Chuen	7	2/10	10/28	Akbal	7
DOUBLE LINES			9/7	Eb	8	2/11	10/29	Kan	8
SEPARATE SECTIONS			9/8	Ben	9	2/12	10/30	Chiccan	9
			9/9	Ix	10	2/13	10/31	Cimi	10
USE SPACE BELOW			9/10	Men	11	2/14	11/1	Manik	11
FOR RECORDING BIRTHDAYS			9/11	Cib	12	2/15	11/2	Lamat	12
			9/12	Caban	13	2/16	11/3	Muluc	13
			9/13	Etznab	1	2/17	11/4	Oc	1
			9/14	Cauac	2	2/18	11/5	Chuen	2
			9/15	Ahau	3	2/19	11/6	Eb	3
			9/16	Imix	4	2/20	11/7	Ben	4
			9/17	Ik	5	2/21	11/8	Ix	5
		1/1	9/18	Akbal	6	2/22	11/9	Men	6
		1/2	9/19	Kan	7	2/23	11/10	Cib	7
		1/3	9/20	Chicchan	8	2/24	11/11	Caban	8
		1/4	9/21	Cimi	9	2/25	11/12	Etznab	9
		1/5	9/22	Manik	10	2/26	11/13	Cauac	10
		1/6	9/23	Lamat	11	2/27	11/14	Ahau	11
		1/7	9/24	Muluc	12	2/28	11/15	Imix	12
		1/8	9/25	Oc	13	3/1	11/16	Ik	13
		1/9	9/26	Chuen	1	3/2	11/17	Akbal	1
		1/10	9/27	Eb	2	3/3	11/18	Kan	2
		1/11	9/28	Ben	3	3/4	11/19	Chicchan	3
		1/12	9/29	Ix	4	3/5	11/20	Cimi	4
		1/13	9/30	Men	5	3/6	11/21	Manik	5
		1/14	10/1	Cib	6	3/7	11/22	Lamat	6
		1/15	10/2	Caban	7	3/8	11/23	Muluc	7
		1/16	10/3	Etznab	8	3/9	11/24	Oc	8
		1/17	10/4	Cauac	9	3/10	11/25	Chuen	9
		1/18	10/5	Ahau	10	3/11	11/26	Eb	10
		1/19	10/6	Imix	11	3/12	11/27	Ben	11
		1/20	10/7	Ik	12	3/13	11/28	Ix	12
		1/21	10/8	Akbal	13	3/14	11/29	Men	13
		1/22	10/9	Kan	1	3/15	11/30	Cib	1
		1/23	10/10	Chicchan	2	3/16	12/1	Caban	2
		1/24	10/11	Cimi	3	3/17	12/2	Etznab	3
		1/25	10/12	Manik	4	3/18	12/3	Cauac	4
		1/26	10/13	Lamat	5	3/19	12/4	Ahau	5
		1/27	10/14	Muluc	6	3/20	12/5	Imix	6
		1/28	10/15	Oc	7	3/21	12/6	Ik	7
		1/29	10/16	Chuen	8	3/22	12/7	Akbal	8
		1/30	10/17	Eb	9	3/23	12/8	Kan	9
		1/31	10/18	Ben	10	3/24	12/9	Chicchan	10
		2/1	10/19	Ix	11	3/25	12/10	Cimi	11
		2/2	10/20	Men	12	3/26	12/11	Manik	12
		2/3	10/21	Cib	13	3/27	12/12	Lamat	13

BIRTHDAY		SOLAR GLYPH	TONE	BIRTHDAY	SOLAR GLYPH	TONE	BIRTHDAY	SOLAR GLYPH	TONE
3/28	12/13	Muluc	1	5/19	Imix	1	7/10	Ben	1
3/29	12/14	Oc	2	5/20	Ik	2	7/11	Ix	2
3/30	12/15	Chuen	3	5/21	Akbal	3	7/12	Men	3
3/31	12/16	Eb	4	5/22	Kan	4	7/13	Cib	4
4/1	12/17	Ben	5	5/23	Chicchan	5	7/14	Caban	5
4/2	12/18	Ix	6	5/24	Cimi	6	7/15	Etznab	6
4/3	12/19	Men	7	5/25	Manik	7	7/16	Cauac	7
4/4	12/20	Cib	8	5/26	Lamat	8	7/17	Ahau	8
4/5	12/21	Caban	9	5/27	Muluc	9	7/18	Imix	9
4/6	12/22	Etznab	10	5/28	Oc	10	7/19	Ik	10
4/7	12/23	Cauac	11	5/29	Chuen	11	7/20	Akbal	11
4/8	12/24	Ahau	12	5/30	Eb	12	7/21	Kan	12
4/9	12/25	Imix	13	5/31	Ben	13	7/22	Chicchan	13
4/10	12/26	Ik	1	6/1	Ix	1	7/23	Cimi	1
4/11	12/27	Akbal	2	6/2	Men	2	7/24	Manik	2
4/12	12/28	Kan	3	6/3	Cib	3	7/25	Lamat	3
4/13	12/29	Chicchan	4	6/4	Caban	4	7/26	Muluc	4
4/14	12/30	Cimi	5	6/5	Etznab	5	7/27	Oc	5
4/15	12/31	Manik	6	6/6	Cauac	6	7/28	Chuen	6
4/16		Lamat	7	6/7	Ahau	7	7/29	Eb	7
4/17		Muluc	8	6/8	Imix	8	7/30	Ben	8
4/18		Oc	9	6/9	Ik	9	7/31	Ix	9
4/19		Chuen	10	6/10	Akbal	10	8/1	Men	10
4/20		Eb	11	6/11	Kan	11	8/2	Cib	11
4/21		Ben	12	6/12	Chicchan	12	8/3	Caban	12
4/22		Ix	13	6/13	Cimi	13	8/4	Etznab	13
4/23		Men	1	6/14	Manik	1	8/5	Cauac	1
4/24		Cib	2	6/15	Lamat	2	8/6	Ahau	2
4/25		Caban	3	6/16	Muluc	3	8/7	Imix	3
4/26		Etznab	4	6/17	Oc	4	8/8	Ik	4
4/27		Cauac	5	6/18	Chuen	5	8/9	Akbal	5
4/28		Ahau	6	6/19	Eb	6	8/10	Kan	6
4/29		Imix	7	6/20	Ben	7	8/11	Chicchan	7
4/30		Ik	8	6/21	Ix	8	8/12	Cimi	8
5/1		Akbal	9	6/22	Men	9	8/13	Manik	9
5/2		Kan	10	6/23	Cib	10	8/14	Lamat	10
5/3		Chicchan	11	6/24	Caban	11	8/15	Muluc	11
5/4		Cimi	12	6/25	Etznab	12	8/16	Oc	12
5/5		Manik	13	6/26	Cauac	13	8/17	Chuen	13
5/6		Lamat	1	6/27	Ahau	1	8/18	Eb	1
5/7		Muluc	2	6/28	Imix	2	8/19	Ben	2
5/8		Oc	3	6/29	Ik	3	8/20	Ix	3
5/9		Chuen	4	6/30	Akbal	4	8/21	Men	4
5/10		Eb	5	7/1	Kan	5	8/22	Cib	5
5/11		Ben	6	7/2	Chicchan	6	8/23	Caban	6
5/12		Ix	7	7/3	Cimi	7	8/24	Etznab	7
5/13		Men	8	7/4	Manik	8	8/25	Cauac	8
5/14		Cib	9	7/5	Lamat	9	8/26	Ahau	9
5/15		Caban	10	7/6	Muluc	10	8/27	Imix	10
5/16		Etznab	11	7/7	Oc	11	8/28	Ik	11
5/17		Cauac	12	7/8	Chuen	12	8/29	Akbal	12
5/18		Ahau	13	7/9	Eb	13	8/30	Kan	13

SAMPLE			BIRTHDAY	SOLAR GLYPH	TONE	BIRTHDAY		SOLAR GLYPH	TONE
			8/30	Muluc	1	2/3	10/21	Imix	1
BIRTHDAY	SOLAR GLYPH	TONE	8/31	Oc	2	2/4	10/22	Ik	2
			9/1	Chuen	3	2/5	10/23	Akbal	3
ALWAYS READ CHART FROM			9/2	Eb	4	2/6	10/24	Kan	4
LEFT TO RIGHT			9/3	Ben	5	2/7	10/25	Chicchan	5
STARTING WITH BIRTHDAY			9/4	Ix	6	2/8	10/26	Cimi	6
			9/5	Men	7	2/9	10/27	Manik	7
DOUBLE LINES			9/6	Cib	8	2/10	10/28	Lamat	8
SEPARATE SECTIONS			9/7	Caban	9	2/11	10/29	Muluc	9
			9/8	Etznab	10	2/12	10/30	Oc	10
USE SPACE BELOW			9/9	Cauac	11	2/13	10/31	Chuen	11
FOR RECORDING BIRTHDAYS			9/10	Ahau	12	2/14	11/1	Eb	12
			9/11	Imix	13	2/15	11/2	Ben	13
			9/12	Ik	1	2/16	11/3	Ix	1
			9/13	Akbal	2	2/17	11/4	Men	2
			9/14	Kan	3	2/18	11/5	Cib	3
			9/15	Chicchan	4	2/19	11/6	Caban	4
			9/16	Cimi	5	2/20	11/7	Etznab	5
			9/17	Manik	6	2/21	11/8	Cauac	6
		1/1	9/18	Lamat	7	2/22	11/9	Ahau	7
		1/2	9/19	Muluc	8	2/23	11/10	Imix	8
		1/3	9/20	Oc	9	2/24	11/11	Ik	9
		1/4	9/21	Chuen	10	2/25	11/12	Akbal	10
		1/5	9/22	Eb	11	2/26	11/13	Kan	11
		1/6	9/23	Ben	12	2/27	11/14	Chicchan	12
		1/7	9/24	Ix	13	2/28	11/15	Cimi	13
		1/8	9/25	Men	1	3/1	11/16	Manik	1
		1/9	9/26	Cib	2	3/2	11/17	Lamat	2
		1/10	9/27	Caban	3	3/3	11/18	Muluc	3
		1/11	9/28	Etznab	4	3/4	11/19	Oc	4
		1/12	9/29	Cauac	5	3/5	11/20	Chuen	5
		1/13	9/30	Ahau	6	3/6	11/21	Eb	6
		1/14	10/1	Imix	7	3/7	11/22	Ben	7
		1/15	10/2	Ik	8	3/8	11/23	Ix	8
		1/16	10/3	Akbal	9	3/9	11/24	Men	9
		1/17	10/4	Kan	10	3/10	11/25	Cib	10
		1/18	10/5	Chicchan	11	3/11	11/26	Caban	11
		1/19	10/6	Cimi	12	3/12	11/27	Etznab	12
		1/20	10/7	Manik	13	3/13	11/28	Cauac	13
		1/21	10/8	Lamat	1	3/14	11/29	Ahau	1
		1/22	10/9	Muluc	2	3/15	11/30	Imix	2
		1/23	10/10	Oc	3	3/16	12/1	Ik	3
		1/24	10/11	Chuen	4	3/17	12/2	Akbal	4
		1/25	10/12	Eb	5	3/18	12/3	Kan	5
		1/26	10/13	Ben	6	3/19	12/4	Chicchan	6
		1/27	10/14	Ix	7	3/20	12/5	Cimi	7
		1/28	10/15	Men	8	3/21	12/6	Manik	8
		1/29	10/16	Cib	9	3/22	12/7	Lamat	9
		1/30	10/17	Caban	10	3/23	12/8	Muluc	10
		1/31	10/18	Etznab	11	3/24	12/9	Oc	11
		2/1	10/19	Cauac	12	3/25	12/10	Chuen	12
		2/2	10/20	Ahau	13	3/26	12/11	Eb	13

BIRTHDAY		SOLAR GLYPH	TONE	BIRTHDAY	SOLAR GLYPH	TONE	BIRTHDAY	SOLAR GLYPH	TONE
3/27	12/12	Ben	1	5/18	Chicchan	1	7/9	Caban	1
3/28	12/13	Ix	2	5/19	Cimi	2	7/10	Etznab	2
3/29	12/14	Men	3	5/20	Manik	3	7/11	Cauac	3
3/30	12/15	Cib	4	5/21	Lamat	4	7/12	Ahau	4
3/31	12/16	Caban	5	5/22	Muluc	5	7/13	Imix	5
4/1	12/17	Etznab	6	5/23	Oc	6	7/14	Ik	6
4/2	12/18	Cauac	7	5/24	Chuen	7	7/15	Akbal	7
4/3	12/19	Ahau	8	5/25	Eb	8	7/16	Kan	8
4/4	12/20	Imix	9	5/26	Ben	9	7/17	Chiccan	9
4/5	12/21	Ik	10	5/27	Ix	10	7/18	Cimi	10
4/6	12/22	Akbal	11	5/28	Men	11	7/19	Manik	11
4/7	12/23	Kan	12	5/29	Cib	12	7/20	Lamat	12
4/8	12/24	Chicchan	13	5/30	Caban	13	7/21	Muluc	13
4/9	12/25	Cimi	1	5/31	Etznab	1	7/22	Oc	1
4/10	12/26	Manik	2	6/1	Cauac	2	7/23	Chuen	2
4/11	12/27	Lamat	3	6/2	Ahau	3	7/24	Eb	3
4/12	12/28	Muluc	4	6/3	Imix	4	7/25	Ben	4
4/13	12/29	Oc	5	6/4	Ik	5	7/26	Ix	5
4/14	12/30	Chuen	6	6/5	Akbal	6	7/27	Men	6
4/15	12/31	Eb	7	6/6	Kan	7	7/28	Cib	7
4/16		Ben	8	6/7	Chicchan	8	7/29	Caban	8
4/17		Ix	9	6/8	Cimi	9	7/30	Etznab	9
4/18		Men	10	6/9	Manik	10	7/31	Cauac	10
4/19		Cib	11	6/10	Lamat	11	8/1	Ahau	11
4/20		Caban	12	6/11	Muluc	12	8/2	Imix	12
4/21		Etznab	13	6/12	Oc	13	8/3	Ik	13
4/22		Cauac	1	6/13	Chuen	1	8/4	Akbal	1
4/23		Ahau	2	6/14	Eb	2	8/5	Kan	2
4/24		Imix	3	6/15	Ben	3	8/6	Chicchan	3
4/25		Ik	4	6/16	Ix	4	8/7	Cimi	4
4/26		Akbal	5	6/17	Men	5	8/8	Manik	5
4/27		Kan	6	6/18	Cib	6	8/9	Lamat	6
4/28		Chicchan	7	6/19	Caban	7	8/10	Muluc	7
4/29		Cimi	8	6/20	Etznab	8	8/11	Oc	8
4/30		Manik	9	6/21	Cauac	9	8/12	Chuen	9
5/1		Lamat	10	6/22	Ahau	10	8/13	Eb	10
5/2		Muluc	11	6/23	Imix	11	8/14	Ben	11
5/3		Oc	12	6/24	Ik	12	8/15	Ix	12
5/4		Chuen	13	6/25	Akbal	13	8/16	Men	13
5/5		Eb	1	6/26	Kan	1	8/17	Cib	1
5/6		Ben	2	6/27	Chicchan	2	8/18	Caban	2
5/7		Ix	3	6/28	Cimi	3	8/19	Etznab	3
5/8		Men	4	6/29	Manik	4	8/20	Cauac	4
5/9		Cib	5	6/30	Lamat	5	8/21	Ahau	5
5/10		Caban	6	7/1	Muluc	6	8/22	Imix	6
5/11		Etznab	7	7/2	Oc	7	8/23	Ik	7
5/12		Cauac	8	7/3	Chuen	8	8/24	Akbal	8
5/13		Ahau	9	7/4	Eb	9	8/25	Kan	9
5/14		Imix	10	7/5	Ben	10	8/26	Chicchan	10
5/15		Ik	11	7/6	Ix	11	8/27	Cimi	11
5/16		Akbal	12	7/7	Men	12	8/28	Manik	12
5/17		Kan	13	7/8	Cib	13	8/29	Lamat	13

SAMPLE			BIRTHDAY		SOLAR GLYPH	TONE	BIRTHDAY		SOLAR GLYPH	TONE
BIRTHDAY	**SOLAR GLYPH**	**TONE**		8/29	Ben	1	2/2	10/20	Chicchan	1
BIRTHDAY	SOLAR GLYPH	TONE		8/30	Ix	2	2/3	10/21	Cimi	2
				8/31	Men	3	2/4	10/22	Manik	3
ALWAYS READ CHART FROM				9/1	Cib	4	2/5	10/23	Lamat	4
LEFT TO RIGHT				9/2	Caban	5	2/6	10/24	Muluc	5
STARTING WITH BIRTHDAY				9/3	Etznab	6	2/7	10/25	Oc	6
				9/4	Cauac	7	2/8	10/26	Chuen	7
DOUBLE LINES				9/5	Ahau	8	2/9	10/27	Eb	8
SEPARATE SECTIONS				9/6	Imix	9	2/10	10/28	Ben	9
				9/7	Ik	10	2/11	10/29	Ix	10
USE SPACE BELOW				9/8	Akbal	11	2/12	10/30	Men	11
FOR RECORDING BIRTHDAYS				9/9	Kan	12	2/13	10/31	Cib	12
				9/10	Chicchan	13	2/14	11/1	Caban	13
				9/11	Cimi	1	2/15	11/2	Etznab	1
				9/12	Manik	2	2/16	11/3	Cauac	2
				9/13	Lamat	3	2/17	11/4	Ahau	3
				9/14	Muluc	4	2/18	11/5	Imix	4
				9/15	Oc	5	2/19	11/6	Ik	5
				9/16	Chuen	6	2/20	11/7	Akbal	6
				9/17	Eb	7	2/21	11/8	Kan	7
			1/1	9/18	Ben	8	2/22	11/9	Chicchan	8
			1/2	9/19	Ix	9	2/23	11/10	Cimi	9
			1/3	9/20	Men	10	2/24	11/11	Manik	10
			1/4	9/21	Cib	11	2/25	11/12	Lamat	11
			1/5	9/22	Caban	12	2/26	11/13	Muluc	12
			1/6	9/23	Etznab	13	2/27	11/14	Oc	13
			1/7	9/24	Cauac	1	2/28	11/15	Chuen	1
			1/8	9/25	Ahau	2	3/1	11/16	Eb	2
			1/9	9/26	Imix	3	3/2	11/17	Ben	3
			1/10	9/27	Ik	4	3/3	11/18	Ix	4
			1/11	9/28	Akbal	5	3/4	11/19	Men	5
			1/12	9/29	Kan	6	3/5	11/20	Cib	6
			1/13	9/30	Chicchan	7	3/6	11/21	Caban	7
			1/14	10/1	Cimi	8	3/7	11/22	Etznab	8
			1/15	10/2	Manik	9	3/8	11/23	Cauac	9
			1/16	10/3	Lamat	10	3/9	11/24	Ahau	10
			1/17	10/4	Muluc	11	3/10	11/25	Imix	11
			1/18	10/5	Oc	12	3/11	11/26	Ik	12
			1/19	10/6	Chuen	13	3/12	11/27	Akbal	13
			1/20	10/7	Eb	1	3/13	11/28	Kan	1
			1/21	10/8	Ben	2	3/14	11/29	Chicchan	2
			1/22	10/9	Ix	3	3/15	11/30	Cimi	3
			1/23	10/10	Men	4	3/16	12/1	Manik	4
			1/24	10/11	Cib	5	3/17	12/2	Lamat	5
			1/25	10/12	Caban	6	3/18	12/3	Muluc	6
			1/26	10/13	Etznab	7	3/19	12/4	Oc	7
			1/27	10/14	Cauac	8	3/20	12/5	Chuen	8
			1/28	10/15	Ahau	9	3/21	12/6	Eb	9
			1/29	10/16	Imix	10	3/22	12/7	Ben	10
			1/30	10/17	Ik	11	3/23	12/8	Ix	11
			1/31	10/18	Akbal	12	3/24	12/9	Men	12
			2/1	10/19	Kan	13	3/25	12/10	Cib	13

BIRTHDAY		SOLAR GLYPH	TONE	BIRTHDAY	SOLAR GLYPH	TONE	BIRTHDAY	SOLAR GLYPH	TONE
3/26	12/11	Caban	1	5/17	Muluc	1	7/8	Imix	1
3/27	12/12	Etznab	2	5/18	Oc	2	7/9	Ik	2
3/28	12/13	Cauac	3	5/19	Chuen	3	7/10	Akbal	3
3/29	12/14	Ahau	4	5/20	Eb	4	7/11	Kan	4
3/30	12/15	Imix	5	5/21	Ben	5	7/12	Chicchan	5
3/31	12/16	Ik	6	5/22	Ix	6	7/13	Cimi	6
4/1	12/17	Akbal	7	5/23	Men	7	7/14	Manik	7
4/2	12/18	Kan	8	5/24	Cib	8	7/15	Lamat	8
4/3	12/19	Chiccan	9	5/25	Caban	9	7/16	Muluc	9
4/4	12/20	Cimi	10	5/26	Etznab	10	7/17	Oc	10
4/5	12/21	Manik	11	5/27	Cauac	11	7/18	Chuen	11
4/6	12/22	Lamat	12	5/28	Ahau	12	7/19	Eb	12
4/7	12/23	Muluc	13	5/29	Imix	13	7/20	Ben	13
4/8	12/24	Oc	1	5/30	Ik	1	7/21	Ix	1
4/9	12/25	Chuen	2	5/31	Akbal	2	7/22	Men	2
4/10	12/26	Eb	3	6/1	Kan	3	7/23	Cib	3
4/11	12/27	Ben	4	6/2	Chicchan	4	7/24	Caban	4
4/12	12/28	Ix	5	6/3	Cimi	5	7/25	Etznab	5
4/13	12/29	Men	6	6/4	Manik	6	7/26	Cauac	6
4/14	12/30	Cib	7	6/5	Lamat	7	7/27	Ahau	7
4/15	12/31	Caban	8	6/6	Muluc	8	7/28	Imix	8
4/16		Etznab	9	6/7	Oc	9	7/29	Ik	9
4/17		Cauac	10	6/8	Chuen	10	7/30	Akbal	10
4/18		Ahau	11	6/9	Eb	11	7/31	Kan	11
4/19		Imix	12	6/10	Ben	12	8/1	Chicchan	12
4/20		Ik	13	6/11	Ix	13	8/2	Cimi	13
4/21		Akbal	1	6/12	Men	1	8/3	Manik	1
4/22		Kan	2	6/13	Cib	2	8/4	Lamat	2
4/23		Chicchan	3	6/14	Caban	3	8/5	Muluc	3
4/24		Cimi	4	6/15	Etznab	4	8/6	Oc	4
4/25		Manik	5	6/16	Cauac	5	8/7	Chuen	5
4/26		Lamat	6	6/17	Ahau	6	8/8	Eb	6
4/27		Muluc	7	6/18	Imix	7	8/9	Ben	7
4/28		Oc	8	6/19	Ik	8	8/10	Ix	8
4/29		Chuen	9	6/20	Akbal	9	8/11	Men	9
4/30		Eb	10	6/21	Kan	10	8/12	Cib	10
5/1		Ben	11	6/22	Chicchan	11	8/13	Caban	11
5/2		Ix	12	6/23	Cimi	12	8/14	Etznab	12
5/3		Men	13	6/24	Manik	13	8/15	Cauac	13
5/4		Cib	1	6/25	Lamat	1	8/16	Ahau	1
5/5		Caban	2	6/26	Muluc	2	8/17	Imix	2
5/6		Etznab	3	6/27	Oc	3	8/18	Ik	3
5/7		Cauac	4	6/28	Chuen	4	8/19	Akbal	4
5/8		Ahau	5	6/29	Eb	5	8/20	Kan	5
5/9		Imix	6	6/30	Ben	6	8/21	Chicchan	6
5/10		Ik	7	7/1	Ix	7	8/22	Cimi	7
5/11		Akbal	8	7/2	Men	8	8/23	Manik	8
5/12		Kan	9	7/3	Cib	9	8/24	Lamat	9
5/13		Chicchan	10	7/4	Caban	10	8/25	Muluc	10
5/14		Cimi	11	7/5	Etznab	11	8/26	Oc	11
5/15		Manik	12	7/6	Cauac	12	8/27	Chuen	12
5/16		Lamat	13	7/7	Ahau	13	8/28	Eb	13

SAMPLE			Record	BIRTHDAY	SOLAR GLYPH	TONE	BIRTHDAY		SOLAR GLYPH	TONE
				8/28	Caban	1	2/1	10/19	Muluc	1
BIRTHDAY	SOLAR GLYPH	TONE		8/29	Etznab	2	2/2	10/20	Oc	2
				8/30	Cauac	3	2/3	10/21	Chuen	3
ALWAYS READ CHART FROM				8/31	Ahau	4	2/4	10/22	Eb	4
LEFT TO RIGHT				9/1	Imix	5	2/5	10/23	Ben	5
STARTING WITH BIRTHDAY				9/2	Ik	6	2/6	10/24	Ix	6
				9/3	Akbal	7	2/7	10/25	Men	7
DOUBLE LINES				9/4	Kan	8	2/8	10/26	Cib	8
SEPARATE SECTIONS				9/5	Chiccan	9	2/9	10/27	Caban	9
				9/6	Cimi	10	2/10	10/28	Etznab	10
USE SPACE BELOW				9/7	Manik	11	2/11	10/29	Cauac	11
FOR RECORDING BIRTHDAYS				9/8	Lamat	12	2/12	10/30	Ahau	12
				9/9	Muluc	13	2/13	10/31	Imix	13
				9/10	Oc	1	2/14	11/1	Ik	1
				9/11	Chuen	2	2/15	11/2	Akbal	2
				9/12	Eb	3	2/16	11/3	Kan	3
				9/13	Ben	4	2/17	11/4	Chiccan	4
				9/14	Ix	5	2/18	11/5	Cimi	5
				9/15	Men	6	2/19	11/6	Manik	6
				9/16	Cib	7	2/20	11/7	Lamat	7
				9/17	Caban	8	2/21	11/8	Muluc	8
			1/1	9/18	Etznab	9	2/22	11/9	Oc	9
			1/2	9/19	Cauac	10	2/23	11/10	Chuen	10
			1/3	9/20	Ahau	11	2/24	11/11	Eb	11
			1/4	9/21	Imix	12	2/25	11/12	Ben	12
			1/5	9/22	Ik	13	2/26	11/13	Ix	13
			1/6	9/23	Akbal	1	2/27	11/14	Men	1
			1/7	9/24	Kan	2	2/28	11/15	Cib	2
			1/8	9/25	Chicchan	3	3/1	11/16	Caban	3
			1/9	9/26	Cimi	4	3/2	11/17	Etznab	4
			1/10	9/27	Manik	5	3/3	11/18	Cauac	5
			1/11	9/28	Lamat	6	3/4	11/19	Ahau	6
			1/12	9/29	Muluc	7	3/5	11/20	Imix	7
			1/13	9/30	Oc	8	3/6	11/21	Ik	8
			1/14	10/1	Chuen	9	3/7	11/22	Akbal	9
			1/15	10/2	Eb	10	3/8	11/23	Kan	10
			1/16	10/3	Ben	11	3/9	11/24	Chicchan	11
			1/17	10/4	Ix	12	3/10	11/25	Cimi	12
			1/18	10/5	Men	13	3/11	11/26	Manik	13
			1/19	10/6	Cib	1	3/12	11/27	Lamat	1
			1/20	10/7	Caban	2	3/13	11/28	Muluc	2
			1/21	10/8	Etznab	3	3/14	11/29	Oc	3
			1/22	10/9	Cauac	4	3/15	11/30	Chuen	4
			1/23	10/10	Ahau	5	3/16	12/1	Eb	5
			1/24	10/11	Imix	6	3/17	12/2	Ben	6
			1/25	10/12	Ik	7	3/18	12/3	Ix	7
			1/26	10/13	Akbal	8	3/19	12/4	Men	8
			1/27	10/14	Kan	9	3/20	12/5	Cib	9
			1/28	10/15	Chicchan	10	3/21	12/6	Caban	10
			1/29	10/16	Cimi	11	3/22	12/7	Etznab	11
			1/30	10/17	Manik	12	3/23	12/8	Cauac	12
			1/31	10/18	Lamat	13	3/24	12/9	Ahau	13

BIRTHDAY		SOLAR GLYPH	TONE	BIRTHDAY	SOLAR GLYPH	TONE	BIRTHDAY	SOLAR GLYPH	TONE
3/25	12/10	Imix	1	5/16	Ben	1	7/7	Chicchan	1
3/26	12/11	Ik	2	5/17	Ix	2	7/8	Cimi	2
3/27	12/12	Akbal	3	5/18	Men	3	7/9	Manik	3
3/28	12/13	Kan	4	5/19	Cib	4	7/10	Lamat	4
3/29	12/14	Chicchan	5	5/20	Caban	5	7/11	Muluc	5
3/30	12/15	Cimi	6	5/21	Etznab	6	7/12	Oc	6
3/31	12/16	Manik	7	5/22	Cauac	7	7/13	Chuen	7
4/1	12/17	Lamat	8	5/23	Ahau	8	7/14	Eb	8
4/2	12/18	Muluc	9	5/24	Imix	9	7/15	Ben	9
4/3	12/19	Oc	10	5/25	Ik	10	7/16	Ix	10
4/4	12/20	Chuen	11	5/26	Akbal	11	7/17	Men	11
4/5	12/21	Eb	12	5/27	Kan	12	7/18	Cib	12
4/6	12/22	Ben	13	5/28	Chicchan	13	7/19	Caban	13
4/7	12/23	Ix	1	5/29	Cimi	1	7/20	Etznab	1
4/8	12/24	Men	2	5/30	Manik	2	7/21	Cauac	2
4/9	12/25	Cib	3	5/31	Lamat	3	7/22	Ahau	3
4/10	12/26	Caban	4	6/1	Muluc	4	7/23	Imix	4
4/11	12/27	Etznab	5	6/2	Oc	5	7/24	Ik	5
4/12	12/28	Cauac	6	6/3	Chuen	6	7/25	Akbal	6
4/13	12/29	Ahau	7	6/4	Eb	7	7/26	Kan	7
4/14	12/30	Imix	8	6/5	Ben	8	7/27	Chicchan	8
4/15	12/31	Ik	9	6/6	Ix	9	7/28	Cimi	9
4/16		Akbal	10	6/7	Men	10	7/29	Manik	10
4/17		Kan	11	6/8	Cib	11	7/30	Lamat	11
4/18		Chicchan	12	6/9	Caban	12	7/31	Muluc	12
4/19		Cimi	13	6/10	Etznab	13	8/1	Oc	13
4/20		Manik	1	6/11	Cauac	1	8/2	Chuen	1
4/21		Lamat	2	6/12	Ahau	2	8/3	Eb	2
4/22		Muluc	3	6/13	Imix	3	8/4	Ben	3
4/23		Oc	4	6/14	Ik	4	8/5	Ix	4
4/24		Chuen	5	6/15	Akbal	5	8/6	Men	5
4/25		Eb	6	6/16	Kan	6	8/7	Cib	6
4/26		Ben	7	6/17	Chicchan	7	8/8	Caban	7
4/27		Ix	8	6/18	Cimi	8	8/9	Etznab	8
4/28		Men	9	6/19	Manik	9	8/10	Cauac	9
4/29		Cib	10	6/20	Lamat	10	8/11	Ahau	10
4/30		Caban	11	6/21	Muluc	11	8/12	Imix	11
5/1		Etznab	12	6/22	Oc	12	8/13	Ik	12
5/2		Cauac	13	6/23	Chuen	13	8/14	Akbal	13
5/3		Ahau	1	6/24	Eb	1	8/15	Kan	1
5/4		Imix	2	6/25	Ben	2	8/16	Chicchan	2
5/5		Ik	3	6/26	Ix	3	8/17	Cimi	3
5/6		Akbal	4	6/27	Men	4	8/18	Manik	4
5/7		Kan	5	6/28	Cib	5	8/19	Lamat	5
5/8		Chicchan	6	6/29	Caban	6	8/20	Muluc	6
5/9		Cimi	7	6/30	Etznab	7	8/21	Oc	7
5/10		Manik	8	7/1	Cauac	8	8/22	Chuen	8
5/11		Lamat	9	7/2	Ahau	9	8/23	Eb	9
5/12		Muluc	10	7/3	Imix	10	8/24	Ben	10
5/13		Oc	11	7/4	Ik	11	8/25	Ix	11
5/14		Chuen	12	7/5	Akbal	12	8/26	Men	12
5/15		Eb	13	7/6	Kan	13	8/27	Cib	13

SAMPLE

BIRTHDAY	SOLAR GLYPH	TONE

ALWAYS READ CHART FROM
LEFT TO RIGHT
STARTING WITH BIRTHDAY

DOUBLE LINES
SEPARATE SECTIONS

USE SPACE BELOW
FOR RECORDING BIRTHDAYS

BIRTHDAY		SOLAR GLYPH	TONE	BIRTHDAY		SOLAR GLYPH	TONE
	8/27	Imix	1	1/31	10/18	Ben	1
	8/28	Ik	2	2/1	10/19	Ix	2
	8/29	Akbal	3	2/2	10/20	Men	3
	8/30	Kan	4	2/3	10/21	Cib	4
	8/31	Chicchan	5	2/4	10/22	Caban	5
	9/1	Cimi	6	2/5	10/23	Etznab	6
	9/2	Manik	7	2/6	10/24	Cauac	7
	9/3	Lamat	8	2/7	10/25	Ahau	8
	9/4	Muluc	9	2/8	10/26	Imix	9
	9/5	Oc	10	2/9	10/27	Ik	10
	9/6	Chuen	11	2/10	10/28	Akbal	11
	9/7	Eb	12	2/11	10/29	Kan	12
	9/8	Ben	13	2/12	10/30	Chicchan	13
	9/9	Ix	1	2/13	10/31	Cimi	1
	9/10	Men	2	2/14	11/1	Manik	2
	9/11	Cib	3	2/15	11/2	Lamat	3
	9/12	Caban	4	2/16	11/3	Muluc	4
	9/13	Etznab	5	2/17	11/4	Oc	5
	9/14	Cauac	6	2/18	11/5	Chuen	6
	9/15	Ahau	7	2/19	11/6	Eb	7
	9/16	Imix	8	2/20	11/7	Ben	8
	9/17	Ik	9	2/21	11/8	Ix	9
1/1	9/18	Akbal	10	2/22	11/9	Men	10
1/2	9/19	Kan	11	2/23	11/10	Cib	11
1/3	9/20	Chicchan	12	2/24	11/11	Caban	12
1/4	9/21	Cimi	13	2/25	11/12	Etznab	13
1/5	9/22	Manik	1	2/26	11/13	Cauac	1
1/6	9/23	Lamat	2	2/27	11/14	Ahau	2
1/7	9/24	Muluc	3	2/28	11/15	Imix	3
1/8	9/25	Oc	4	3/1	11/16	Ik	4
1/9	9/26	Chuen	5	3/2	11/17	Akbal	5
1/10	9/27	Eb	6	3/3	11/18	Kan	6
1/11	9/28	Ben	7	3/4	11/19	Chicchan	7
1/12	9/29	Ix	8	3/5	11/20	Cimi	8
1/13	9/30	Men	9	3/6	11/21	Manik	9
1/14	10/1	Cib	10	3/7	11/22	Lamat	10
1/15	10/2	Caban	11	3/8	11/23	Muluc	11
1/16	10/3	Etznab	12	3/9	11/24	Oc	12
1/17	10/4	Cauac	13	3/10	11/25	Chuen	13
1/18	10/5	Ahau	1	3/11	11/26	Eb	1
1/19	10/6	Imix	2	3/12	11/27	Ben	2
1/20	10/7	Ik	3	3/13	11/28	Ix	3
1/21	10/8	Akbal	4	3/14	11/29	Men	4
1/22	10/9	Kan	5	3/15	11/30	Cib	5
1/23	10/10	Chicchan	6	3/16	12/1	Caban	6
1/24	10/11	Cimi	7	3/17	12/2	Etznab	7
1/25	10/12	Manik	8	3/18	12/3	Cauac	8
1/26	10/13	Lamat	9	3/19	12/4	Ahau	9
1/27	10/14	Muluc	10	3/20	12/5	Imix	10
1/28	10/15	Oc	11	3/21	12/6	Ik	11
1/29	10/16	Chuen	12	3/22	12/7	Akbal	12
1/30	10/17	Eb	13	3/23	12/8	Kan	13

BIRTHDAY		SOLAR GLYPH	TONE	BIRTHDAY	SOLAR GLYPH	TONE	BIRTHDAY	SOLAR GLYPH	TONE
3/24	12/9	Chicchan	1	5/15	Caban	1	7/6	Muluc	1
3/25	12/10	Cimi	2	5/16	Etznab	2	7/7	Oc	2
3/26	12/11	Manik	3	5/17	Cauac	3	7/8	Chuen	3
3/27	12/12	Lamat	4	5/18	Ahau	4	7/9	Eb	4
3/28	12/13	Muluc	5	5/19	Imix	5	7/10	Ben	5
3/29	12/14	Oc	6	5/20	Ik	6	7/11	Ix	6
3/30	12/15	Chuen	7	5/21	Akbal	7	7/12	Men	7
3/31	12/16	Eb	8	5/22	Kan	8	7/13	Cib	8
4/1	12/17	Ben	9	5/23	Chiccan	9	7/14	Caban	9
4/2	12/18	Ix	10	5/24	Cimi	10	7/15	Etznab	10
4/3	12/19	Men	11	5/25	Manik	11	7/16	Cauac	11
4/4	12/20	Cib	12	5/26	Lamat	12	7/17	Ahau	12
4/5	12/21	Caban	13	5/27	Muluc	13	7/18	Imix	13
4/6	12/22	Etznab	1	5/28	Oc	1	7/19	Ik	1
4/7	12/23	Cauac	2	5/29	Chuen	2	7/20	Akbal	2
4/8	12/24	Ahau	3	5/30	Eb	3	7/21	Kan	3
4/9	12/25	Imix	4	5/31	Ben	4	7/22	Chicchan	4
4/10	12/26	Ik	5	6/1	Ix	5	7/23	Cimi	5
4/11	12/27	Akbal	6	6/2	Men	6	7/24	Manik	6
4/12	12/28	Kan	7	6/3	Cib	7	7/25	Lamat	7
4/13	12/29	Chicchan	8	6/4	Caban	8	7/26	Muluc	8
4/14	12/30	Cimi	9	6/5	Etznab	9	7/27	Oc	9
4/15	12/31	Manik	10	6/6	Cauac	10	7/28	Chuen	10
4/16		Lamat	11	6/7	Ahau	11	7/29	Eb	11
4/17		Muluc	12	6/8	Imix	12	7/30	Ben	12
4/18		Oc	13	6/9	Ik	13	7/31	Ix	13
4/19		Chuen	1	6/10	Akbal	1	8/1	Men	1
4/20		Eb	2	6/11	Kan	2	8/2	Cib	2
4/21		Ben	3	6/12	Chicchan	3	8/3	Caban	3
4/22		Ix	4	6/13	Cimi	4	8/4	Etznab	4
4/23		Men	5	6/14	Manik	5	8/5	Cauac	5
4/24		Cib	6	6/15	Lamat	6	8/6	Ahau	6
4/25		Caban	7	6/16	Muluc	7	8/7	Imix	7
4/26		Etznab	8	6/17	Oc	8	8/8	Ik	8
4/27		Cauac	9	6/18	Chuen	9	8/9	Akbal	9
4/28		Ahau	10	6/19	Eb	10	8/10	Kan	10
4/29		Imix	11	6/20	Ben	11	8/11	Chicchan	11
4/30		Ik	12	6/21	Ix	12	8/12	Cimi	12
5/1		Akbal	13	6/22	Men	13	8/13	Manik	13
5/2		Kan	1	6/23	Cib	1	8/14	Lamat	1
5/3		Chicchan	2	6/24	Caban	2	8/15	Muluc	2
5/4		Cimi	3	6/25	Etznab	3	8/16	Oc	3
5/5		Manik	4	6/26	Cauac	4	8/17	Chuen	4
5/6		Lamat	5	6/27	Ahau	5	8/18	Eb	5
5/7		Muluc	6	6/28	Imix	6	8/19	Ben	6
5/8		Oc	7	6/29	Ik	7	8/20	Ix	7
5/9		Chuen	8	6/30	Akbal	8	8/21	Men	8
5/10		Eb	9	7/1	Kan	9	8/22	Cib	9
5/11		Ben	10	7/2	Chicchan	10	8/23	Caban	10
5/12		Ix	11	7/3	Cimi	11	8/24	Etznab	11
5/13		Men	12	7/4	Manik	12	8/25	Cauac	12
5/14		Cib	13	7/5	Lamat	13	8/26	Ahau	13

SAMPLE

BIRTHDAY	SOLAR GLYPH	TONE
ALWAYS READ CHART FROM		
LEFT TO RIGHT		
STARTING WITH BIRTHDAY		
DOUBLE LINES		
SEPARATE SECTIONS		
USE SPACE BELOW		
FOR RECORDING BIRTHDAYS		

	BIRTHDAY	SOLAR GLYPH	TONE
	8/26	Chicchan	1
	8/27	Cimi	2
	8/28	Manik	3
	8/29	Lamat	4
	8/30	Muluc	5
	8/31	Oc	6
	9/1	Chuen	7
	9/2	Eb	8
	9/3	Ben	9
	9/4	Ix	10
	9/5	Men	11
	9/6	Cib	12
	9/7	Caban	13
	9/8	Etznab	1
	9/9	Cauac	2
	9/10	Ahau	3
	9/11	Imix	4
	9/12	Ik	5
	9/13	Akbal	6
	9/14	Kan	7
	9/15	Chicchan	8
	9/16	Cimi	9
	9/17	Manik	10
1/1	9/18	Lamat	11
1/2	9/19	Muluc	12
1/3	9/20	Oc	13
1/4	9/21	Chuen	1
1/5	9/22	Eb	2
1/6	9/23	Ben	3
1/7	9/24	Ix	4
1/8	9/25	Men	5
1/9	9/26	Cib	6
1/10	9/27	Caban	7
1/11	9/28	Etznab	8
1/12	9/29	Cauac	9
1/13	9/30	Ahau	10
1/14	10/1	Imix	11
1/15	10/2	Ik	12
1/16	10/3	Akbal	13
1/17	10/4	Kan	1
1/18	10/5	Chicchan	2
1/19	10/6	Cimi	3
1/20	10/7	Manik	4
1/21	10/8	Lamat	5
1/22	10/9	Muluc	6
1/23	10/10	Oc	7
1/24	10/11	Chuen	8
1/25	10/12	Eb	9
1/26	10/13	Ben	10
1/27	10/14	Ix	11
1/28	10/15	Men	12
1/29	10/16	Cib	13

BIRTHDAY		SOLAR GLYPH	TONE
1/30	10/17	Caban	1
1/31	10/18	Etznab	2
2/1	10/19	Cauac	3
2/2	10/20	Ahau	4
2/3	10/21	Imix	5
2/4	10/22	Ik	6
2/5	10/23	Akbal	7
2/6	10/24	Kan	8
2/7	10/25	Chiccan	9
2/8	10/26	Cimi	10
2/9	10/27	Manik	11
2/10	10/28	Lamat	12
2/11	10/29	Muluc	13
2/12	10/30	Oc	1
2/13	10/31	Chuen	2
2/14	11/1	Eb	3
2/15	11/2	Ben	4
2/16	11/3	Ix	5
2/17	11/4	Men	6
2/18	11/5	Cib	7
2/19	11/6	Caban	8
2/20	11/7	Etznab	9
2/21	11/8	Cauac	10
2/22	11/9	Ahau	11
2/23	11/10	Imix	12
2/24	11/11	Ik	13
2/25	11/12	Akbal	1
2/26	11/13	Kan	2
2/27	11/14	Chicchan	3
2/28	11/15	Cimi	4
3/1	11/16	Manik	5
3/2	11/17	Lamat	6
3/3	11/18	Muluc	7
3/4	11/19	Oc	8
3/5	11/20	Chuen	9
3/6	11/21	Eb	10
3/7	11/22	Ben	11
3/8	11/23	Ix	12
3/9	11/24	Men	13
3/10	11/25	Cib	1
3/11	11/26	Caban	2
3/12	11/27	Etznab	3
3/13	11/28	Cauac	4
3/14	11/29	Ahau	5
3/15	11/30	Imix	6
3/16	12/1	Ik	7
3/17	12/2	Akbal	8
3/18	12/3	Kan	9
3/19	12/4	Chicchan	10
3/20	12/5	Cimi	11
3/21	12/6	Manik	12
3/22	12/7	Lamat	13

BIRTHDAY		SOLAR GLYPH	TONE	BIRTHDAY	SOLAR GLYPH	TONE	BIRTHDAY	SOLAR GLYPH	TONE
3/23	12/8	Muluc	1	5/14	Imix	1	7/5	Ben	1
3/24	12/9	Oc	2	5/15	Ik	2	7/6	Ix	2
3/25	12/10	Chuen	3	5/16	Akbal	3	7/7	Men	3
3/26	12/11	Eb	4	5/17	Kan	4	7/8	Cib	4
3/27	12/12	Ben	5	5/18	Chicchan	5	7/9	Caban	5
3/28	12/13	Ix	6	5/19	Cimi	6	7/10	Etznab	6
3/29	12/14	Men	7	5/20	Manik	7	7/11	Cauac	7
3/30	12/15	Cib	8	5/21	Lamat	8	7/12	Ahau	8
3/31	12/16	Caban	9	5/22	Muluc	9	7/13	Imix	9
4/1	12/17	Etznab	10	5/23	Oc	10	7/14	Ik	10
4/2	12/18	Cauac	11	5/24	Chuen	11	7/15	Akbal	11
4/3	12/19	Ahau	12	5/25	Eb	12	7/16	Kan	12
4/4	12/20	Imix	13	5/26	Ben	13	7/17	Chicchan	13
4/5	12/21	Ik	1	5/27	Ix	1	7/18	Cimi	1
4/6	12/22	Akbal	2	5/28	Men	2	7/19	Manik	2
4/7	12/23	Kan	3	5/29	Cib	3	7/20	Lamat	3
4/8	12/24	Chicchan	4	5/30	Caban	4	7/21	Muluc	4
4/9	12/25	Cimi	5	5/31	Etznab	5	7/22	Oc	5
4/10	12/26	Manik	6	6/1	Cauac	6	7/23	Chuen	6
4/11	12/27	Lamat	7	6/2	Ahau	7	7/24	Eb	7
4/12	12/28	Muluc	8	6/3	Imix	8	7/25	Ben	8
4/13	12/29	Oc	9	6/4	Ik	9	7/26	Ix	9
4/14	12/30	Chuen	10	6/5	Akbal	10	7/27	Men	10
4/15	12/31	Eb	11	6/6	Kan	11	7/28	Cib	11
4/16		Ben	12	6/7	Chicchan	12	7/29	Caban	12
4/17		Ix	13	6/8	Cimi	13	7/30	Etznab	13
4/18		Men	1	6/9	Manik	1	7/31	Cauac	1
4/19		Cib	2	6/10	Lamat	2	8/1	Ahau	2
4/20		Caban	3	6/11	Muluc	3	8/2	Imix	3
4/21		Etznab	4	6/12	Oc	4	8/3	Ik	4
4/22		Cauac	5	6/13	Chuen	5	8/4	Akbal	5
4/23		Ahau	6	6/14	Eb	6	8/5	Kan	6
4/24		Imix	7	6/15	Ben	7	8/6	Chicchan	7
4/25		Ik	8	6/16	Ix	8	8/7	Cimi	8
4/26		Akbal	9	6/17	Men	9	8/8	Manik	9
4/27		Kan	10	6/18	Cib	10	8/9	Lamat	10
4/28		Chicchan	11	6/19	Caban	11	8/10	Muluc	11
4/29		Cimi	12	6/20	Etznab	12	8/11	Oc	12
4/30		Manik	13	6/21	Cauac	13	8/12	Chuen	13
5/1		Lamat	1	6/22	Ahau	1	8/13	Eb	1
5/2		Muluc	2	6/23	Imix	2	8/14	Ben	2
5/3		Oc	3	6/24	Ik	3	8/15	Ix	3
5/4		Chuen	4	6/25	Akbal	4	8/16	Men	4
5/5		Eb	5	6/26	Kan	5	8/17	Cib	5
5/6		Ben	6	6/27	Chicchan	6	8/18	Caban	6
5/7		Ix	7	6/28	Cimi	7	8/19	Etznab	7
5/8		Men	8	6/29	Manik	8	8/20	Cauac	8
5/9		Cib	9	6/30	Lamat	9	8/21	Ahau	9
5/10		Caban	10	7/1	Muluc	10	8/22	Imix	10
5/11		Etznab	11	7/2	Oc	11	8/23	Ik	11
5/12		Cauac	12	7/3	Chuen	12	8/24	Akbal	12
5/13		Ahau	13	7/4	Eb	13	8/25	Kan	13

SAMPLE			BIRTHDAY		SOLAR GLYPH	TONE	BIRTHDAY		SOLAR GLYPH	TONE
				8/25	Muluc	1	1/29	10/16	Imix	1
BIRTHDAY	SOLAR GLYPH	TONE		8/26	Oc	2	1/30	10/17	Ik	2
				8/27	Chuen	3	1/31	10/18	Akbal	3
ALWAYS READ CHART FROM				8/28	Eb	4	2/1	10/19	Kan	4
LEFT TO RIGHT				8/29	Ben	5	2/2	10/20	Chicchan	5
STARTING WITH BIRTHDAY				8/30	Ix	6	2/3	10/21	Cimi	6
				8/31	Men	7	2/4	10/22	Manik	7
DOUBLE LINES				9/1	Cib	8	2/5	10/23	Lamat	8
SEPARATE SECTIONS				9/2	Caban	9	2/6	10/24	Muluc	9
				9/3	Etznab	10	2/7	10/25	Oc	10
USE SPACE BELOW				9/4	Cauac	11	2/8	10/26	Chuen	11
FOR RECORDING BIRTHDAYS				9/5	Ahau	12	2/9	10/27	Eb	12
				9/6	Imix	13	2/10	10/28	Ben	13
				9/7	Ik	1	2/11	10/29	Ix	1
				9/8	Akbal	2	2/12	10/30	Men	2
				9/9	Kan	3	2/13	10/31	Cib	3
				9/10	Chicchan	4	2/14	11/1	Caban	4
				9/11	Cimi	5	2/15	11/2	Etznab	5
				9/12	Manik	6	2/16	11/3	Cauac	6
				9/13	Lamat	7	2/17	11/4	Ahau	7
				9/14	Muluc	8	2/18	11/5	Imix	8
				9/15	Oc	9	2/19	11/6	Ik	9
				9/16	Chuen	10	2/20	11/7	Akbal	10
				9/17	Eb	11	2/21	11/8	Kan	11
			1/1	9/18	Ben	12	2/22	11/9	Chicchan	12
			1/2	9/19	Ix	13	2/23	11/10	Cimi	13
			1/3	9/20	Men	1	2/24	11/11	Manik	1
			1/4	9/21	Cib	2	2/25	11/12	Lamat	2
			1/5	9/22	Caban	3	2/26	11/13	Muluc	3
			1/6	9/23	Etznab	4	2/27	11/14	Oc	4
			1/7	9/24	Cauac	5	2/28	11/15	Chuen	5
			1/8	9/25	Ahau	6	3/1	11/16	Eb	6
			1/9	9/26	Imix	7	3/2	11/17	Ben	7
			1/10	9/27	Ik	8	3/3	11/18	Ix	8
			1/11	9/28	Akbal	9	3/4	11/19	Men	9
			1/12	9/29	Kan	10	3/5	11/20	Cib	10
			1/13	9/30	Chicchan	11	3/6	11/21	Caban	11
			1/14	10/1	Cimi	12	3/7	11/22	Etznab	12
			1/15	10/2	Manik	13	3/8	11/23	Cauac	13
			1/16	10/3	Lamat	1	3/9	11/24	Ahau	1
			1/17	10/4	Muluc	2	3/10	11/25	Imix	2
			1/18	10/5	Oc	3	3/11	11/26	Ik	3
			1/19	10/6	Chuen	4	3/12	11/27	Akbal	4
			1/20	10/7	Eb	5	3/13	11/28	Kan	5
			1/21	10/8	Ben	6	3/14	11/29	Chicchan	6
			1/22	10/9	Ix	7	3/15	11/30	Cimi	7
			1/23	10/10	Men	8	3/16	12/1	Manik	8
			1/24	10/11	Cib	9	3/17	12/2	Lamat	9
			1/25	10/12	Caban	10	3/18	12/3	Muluc	10
			1/26	10/13	Etznab	11	3/19	12/4	Oc	11
			1/27	10/14	Cauac	12	3/20	12/5	Chuen	12
			1/28	10/15	Ahau	13	3/21	12/6	Eb	13

BIRTHDAY		SOLAR GLYPH	TONE	BIRTHDAY	SOLAR GLYPH	TONE	BIRTHDAY	SOLAR GLYPH	TONE
3/22	12/7	Ben	1	5/13	Chicchan	1	7/4	Caban	1
3/23	12/8	Ix	2	5/14	Cimi	2	7/5	Etznab	2
3/24	12/9	Men	3	5/15	Manik	3	7/6	Cauac	3
3/25	12/10	Cib	4	5/16	Lamat	4	7/7	Ahau	4
3/26	12/11	Caban	5	5/17	Muluc	5	7/8	Imix	5
3/27	12/12	Etznab	6	5/18	Oc	6	7/9	Ik	6
3/28	12/13	Cauac	7	5/19	Chuen	7	7/10	Akbal	7
3/29	12/14	Ahau	8	5/20	Eb	8	7/11	Kan	8
3/30	12/15	Imix	9	5/21	Ben	9	7/12	Chiccan	9
3/31	12/16	Ik	10	5/22	Ix	10	7/13	Cimi	10
4/1	12/17	Akbal	11	5/23	Men	11	7/14	Manik	11
4/2	12/18	Kan	12	5/24	Cib	12	7/15	Lamat	12
4/3	12/19	Chicchan	13	5/25	Caban	13	7/16	Muluc	13
4/4	12/20	Cimi	1	5/26	Etznab	1	7/17	Oc	1
4/5	12/21	Manik	2	5/27	Cauac	2	7/18	Chuen	2
4/6	12/22	Lamat	3	5/28	Ahau	3	7/19	Eb	3
4/7	12/23	Muluc	4	5/29	Imix	4	7/20	Ben	4
4/8	12/24	Oc	5	5/30	Ik	5	7/21	Ix	5
4/9	12/25	Chuen	6	5/31	Akbal	6	7/22	Men	6
4/10	12/26	Eb	7	6/1	Kan	7	7/23	Cib	7
4/11	12/27	Ben	8	6/2	Chicchan	8	7/24	Caban	8
4/12	12/28	Ix	9	6/3	Cimi	9	7/25	Etznab	9
4/13	12/29	Men	10	6/4	Manik	10	7/26	Cauac	10
4/14	12/30	Cib	11	6/5	Lamat	11	7/27	Ahau	11
4/15	12/31	Caban	12	6/6	Muluc	12	7/28	Imix	12
4/16		Etznab	13	6/7	Oc	13	7/29	Ik	13
4/17		Cauac	1	6/8	Chuen	1	7/30	Akbal	1
4/18		Ahau	2	6/9	Eb	2	7/31	Kan	2
4/19		Imix	3	6/10	Ben	3	8/1	Chicchan	3
4/20		Ik	4	6/11	Ix	4	8/2	Cimi	4
4/21		Akbal	5	6/12	Men	5	8/3	Manik	5
4/22		Kan	6	6/13	Cib	6	8/4	Lamat	6
4/23		Chicchan	7	6/14	Caban	7	8/5	Muluc	7
4/24		Cimi	8	6/15	Etznab	8	8/6	Oc	8
4/25		Manik	9	6/16	Cauac	9	8/7	Chuen	9
4/26		Lamat	10	6/17	Ahau	10	8/8	Eb	10
4/27		Muluc	11	6/18	Imix	11	8/9	Ben	11
4/28		Oc	12	6/19	Ik	12	8/10	Ix	12
4/29		Chuen	13	6/20	Akbal	13	8/11	Men	13
4/30		Eb	1	6/21	Kan	1	8/12	Cib	1
5/1		Ben	2	6/22	Chicchan	2	8/13	Caban	2
5/2		Ix	3	6/23	Cimi	3	8/14	Etznab	3
5/3		Men	4	6/24	Manik	4	8/15	Cauac	4
5/4		Cib	5	6/25	Lamat	5	8/16	Ahau	5
5/5		Caban	6	6/26	Muluc	6	8/17	Imix	6
5/6		Etznab	7	6/27	Oc	7	8/18	Ik	7
5/7		Cauac	8	6/28	Chuen	8	8/19	Akbal	8
5/8		Ahau	9	6/29	Eb	9	8/20	Kan	9
5/9		Imix	10	6/30	Ben	10	8/21	Chicchan	10
5/10		Ik	11	7/1	Ix	11	8/22	Cimi	11
5/11		Akbal	12	7/2	Men	12	8/23	Manik	12
5/12		Kan	13	7/3	Cib	13	8/24	Lamat	13

SAMPLE

BIRTHDAY	SOLAR GLYPH	TONE

ALWAYS READ CHART FROM
LEFT TO RIGHT
STARTING WITH BIRTHDAY

DOUBLE LINES
SEPARATE SECTIONS

USE SPACE BELOW
FOR RECORDING BIRTHDAYS

BIRTHDAY		SOLAR GLYPH	TONE	BIRTHDAY		SOLAR GLYPH	TONE
	8/24	Ben	1	1/28	10/15	Chicchan	1
	8/25	Ix	2	1/29	10/16	Cimi	2
	8/26	Men	3	1/30	10/17	Manik	3
	8/27	Cib	4	1/31	10/18	Lamat	4
	8/28	Caban	5	2/1	10/19	Muluc	5
	8/29	Etznab	6	2/2	10/20	Oc	6
	8/30	Cauac	7	2/3	10/21	Chuen	7
	8/31	Ahau	8	2/4	10/22	Eb	8
	9/1	Imix	9	2/5	10/23	Ben	9
	9/2	Ik	10	2/6	10/24	Ix	10
	9/3	Akbal	11	2/7	10/25	Men	11
	9/4	Kan	12	2/8	10/26	Cib	12
	9/5	Chicchan	13	2/9	10/27	Caban	13
	9/6	Cimi	1	2/10	10/28	Etznab	1
	9/7	Manik	2	2/11	10/29	Cauac	2
	9/8	Lamat	3	2/12	10/30	Ahau	3
	9/9	Muluc	4	2/13	10/31	Imix	4
	9/10	Oc	5	2/14	11/1	Ik	5
	9/11	Chuen	6	2/15	11/2	Akbal	6
	9/12	Eb	7	2/16	11/3	Kan	7
	9/13	Ben	8	2/17	11/4	Chicchan	8
	9/14	Ix	9	2/18	11/5	Cimi	9
	9/15	Men	10	2/19	11/6	Manik	10
	9/16	Cib	11	2/20	11/7	Lamat	11
	9/17	Caban	12	2/21	11/8	Muluc	12
1/1	9/18	Etznab	13	2/22	11/9	Oc	13
1/2	9/19	Cauac	1	2/23	11/10	Chuen	1
1/3	9/20	Ahau	2	2/24	11/11	Eb	2
1/4	9/21	Imix	3	2/25	11/12	Ben	3
1/5	9/22	Ik	4	2/26	11/13	Ix	4
1/6	9/23	Akbal	5	2/27	11/14	Men	5
1/7	9/24	Kan	6	2/28	11/15	Cib	6
1/8	9/25	Chicchan	7	3/1	11/16	Caban	7
1/9	9/26	Cimi	8	3/2	11/17	Etznab	8
1/10	9/27	Manik	9	3/3	11/18	Cauac	9
1/11	9/28	Lamat	10	3/4	11/19	Ahau	10
1/12	9/29	Muluc	11	3/5	11/20	Imix	11
1/13	9/30	Oc	12	3/6	11/21	Ik	12
1/14	10/1	Chuen	13	3/7	11/22	Akbal	13
1/15	10/2	Eb	1	3/8	11/23	Kan	1
1/16	10/3	Ben	2	3/9	11/24	Chicchan	2
1/17	10/4	Ix	3	3/10	11/25	Cimi	3
1/18	10/5	Men	4	3/11	11/26	Manik	4
1/19	10/6	Cib	5	3/12	11/27	Lamat	5
1/20	10/7	Caban	6	3/13	11/28	Muluc	6
1/21	10/8	Etznab	7	3/14	11/29	Oc	7
1/22	10/9	Cauac	8	3/15	11/30	Chuen	8
1/23	10/10	Ahau	9	3/16	12/1	Eb	9
1/24	10/11	Imix	10	3/17	12/2	Ben	10
1/25	10/12	Ik	11	3/18	12/3	Ix	11
1/26	10/13	Akbal	12	3/19	12/4	Men	12
1/27	10/14	Kan	13	3/20	12/5	Cib	13

BIRTHDAY		SOLAR GLYPH	TONE	BIRTHDAY	SOLAR GLYPH	TONE	BIRTHDAY	SOLAR GLYPH	TONE
3/21	12/6	Caban	1	5/12	Muluc	1	7/3	Imix	1
3/22	12/7	Etznab	2	5/13	Oc	2	7/4	Ik	2
3/23	12/8	Cauac	3	5/14	Chuen	3	7/5	Akbal	3
3/24	12/9	Ahau	4	5/15	Eb	4	7/6	Kan	4
3/25	12/10	Imix	5	5/16	Ben	5	7/7	Chicchan	5
3/26	12/11	Ik	6	5/17	Ix	6	7/8	Cimi	6
3/27	12/12	Akbal	7	5/18	Men	7	7/9	Manik	7
3/28	12/13	Kan	8	5/19	Cib	8	7/10	Lamat	8
3/29	12/14	Chiccan	9	5/20	Caban	9	7/11	Muluc	9
3/30	12/15	Cimi	10	5/21	Etznab	10	7/12	Oc	10
3/31	12/16	Manik	11	5/22	Cauac	11	7/13	Chuen	11
4/1	12/17	Lamat	12	5/23	Ahau	12	7/14	Eb	12
4/2	12/18	Muluc	13	5/24	Imix	13	7/15	Ben	13
4/3	12/19	Oc	1	5/25	Ik	1	7/16	Ix	1
4/4	12/20	Chuen	2	5/26	Akbal	2	7/17	Men	2
4/5	12/21	Eb	3	5/27	Kan	3	7/18	Cib	3
4/6	12/22	Ben	4	5/28	Chicchan	4	7/19	Caban	4
4/7	12/23	Ix	5	5/29	Cimi	5	7/20	Etznab	5
4/8	12/24	Men	6	5/30	Manik	6	7/21	Cauac	6
4/9	12/25	Cib	7	5/31	Lamat	7	7/22	Ahau	7
4/10	12/26	Caban	8	6/1	Muluc	8	7/23	Imix	8
4/11	12/27	Etznab	9	6/2	Oc	9	7/24	Ik	9
4/12	12/28	Cauac	10	6/3	Chuen	10	7/25	Akbal	10
4/13	12/29	Ahau	11	6/4	Eb	11	7/26	Kan	11
4/14	12/30	Imix	12	6/5	Ben	12	7/27	Chicchan	12
4/15	12/31	Ik	13	6/6	Ix	13	7/28	Cimi	13
4/16		Akbal	1	6/7	Men	1	7/29	Manik	1
4/17		Kan	2	6/8	Cib	2	7/30	Lamat	2
4/18		Chicchan	3	6/9	Caban	3	7/31	Muluc	3
4/19		Cimi	4	6/10	Etznab	4	8/1	Oc	4
4/20		Manik	5	6/11	Cauac	5	8/2	Chuen	5
4/21		Lamat	6	6/12	Ahau	6	8/3	Eb	6
4/22		Muluc	7	6/13	Imix	7	8/4	Ben	7
4/23		Oc	8	6/14	Ik	8	8/5	Ix	8
4/24		Chuen	9	6/15	Akbal	9	8/6	Men	9
4/25		Eb	10	6/16	Kan	10	8/7	Cib	10
4/26		Ben	11	6/17	Chicchan	11	8/8	Caban	11
4/27		Ix	12	6/18	Cimi	12	8/9	Etznab	12
4/28		Men	13	6/19	Manik	13	8/10	Cauac	13
4/29		Cib	1	6/20	Lamat	1	8/11	Ahau	1
4/30		Caban	2	6/21	Muluc	2	8/12	Imix	2
5/1		Etznab	3	6/22	Oc	3	8/13	Ik	3
5/2		Cauac	4	6/23	Chuen	4	8/14	Akbal	4
5/3		Ahau	5	6/24	Eb	5	8/15	Kan	5
5/4		Imix	6	6/25	Ben	6	8/16	Chicchan	6
5/5		Ik	7	6/26	Ix	7	8/17	Cimi	7
5/6		Akbal	8	6/27	Men	8	8/18	Manik	8
5/7		Kan	9	6/28	Cib	9	8/19	Lamat	9
5/8		Chicchan	10	6/29	Caban	10	8/20	Muluc	10
5/9		Cimi	11	6/30	Etznab	11	8/21	Oc	11
5/10		Manik	12	7/1	Cauac	12	8/22	Chuen	12
5/11		Lamat	13	7/2	Ahau	13	8/23	Eb	13

	SAMPLE	
BIRTHDAY	SOLAR GLYPH	TONE
ALWAYS READ CHART FROM		
LEFT TO RIGHT		
STARTING WITH BIRTHDAY		
DOUBLE LINES		
SEPARATE SECTIONS		
USE SPACE BELOW		
FOR RECORDING BIRTHDAYS		

BIRTHDAY	BIRTHDAY	SOLAR GLYPH	TONE	BIRTHDAY	BIRTHDAY	SOLAR GLYPH	TONE
	8/23	Caban	1	1/27	10/14	Muluc	1
	8/24	Etznab	2	1/28	10/15	Oc	2
	8/25	Cauac	3	1/29	10/16	Chuen	3
	8/26	Ahau	4	1/30	10/17	Eb	4
	8/27	Imix	5	1/31	10/18	Ben	5
	8/28	Ik	6	2/1	10/19	Ix	6
	8/29	Akbal	7	2/2	10/20	Men	7
	8/30	Kan	8	2/3	10/21	Cib	8
	8/31	Chiccan	9	2/4	10/22	Caban	9
	9/1	Cimi	10	2/5	10/23	Etznab	10
	9/2	Manik	11	2/6	10/24	Cauac	11
	9/3	Lamat	12	2/7	10/25	Ahau	12
	9/4	Muluc	13	2/8	10/26	Imix	13
	9/5	Oc	1	2/9	10/27	Ik	1
	9/6	Chuen	2	2/10	10/28	Akbal	2
	9/7	Eb	3	2/11	10/29	Kan	3
	9/8	Ben	4	2/12	10/30	Chicchan	4
	9/9	Ix	5	2/13	10/31	Cimi	5
	9/10	Men	6	2/14	11/1	Manik	6
	9/11	Cib	7	2/15	11/2	Lamat	7
	9/12	Caban	8	2/16	11/3	Muluc	8
	9/13	Etznab	9	2/17	11/4	Oc	9
	9/14	Cauac	10	2/18	11/5	Chuen	10
	9/15	Ahau	11	2/19	11/6	Eb	11
	9/16	Imix	12	2/20	11/7	Ben	12
	9/17	Ik	13	2/21	11/8	Ix	13
1/1	9/18	Akbal	1	2/22	11/9	Men	1
1/2	9/19	Kan	2	2/23	11/10	Cib	2
1/3	9/20	Chicchan	3	2/24	11/11	Caban	3
1/4	9/21	Cimi	4	2/25	11/12	Etznab	4
1/5	9/22	Manik	5	2/26	11/13	Cauac	5
1/6	9/23	Lamat	6	2/27	11/14	Ahau	6
1/7	9/24	Muluc	7	2/28	11/15	Imix	7
1/8	9/25	Oc	8	3/1	11/16	Ik	8
1/9	9/26	Chuen	9	3/2	11/17	Akbal	9
1/10	9/27	Eb	10	3/3	11/18	Kan	10
1/11	9/28	Ben	11	3/4	11/19	Chicchan	11
1/12	9/29	Ix	12	3/5	11/20	Cimi	12
1/13	9/30	Men	13	3/6	11/21	Manik	13
1/14	10/1	Cib	1	3/7	11/22	Lamat	1
1/15	10/2	Caban	2	3/8	11/23	Muluc	2
1/16	10/3	Etznab	3	3/9	11/24	Oc	3
1/17	10/4	Cauac	4	3/10	11/25	Chuen	4
1/18	10/5	Ahau	5	3/11	11/26	Eb	5
1/19	10/6	Imix	6	3/12	11/27	Ben	6
1/20	10/7	Ik	7	3/13	11/28	Ix	7
1/21	10/8	Akbal	8	3/14	11/29	Men	8
1/22	10/9	Kan	9	3/15	11/30	Cib	9
1/23	10/10	Chicchan	10	3/16	12/1	Caban	10
1/24	10/11	Cimi	11	3/17	12/2	Etznab	11
1/25	10/12	Manik	12	3/18	12/3	Cauac	12
1/26	10/13	Lamat	13	3/19	12/4	Ahau	13

BIRTHDAY	SOLAR GLYPH	TONE	BIRTHDAY	SOLAR GLYPH	TONE	BIRTHDAY	SOLAR GLYPH	TONE
3/20 12/5	Imix	1	5/11	Ben	1	7/2	Chicchan	1
3/21 12/6	Ik	2	5/12	Ix	2	7/3	Cimi	2
3/22 12/7	Akbal	3	5/13	Men	3	7/4	Manik	3
3/23 12/8	Kan	4	5/14	Cib	4	7/5	Lamat	4
3/24 12/9	Chicchan	5	5/15	Caban	5	7/6	Muluc	5
3/25 12/10	Cimi	6	5/16	Etznab	6	7/7	Oc	6
3/26 12/11	Manik	7	5/17	Cauac	7	7/8	Chuen	7
3/27 12/12	Lamat	8	5/18	Ahau	8	7/9	Eb	8
3/28 12/13	Muluc	9	5/19	Imix	9	7/10	Ben	9
3/29 12/14	Oc	10	5/20	Ik	10	7/11	Ix	10
3/30 12/15	Chuen	11	5/21	Akbal	11	7/12	Men	11
3/31 12/16	Eb	12	5/22	Kan	12	7/13	Cib	12
4/1 12/17	Ben	13	5/23	Chicchan	13	7/14	Caban	13
4/2 12/18	Ix	1	5/24	Cimi	1	7/15	Etznab	1
4/3 12/19	Men	2	5/25	Manik	2	7/16	Cauac	2
4/4 12/20	Cib	3	5/26	Lamat	3	7/17	Ahau	3
4/5 12/21	Caban	4	5/27	Muluc	4	7/18	Imix	4
4/6 12/22	Etznab	5	5/28	Oc	5	7/19	Ik	5
4/7 12/23	Cauac	6	5/29	Chuen	6	7/20	Akbal	6
4/8 12/24	Ahau	7	5/30	Eb	7	7/21	Kan	7
4/9 12/25	Imix	8	5/31	Ben	8	7/22	Chicchan	8
4/10 12/26	Ik	9	6/1	Ix	9	7/23	Cimi	9
4/11 12/27	Akbal	10	6/2	Men	10	7/24	Manik	10
4/12 12/28	Kan	11	6/3	Cib	11	7/25	Lamat	11
4/13 12/29	Chicchan	12	6/4	Caban	12	7/26	Muluc	12
4/14 12/30	Cimi	13	6/5	Etznab	13	7/27	Oc	13
4/15 12/31	Manik	1	6/6	Cauac	1	7/28	Chuen	1
4/16	Lamat	2	6/7	Ahau	2	7/29	Eb	2
4/17	Muluc	3	6/8	Imix	3	7/30	Ben	3
4/18	Oc	4	6/9	Ik	4	7/31	Ix	4
4/19	Chuen	5	6/10	Akbal	5	8/1	Men	5
4/20	Eb	6	6/11	Kan	6	8/2	Cib	6
4/21	Ben	7	6/12	Chicchan	7	8/3	Caban	7
4/22	Ix	8	6/13	Cimi	8	8/4	Etznab	8
4/23	Men	9	6/14	Manik	9	8/5	Cauac	9
4/24	Cib	10	6/15	Lamat	10	8/6	Ahau	10
4/25	Caban	11	6/16	Muluc	11	8/7	Imix	11
4/26	Etznab	12	6/17	Oc	12	8/8	Ik	12
4/27	Cauac	13	6/18	Chuen	13	8/9	Akbal	13
4/28	Ahau	1	6/19	Eb	1	8/10	Kan	1
4/29	Imix	2	6/20	Ben	2	8/11	Chicchan	2
4/30	Ik	3	6/21	Ix	3	8/12	Cimi	3
5/1	Akbal	4	6/22	Men	4	8/13	Manik	4
5/2	Kan	5	6/23	Cib	5	8/14	Lamat	5
5/3	Chicchan	6	6/24	Caban	6	8/15	Muluc	6
5/4	Cimi	7	6/25	Etznab	7	8/16	Oc	7
5/5	Manik	8	6/26	Cauac	8	8/17	Chuen	8
5/6	Lamat	9	6/27	Ahau	9	8/18	Eb	9
5/7	Muluc	10	6/28	Imix	10	8/19	Ben	10
5/8	Oc	11	6/29	Ik	11	8/20	Ix	11
5/9	Chuen	12	6/30	Akbal	12	8/21	Men	12
5/10	Eb	13	7/1	Kan	13	8/22	Cib	13

SAMPLE			BIRTHDAY	SOLAR GLYPH	TONE	BIRTHDAY		SOLAR GLYPH	TONE
			8/22	Imix	1	1/26	10/13	Ben	1
BIRTHDAY	SOLAR GLYPH	TONE	8/23	Ik	2	1/27	10/14	Ix	2
			8/24	Akbal	3	1/28	10/15	Men	3
ALWAYS READ CHART FROM			8/25	Kan	4	1/29	10/16	Cib	4
LEFT TO RIGHT			8/26	Chicchan	5	1/30	10/17	Caban	5
STARTING WITH BIRTHDAY			8/27	Cimi	6	1/31	10/18	Etznab	6
			8/28	Manik	7	2/1	10/19	Cauac	7
DOUBLE LINES			8/29	Lamat	8	2/2	10/20	Ahau	8
SEPARATE SECTIONS			8/30	Muluc	9	2/3	10/21	Imix	9
			8/31	Oc	10	2/4	10/22	Ik	10
USE SPACE BELOW			9/1	Chuen	11	2/5	10/23	Akbal	11
FOR RECORDING BIRTHDAYS			9/2	Eb	12	2/6	10/24	Kan	12
			9/3	Ben	13	2/7	10/25	Chicchan	13
			9/4	Ix	1	2/8	10/26	Cimi	1
			9/5	Men	2	2/9	10/27	Manik	2
			9/6	Cib	3	2/10	10/28	Lamat	3
			9/7	Caban	4	2/11	10/29	Muluc	4
			9/8	Etznab	5	2/12	10/30	Oc	5
			9/9	Cauac	6	2/13	10/31	Chuen	6
			9/10	Ahau	7	2/14	11/1	Eb	7
			9/11	Imix	8	2/15	11/2	Ben	8
			9/12	Ik	9	2/16	11/3	Ix	9
			9/13	Akbal	10	2/17	11/4	Men	10
			9/14	Kan	11	2/18	11/5	Cib	11
			9/15	Chicchan	12	2/19	11/6	Caban	12
			9/16	Cimi	13	2/20	11/7	Etznab	13
			9/17	Manik	1	2/21	11/8	Cauac	1
		1/1	9/18	Lamat	2	2/22	11/9	Ahau	2
		1/2	9/19	Muluc	3	2/23	11/10	Imix	3
		1/3	9/20	Oc	4	2/24	11/11	Ik	4
		1/4	9/21	Chuen	5	2/25	11/12	Akbal	5
		1/5	9/22	Eb	6	2/26	11/13	Kan	6
		1/6	9/23	Ben	7	2/27	11/14	Chicchan	7
		1/7	9/24	Ix	8	2/28	11/15	Cimi	8
		1/8	9/25	Men	9	3/1	11/16	Manik	9
		1/9	9/26	Cib	10	3/2	11/17	Lamat	10
		1/10	9/27	Caban	11	3/3	11/18	Muluc	11
		1/11	9/28	Etznab	12	3/4	11/19	Oc	12
		1/12	9/29	Cauac	13	3/5	11/20	Chuen	13
		1/13	9/30	Ahau	1	3/6	11/21	Eb	1
		1/14	10/1	Imix	2	3/7	11/22	Ben	2
		1/15	10/2	Ik	3	3/8	11/23	Ix	3
		1/16	10/3	Akbal	4	3/9	11/24	Men	4
		1/17	10/4	Kan	5	3/10	11/25	Cib	5
		1/18	10/5	Chicchan	6	3/11	11/26	Caban	6
		1/19	10/6	Cimi	7	3/12	11/27	Etznab	7
		1/20	10/7	Manik	8	3/13	11/28	Cauac	8
		1/21	10/8	Lamat	9	3/14	11/29	Ahau	9
		1/22	10/9	Muluc	10	3/15	11/30	Imix	10
		1/23	10/10	Oc	11	3/16	12/1	Ik	11
		1/24	10/11	Chuen	12	3/17	12/2	Akbal	12
		1/25	10/12	Eb	13	3/18	12/3	Kan	13

BIRTHDAY		SOLAR GLYPH	TONE	BIRTHDAY	SOLAR GLYPH	TONE	BIRTHDAY	SOLAR GLYPH	TONE
3/19	12/4	Chicchan	1	5/10	Caban	1	7/1	Muluc	1
3/20	12/5	Cimi	2	5/11	Etznab	2	7/2	Oc	2
3/21	12/6	Manik	3	5/12	Cauac	3	7/3	Chuen	3
3/22	12/7	Lamat	4	5/13	Ahau	4	7/4	Eb	4
3/23	12/8	Muluc	5	5/14	Imix	5	7/5	Ben	5
3/24	12/9	Oc	6	5/15	Ik	6	7/6	Ix	6
3/25	12/10	Chuen	7	5/16	Akbal	7	7/7	Men	7
3/26	12/11	Eb	8	5/17	Kan	8	7/8	Cib	8
3/27	12/12	Ben	9	5/18	Chiccan	9	7/9	Caban	9
3/28	12/13	Ix	10	5/19	Cimi	10	7/10	Etznab	10
3/29	12/14	Men	11	5/20	Manik	11	7/11	Cauac	11
3/30	12/15	Cib	12	5/21	Lamat	12	7/12	Ahau	12
3/31	12/16	Caban	13	5/22	Muluc	13	7/13	Imix	13
4/1	12/17	Etznab	1	5/23	Oc	1	7/14	Ik	1
4/2	12/18	Cauac	2	5/24	Chuen	2	7/15	Akbal	2
4/3	12/19	Ahau	3	5/25	Eb	3	7/16	Kan	3
4/4	12/20	Imix	4	5/26	Ben	4	7/17	Chicchan	4
4/5	12/21	Ik	5	5/27	Ix	5	7/18	Cimi	5
4/6	12/22	Akbal	6	5/28	Men	6	7/19	Manik	6
4/7	12/23	Kan	7	5/29	Cib	7	7/20	Lamat	7
4/8	12/24	Chicchan	8	5/30	Caban	8	7/21	Muluc	8
4/9	12/25	Cimi	9	5/31	Etznab	9	7/22	Oc	9
4/10	12/26	Manik	10	6/1	Cauac	10	7/23	Chuen	10
4/11	12/27	Lamat	11	6/2	Ahau	11	7/24	Eb	11
4/12	12/28	Muluc	12	6/3	Imix	12	7/25	Ben	12
4/13	12/29	Oc	13	6/4	Ik	13	7/26	Ix	13
4/14	12/30	Chuen	1	6/5	Akbal	1	7/27	Men	1
4/15	12/31	Eb	2	6/6	Kan	2	7/28	Cib	2
4/16		Ben	3	6/7	Chicchan	3	7/29	Caban	3
4/17		Ix	4	6/8	Cimi	4	7/30	Etznab	4
4/18		Men	5	6/9	Manik	5	7/31	Cauac	5
4/19		Cib	6	6/10	Lamat	6	8/1	Ahau	6
4/20		Caban	7	6/11	Muluc	7	8/2	Imix	7
4/21		Etznab	8	6/12	Oc	8	8/3	Ik	8
4/22		Cauac	9	6/13	Chuen	9	8/4	Akbal	9
4/23		Ahau	10	6/14	Eb	10	8/5	Kan	10
4/24		Imix	11	6/15	Ben	11	8/6	Chicchan	11
4/25		Ik	12	6/16	Ix	12	8/7	Cimi	12
4/26		Akbal	13	6/17	Men	13	8/8	Manik	13
4/27		Kan	1	6/18	Cib	1	8/9	Lamat	1
4/28		Chicchan	2	6/19	Caban	2	8/10	Muluc	2
4/29		Cimi	3	6/20	Etznab	3	8/11	Oc	3
4/30		Manik	4	6/21	Cauac	4	8/12	Chuen	4
5/1		Lamat	5	6/22	Ahau	5	8/13	Eb	5
5/2		Muluc	6	6/23	Imix	6	8/14	Ben	6
5/3		Oc	7	6/24	Ik	7	8/15	Ix	7
5/4		Chuen	8	6/25	Akbal	8	8/16	Men	8
5/5		Eb	9	6/26	Kan	9	8/17	Cib	9
5/6		Ben	10	6/27	Chicchan	10	8/18	Caban	10
5/7		Ix	11	6/28	Cimi	11	8/19	Etznab	11
5/8		Men	12	6/29	Manik	12	8/20	Cauac	12
5/9		Cib	13	6/30	Lamat	13	8/21	Ahau	13

SAMPLE

BIRTHDAY	SOLAR GLYPH	TONE

ALWAYS READ CHART FROM
LEFT TO RIGHT
STARTING WITH BIRTHDAY

DOUBLE LINES
SEPARATE SECTIONS

USE SPACE BELOW
FOR RECORDING BIRTHDAYS

		BIRTHDAY	SOLAR GLYPH	TONE	BIRTHDAY		SOLAR GLYPH	TONE
		8/21	Chicchan	1	1/25	10/12	Caban	1
		8/22	Cimi	2	1/26	10/13	Etznab	2
		8/23	Manik	3	1/27	10/14	Cauac	3
		8/24	Lamat	4	1/28	10/15	Ahau	4
		8/25	Muluc	5	1/29	10/16	Imix	5
		8/26	Oc	6	1/30	10/17	Ik	6
		8/27	Chuen	7	1/31	10/18	Akbal	7
		8/28	Eb	8	2/1	10/19	Kan	8
		8/29	Ben	9	2/2	10/20	Chiccan	9
		8/30	Ix	10	2/3	10/21	Cimi	10
		8/31	Men	11	2/4	10/22	Manik	11
		9/1	Cib	12	2/5	10/23	Lamat	12
		9/2	Caban	13	2/6	10/24	Muluc	13
		9/3	Etznab	1	2/7	10/25	Oc	1
		9/4	Cauac	2	2/8	10/26	Chuen	2
		9/5	Ahau	3	2/9	10/27	Eb	3
		9/6	Imix	4	2/10	10/28	Ben	4
		9/7	Ik	5	2/11	10/29	Ix	5
		9/8	Akbal	6	2/12	10/30	Men	6
		9/9	Kan	7	2/13	10/31	Cib	7
		9/10	Chicchan	8	2/14	11/1	Caban	8
		9/11	Cimi	9	2/15	11/2	Etznab	9
		9/12	Manik	10	2/16	11/3	Cauac	10
		9/13	Lamat	11	2/17	11/4	Ahau	11
		9/14	Muluc	12	2/18	11/5	Imix	12
		9/15	Oc	13	2/19	11/6	Ik	13
		9/16	Chuen	1	2/20	11/7	Akbal	1
		9/17	Eb	2	2/21	11/8	Kan	2
1/1	9/18	Ben	3	2/22	11/9	Chiccan	3	
1/2	9/19	Ix	4	2/23	11/10	Cimi	4	
1/3	9/20	Men	5	2/24	11/11	Manik	5	
1/4	9/21	Cib	6	2/25	11/12	Lamat	6	
1/5	9/22	Caban	7	2/26	11/13	Muluc	7	
1/6	9/23	Etznab	8	2/27	11/14	Oc	8	
1/7	9/24	Cauac	9	2/28	11/15	Chuen	9	
1/8	9/25	Ahau	10	3/1	11/16	Eb	10	
1/9	9/26	Imix	11	3/2	11/17	Ben	11	
1/10	9/27	Ik	12	3/3	11/18	Ix	12	
1/11	9/28	Akbal	13	3/4	11/19	Men	13	
1/12	9/29	Kan	1	3/5	11/20	Cib	1	
1/13	9/30	Chicchan	2	3/6	11/21	Caban	2	
1/14	10/1	Cimi	3	3/7	11/22	Etznab	3	
1/15	10/2	Manik	4	3/8	11/23	Cauac	4	
1/16	10/3	Lamat	5	3/9	11/24	Ahau	5	
1/17	10/4	Muluc	6	3/10	11/25	Imix	6	
1/18	10/5	Oc	7	3/11	11/26	Ik	7	
1/19	10/6	Chuen	8	3/12	11/27	Akbal	8	
1/20	10/7	Eb	9	3/13	11/28	Kan	9	
1/21	10/8	Ben	10	3/14	11/29	Chiccan	10	
1/22	10/9	Ix	11	3/15	11/30	Cimi	11	
1/23	10/10	Men	12	3/16	12/1	Manik	12	
1/24	10/11	Cib	13	3/17	12/2	Lamat	13	

BIRTHDAY		SOLAR GLYPH	TONE	BIRTHDAY	SOLAR GLYPH	TONE	BIRTHDAY	SOLAR GLYPH	TONE
3/18	12/3	Muluc	1	5/9	Imix	1	6/30	Ben	1
3/19	12/4	Oc	2	5/10	Ik	2	7/1	Ix	2
3/20	12/5	Chuen	3	5/11	Akbal	3	7/2	Men	3
3/21	12/6	Eb	4	5/12	Kan	4	7/3	Cib	4
3/22	12/7	Ben	5	5/13	Chicchan	5	7/4	Caban	5
3/23	12/8	Ix	6	5/14	Cimi	6	7/5	Etznab	6
3/24	12/9	Men	7	5/15	Manik	7	7/6	Cauac	7
3/25	12/10	Cib	8	5/16	Lamat	8	7/7	Ahau	8
3/26	12/11	Caban	9	5/17	Muluc	9	7/8	Imix	9
3/27	12/12	Etznab	10	5/18	Oc	10	7/9	Ik	10
3/28	12/13	Cauac	11	5/19	Chuen	11	7/10	Akbal	11
3/29	12/14	Ahau	12	5/20	Eb	12	7/11	Kan	12
3/30	12/15	Imix	13	5/21	Ben	13	7/12	Chicchan	13
3/31	12/16	Ik	1	5/22	Ix	1	7/13	Cimi	1
4/1	12/17	Akbal	2	5/23	Men	2	7/14	Manik	2
4/2	12/18	Kan	3	5/24	Cib	3	7/15	Lamat	3
4/3	12/19	Chicchan	4	5/25	Caban	4	7/16	Muluc	4
4/4	12/20	Cimi	5	5/26	Etznab	5	7/17	Oc	5
4/5	12/21	Manik	6	5/27	Cauac	6	7/18	Chuen	6
4/6	12/22	Lamat	7	5/28	Ahau	7	7/19	Eb	7
4/7	12/23	Muluc	8	5/29	Imix	8	7/20	Ben	8
4/8	12/24	Oc	9	5/30	Ik	9	7/21	Ix	9
4/9	12/25	Chuen	10	5/31	Akbal	10	7/22	Men	10
4/10	12/26	Eb	11	6/1	Kan	11	7/23	Cib	11
4/11	12/27	Ben	12	6/2	Chicchan	12	7/24	Caban	12
4/12	12/28	Ix	13	6/3	Cimi	13	7/25	Etznab	13
4/13	12/29	Men	1	6/4	Manik	1	7/26	Cauac	1
4/14	12/30	Cib	2	6/5	Lamat	2	7/27	Ahau	2
4/15	12/31	Caban	3	6/6	Muluc	3	7/28	Imix	3
4/16		Etznab	4	6/7	Oc	4	7/29	Ik	4
4/17		Cauac	5	6/8	Chuen	5	7/30	Akbal	5
4/18		Ahau	6	6/9	Eb	6	7/31	Kan	6
4/19		Imix	7	6/10	Ben	7	8/1	Chicchan	7
4/20		Ik	8	6/11	Ix	8	8/2	Cimi	8
4/21		Akbal	9	6/12	Men	9	8/3	Manik	9
4/22		Kan	10	6/13	Cib	10	8/4	Lamat	10
4/23		Chicchan	11	6/14	Caban	11	8/5	Muluc	11
4/24		Cimi	12	6/15	Etznab	12	8/6	Oc	12
4/25		Manik	13	6/16	Cauac	13	8/7	Chuen	13
4/26		Lamat	1	6/17	Ahau	1	8/8	Eb	1
4/27		Muluc	2	6/18	Imix	2	8/9	Ben	2
4/28		Oc	3	6/19	Ik	3	8/10	Ix	3
4/29		Chuen	4	6/20	Akbal	4	8/11	Men	4
4/30		Eb	5	6/21	Kan	5	8/12	Cib	5
5/1		Ben	6	6/22	Chicchan	6	8/13	Caban	6
5/2		Ix	7	6/23	Cimi	7	8/14	Etznab	7
5/3		Men	8	6/24	Manik	8	8/15	Cauac	8
5/4		Cib	9	6/25	Lamat	9	8/16	Ahau	9
5/5		Caban	10	6/26	Muluc	10	8/17	Imix	10
5/6		Etznab	11	6/27	Oc	11	8/18	Ik	11
5/7		Cauac	12	6/28	Chuen	12	8/19	Akbal	12
5/8		Ahau	13	6/29	Eb	13	8/20	Kan	13

SAMPLE

BIRTHDAY	SOLAR GLYPH	TONE
ALWAYS READ CHART FROM		
LEFT TO RIGHT		
STARTING WITH BIRTHDAY		
DOUBLE LINES		
SEPARATE SECTIONS		
USE SPACE BELOW		
FOR RECORDING BIRTHDAYS		

BIRTHDAY	BIRTHDAY	SOLAR GLYPH	TONE	BIRTHDAY	BIRTHDAY	SOLAR GLYPH	TONE
	8/20	Muluc	1	1/24	10/11	Imix	1
	8/21	Oc	2	1/25	10/12	Ik	2
	8/22	Chuen	3	1/26	10/13	Akbal	3
	8/23	Eb	4	1/27	10/14	Kan	4
	8/24	Ben	5	1/28	10/15	Chicchan	5
	8/25	Ix	6	1/29	10/16	Cimi	6
	8/26	Men	7	1/30	10/17	Manik	7
	8/27	Cib	8	1/31	10/18	Lamat	8
	8/28	Caban	9	2/1	10/19	Muluc	9
	8/29	Etznab	10	2/2	10/20	Oc	10
	8/30	Cauac	11	2/3	10/21	Chuen	11
	8/31	Ahau	12	2/4	10/22	Eb	12
	9/1	Imix	13	2/5	10/23	Ben	13
	9/2	Ik	1	2/6	10/24	Ix	1
	9/3	Akbal	2	2/7	10/25	Men	2
	9/4	Kan	3	2/8	10/26	Cib	3
	9/5	Chicchan	4	2/9	10/27	Caban	4
	9/6	Cimi	5	2/10	10/28	Etznab	5
	9/7	Manik	6	2/11	10/29	Cauac	6
	9/8	Lamat	7	2/12	10/30	Ahau	7
	9/9	Muluc	8	2/13	10/31	Imix	8
	9/10	Oc	9	2/14	11/1	Ik	9
	9/11	Chuen	10	2/15	11/2	Akbal	10
	9/12	Eb	11	2/16	11/3	Kan	11
	9/13	Ben	12	2/17	11/4	Chicchan	12
	9/14	Ix	13	2/18	11/5	Cimi	13
	9/15	Men	1	2/19	11/6	Manik	1
	9/16	Cib	2	2/20	11/7	Lamat	2
	9/17	Caban	3	2/21	11/8	Muluc	3
1/1	9/18	Etznab	4	2/22	11/9	Oc	4
1/2	9/19	Cauac	5	2/23	11/10	Chuen	5
1/3	9/20	Ahau	6	2/24	11/11	Eb	6
1/4	9/21	Imix	7	2/25	11/12	Ben	7
1/5	9/22	Ik	8	2/26	11/13	Ix	8
1/6	9/23	Akbal	9	2/27	11/14	Men	9
1/7	9/24	Kan	10	2/28	11/15	Cib	10
1/8	9/25	Chicchan	11	3/1	11/16	Caban	11
1/9	9/26	Cimi	12	3/2	11/17	Etznab	12
1/10	9/27	Manik	13	3/3	11/18	Cauac	13
1/11	9/28	Lamat	1	3/4	11/19	Ahau	1
1/12	9/29	Muluc	2	3/5	11/20	Imix	2
1/13	9/30	Oc	3	3/6	11/21	Ik	3
1/14	10/1	Chuen	4	3/7	11/22	Akbal	4
1/15	10/2	Eb	5	3/8	11/23	Kan	5
1/16	10/3	Ben	6	3/9	11/24	Chicchan	6
1/17	10/4	Ix	7	3/10	11/25	Cimi	7
1/18	10/5	Men	8	3/11	11/26	Manik	8
1/19	10/6	Cib	9	3/12	11/27	Lamat	9
1/20	10/7	Caban	10	3/13	11/28	Muluc	10
1/21	10/8	Etznab	11	3/14	11/29	Oc	11
1/22	10/9	Cauac	12	3/15	11/30	Chuen	12
1/23	10/10	Ahau	13	3/16	12/1	Eb	13

BIRTHDAY		SOLAR GLYPH	TONE	BIRTHDAY	SOLAR GLYPH	TONE	BIRTHDAY	SOLAR GLYPH	TONE
3/17	12/2	Ben	1	5/8	Chicchan	1	6/29	Caban	1
3/18	12/3	Ix	2	5/9	Cimi	2	6/30	Etznab	2
3/19	12/4	Men	3	5/10	Manik	3	7/1	Cauac	3
3/20	12/5	Cib	4	5/11	Lamat	4	7/2	Ahau	4
3/21	12/6	Caban	5	5/12	Muluc	5	7/3	Imix	5
3/22	12/7	Etznab	6	5/13	Oc	6	7/4	Ik	6
3/23	12/8	Cauac	7	5/14	Chuen	7	7/5	Akbal	7
3/24	12/9	Ahau	8	5/15	Eb	8	7/6	Kan	8
3/25	12/10	Imix	9	5/16	Ben	9	7/7	Chiccan	9
3/26	12/11	Ik	10	5/17	Ix	10	7/8	Cimi	10
3/27	12/12	Akbal	11	5/18	Men	11	7/9	Manik	11
3/28	12/13	Kan	12	5/19	Cib	12	7/10	Lamat	12
3/29	12/14	Chicchan	13	5/20	Caban	13	7/11	Muluc	13
3/30	12/15	Cimi	1	5/21	Etznab	1	7/12	Oc	1
3/31	12/16	Manik	2	5/22	Cauac	2	7/13	Chuen	2
4/1	12/17	Lamat	3	5/23	Ahau	3	7/14	Eb	3
4/2	12/18	Muluc	4	5/24	Imix	4	7/15	Ben	4
4/3	12/19	Oc	5	5/25	Ik	5	7/16	Ix	5
4/4	12/20	Chuen	6	5/26	Akbal	6	7/17	Men	6
4/5	12/21	Eb	7	5/27	Kan	7	7/18	Cib	7
4/6	12/22	Ben	8	5/28	Chicchan	8	7/19	Caban	8
4/7	12/23	Ix	9	5/29	Cimi	9	7/20	Etznab	9
4/8	12/24	Men	10	5/30	Manik	10	7/21	Cauac	10
4/9	12/25	Cib	11	5/31	Lamat	11	7/22	Ahau	11
4/10	12/26	Caban	12	6/1	Muluc	12	7/23	Imix	12
4/11	12/27	Etznab	13	6/2	Oc	13	7/24	Ik	13
4/12	12/28	Cauac	1	6/3	Chuen	1	7/25	Akbal	1
4/13	12/29	Ahau	2	6/4	Eb	2	7/26	Kan	2
4/14	12/30	Imix	3	6/5	Ben	3	7/27	Chicchan	3
4/15	12/31	Ik	4	6/6	Ix	4	7/28	Cimi	4
4/16		Akbal	5	6/7	Men	5	7/29	Manik	5
4/17		Kan	6	6/8	Cib	6	7/30	Lamat	6
4/18		Chicchan	7	6/9	Caban	7	7/31	Muluc	7
4/19		Cimi	8	6/10	Etznab	8	8/1	Oc	8
4/20		Manik	9	6/11	Cauac	9	8/2	Chuen	9
4/21		Lamat	10	6/12	Ahau	10	8/3	Eb	10
4/22		Muluc	11	6/13	Imix	11	8/4	Ben	11
4/23		Oc	12	6/14	Ik	12	8/5	Ix	12
4/24		Chuen	13	6/15	Akbal	13	8/6	Men	13
4/25		Eb	1	6/16	Kan	1	8/7	Cib	1
4/26		Ben	2	6/17	Chicchan	2	8/8	Caban	2
4/27		Ix	3	6/18	Cimi	3	8/9	Etznab	3
4/28		Men	4	6/19	Manik	4	8/10	Cauac	4
4/29		Cib	5	6/20	Lamat	5	8/11	Ahau	5
4/30		Caban	6	6/21	Muluc	6	8/12	Imix	6
5/1		Etznab	7	6/22	Oc	7	8/13	Ik	7
5/2		Cauac	8	6/23	Chuen	8	8/14	Akbal	8
5/3		Ahau	9	6/24	Eb	9	8/15	Kan	9
5/4		Imix	10	6/25	Ben	10	8/16	Chicchan	10
5/5		Ik	11	6/26	Ix	11	8/17	Cimi	11
5/6		Akbal	12	6/27	Men	12	8/18	Manik	12
5/7		Kan	13	6/28	Cib	13	8/19	Lamat	13

SAMPLE			BIRTHDAY	SOLAR GLYPH	TONE	BIRTHDAY		SOLAR GLYPH	TONE
			8/19	Ben	1	1/23	10/10	Chicchan	1
BIRTHDAY	SOLAR GLYPH	TONE	8/20	Ix	2	1/24	10/11	Cimi	2
			8/21	Men	3	1/25	10/12	Manik	3
ALWAYS READ CHART FROM			8/22	Cib	4	1/26	10/13	Lamat	4
LEFT TO RIGHT			8/23	Caban	5	1/27	10/14	Muluc	5
STARTING WITH BIRTHDAY			8/24	Etznab	6	1/28	10/15	Oc	6
			8/25	Cauac	7	1/29	10/16	Chuen	7
DOUBLE LINES			8/26	Ahau	8	1/30	10/17	Eb	8
SEPARATE SECTIONS			8/27	Imix	9	1/31	10/18	Ben	9
			8/28	Ik	10	2/1	10/19	Ix	10
USE SPACE BELOW			8/29	Akbal	11	2/2	10/20	Men	11
FOR RECORDING BIRTHDAYS			8/30	Kan	12	2/3	10/21	Cib	12
			8/31	Chicchan	13	2/4	10/22	Caban	13
			9/1	Cimi	1	2/5	10/23	Etznab	1
			9/2	Manik	2	2/6	10/24	Cauac	2
			9/3	Lamat	3	2/7	10/25	Ahau	3
			9/4	Muluc	4	2/8	10/26	Imix	4
			9/5	Oc	5	2/9	10/27	Ik	5
			9/6	Chuen	6	2/10	10/28	Akbal	6
			9/7	Eb	7	2/11	10/29	Kan	7
			9/8	Ben	8	2/12	10/30	Chicchan	8
			9/9	Ix	9	2/13	10/31	Cimi	9
			9/10	Men	10	2/14	11/1	Manik	10
			9/11	Cib	11	2/15	11/2	Lamat	11
			9/12	Caban	12	2/16	11/3	Muluc	12
			9/13	Etznab	13	2/17	11/4	Oc	13
			9/14	Cauac	1	2/18	11/5	Chuen	1
			9/15	Ahau	2	2/19	11/6	Eb	2
			9/16	Imix	3	2/20	11/7	Ben	3
			9/17	Ik	4	2/21	11/8	Ix	4
		1/1	9/18	Akbal	5	2/22	11/9	Men	5
		1/2	9/19	Kan	6	2/23	11/10	Cib	6
		1/3	9/20	Chicchan	7	2/24	11/11	Caban	7
		1/4	9/21	Cimi	8	2/25	11/12	Etznab	8
		1/5	9/22	Manik	9	2/26	11/13	Cauac	9
		1/6	9/23	Lamat	10	2/27	11/14	Ahau	10
		1/7	9/24	Muluc	11	2/28	11/15	Imix	11
		1/8	9/25	Oc	12	3/1	11/16	Ik	12
		1/9	9/26	Chuen	13	3/2	11/17	Akbal	13
		1/10	9/27	Eb	1	3/3	11/18	Kan	1
		1/11	9/28	Ben	2	3/4	11/19	Chicchan	2
		1/12	9/29	Ix	3	3/5	11/20	Cimi	3
		1/13	9/30	Men	4	3/6	11/21	Manik	4
		1/14	10/1	Cib	5	3/7	11/22	Lamat	5
		1/15	10/2	Caban	6	3/8	11/23	Muluc	6
		1/16	10/3	Etznab	7	3/9	11/24	Oc	7
		1/17	10/4	Cauac	8	3/10	11/25	Chuen	8
		1/18	10/5	Ahau	9	3/11	11/26	Eb	9
		1/19	10/6	Imix	10	3/12	11/27	Ben	10
		1/20	10/7	Ik	11	3/13	11/28	Ix	11
		1/21	10/8	Akbal	12	3/14	11/29	Men	12
		1/22	10/9	Kan	13	3/15	11/30	Cib	13

BIRTHDAY		SOLAR GLYPH	TONE	BIRTHDAY	SOLAR GLYPH	TONE	BIRTHDAY	SOLAR GLYPH	TONE
3/16	12/1	Caban	1	5/7	Muluc	1	6/28	Imix	1
3/17	12/2	Etznab	2	5/8	Oc	2	6/29	Ik	2
3/18	12/3	Cauac	3	5/9	Chuen	3	6/30	Akbal	3
3/19	12/4	Ahau	4	5/10	Eb	4	7/1	Kan	4
3/20	12/5	Imix	5	5/11	Ben	5	7/2	Chicchan	5
3/21	12/6	Ik	6	5/12	Ix	6	7/3	Cimi	6
3/22	12/7	Akbal	7	5/13	Men	7	7/4	Manik	7
3/23	12/8	Kan	8	5/14	Cib	8	7/5	Lamat	8
3/24	12/9	Chiccan	9	5/15	Caban	9	7/6	Muluc	9
3/25	12/10	Cimi	10	5/16	Etznab	10	7/7	Oc	10
3/26	12/11	Manik	11	5/17	Cauac	11	7/8	Chuen	11
3/27	12/12	Lamat	12	5/18	Ahau	12	7/9	Eb	12
3/28	12/13	Muluc	13	5/19	Imix	13	7/10	Ben	13
3/29	12/14	Oc	1	5/20	Ik	1	7/11	Ix	1
3/30	12/15	Chuen	2	5/21	Akbal	2	7/12	Men	2
3/31	12/16	Eb	3	5/22	Kan	3	7/13	Cib	3
4/1	12/17	Ben	4	5/23	Chicchan	4	7/14	Caban	4
4/2	12/18	Ix	5	5/24	Cimi	5	7/15	Etznab	5
4/3	12/19	Men	6	5/25	Manik	6	7/16	Cauac	6
4/4	12/20	Cib	7	5/26	Lamat	7	7/17	Ahau	7
4/5	12/21	Caban	8	5/27	Muluc	8	7/18	Imix	8
4/6	12/22	Etznab	9	5/28	Oc	9	7/19	Ik	9
4/7	12/23	Cauac	10	5/29	Chuen	10	7/20	Akbal	10
4/8	12/24	Ahau	11	5/30	Eb	11	7/21	Kan	11
4/9	12/25	Imix	12	5/31	Ben	12	7/22	Chicchan	12
4/10	12/26	Ik	13	6/1	Ix	13	7/23	Cimi	13
4/11	12/27	Akbal	1	6/2	Men	1	7/24	Manik	1
4/12	12/28	Kan	2	6/3	Cib	2	7/25	Lamat	2
4/13	12/29	Chicchan	3	6/4	Caban	3	7/26	Muluc	3
4/14	12/30	Cimi	4	6/5	Etznab	4	7/27	Oc	4
4/15	12/31	Manik	5	6/6	Cauac	5	7/28	Chuen	5
4/16		Lamat	6	6/7	Ahau	6	7/29	Eb	6
4/17		Muluc	7	6/8	Imix	7	7/30	Ben	7
4/18		Oc	8	6/9	Ik	8	7/31	Ix	8
4/19		Chuen	9	6/10	Akbal	9	8/1	Men	9
4/20		Eb	10	6/11	Kan	10	8/2	Cib	10
4/21		Ben	11	6/12	Chicchan	11	8/3	Caban	11
4/22		Ix	12	6/13	Cimi	12	8/4	Etznab	12
4/23		Men	13	6/14	Manik	13	8/5	Cauac	13
4/24		Cib	1	6/15	Lamat	1	8/6	Ahau	1
4/25		Caban	2	6/16	Muluc	2	8/7	Imix	2
4/26		Etznab	3	6/17	Oc	3	8/8	Ik	3
4/27		Cauac	4	6/18	Chuen	4	8/9	Akbal	4
4/28		Ahau	5	6/19	Eb	5	8/10	Kan	5
4/29		Imix	6	6/20	Ben	6	8/11	Chicchan	6
4/30		Ik	7	6/21	Ix	7	8/12	Cimi	7
5/1		Akbal	8	6/22	Men	8	8/13	Manik	8
5/2		Kan	9	6/23	Cib	9	8/14	Lamat	9
5/3		Chicchan	10	6/24	Caban	10	8/15	Muluc	10
5/4		Cimi	11	6/25	Etznab	11	8/16	Oc	11
5/5		Manik	12	6/26	Cauac	12	8/17	Chuen	12
5/6		Lamat	13	6/27	Ahau	13	8/18	Eb	13

SAMPLE

BIRTHDAY	SOLAR GLYPH	TONE
ALWAYS READ CHART FROM		
LEFT TO RIGHT		
STARTING WITH BIRTHDAY		
DOUBLE LINES		
SEPARATE SECTIONS		
USE SPACE BELOW		
FOR RECORDING BIRTHDAYS		

	BIRTHDAY	SOLAR GLYPH	TONE		BIRTHDAY	SOLAR GLYPH	TONE
	8/18	Caban	1	1/22	10/9	Muluc	1
	8/19	Etznab	2	1/23	10/10	Oc	2
	8/20	Cauac	3	1/24	10/11	Chuen	3
	8/21	Ahau	4	1/25	10/12	Eb	4
	8/22	Imix	5	1/26	10/13	Ben	5
	8/23	Ik	6	1/27	10/14	Ix	6
	8/24	Akbal	7	1/28	10/15	Men	7
	8/25	Kan	8	1/29	10/16	Cib	8
	8/26	Chiccan	9	1/30	10/17	Caban	9
	8/27	Cimi	10	1/31	10/18	Etznab	10
	8/28	Manik	11	2/1	10/19	Cauac	11
	8/29	Lamat	12	2/2	10/20	Ahau	12
	8/30	Muluc	13	2/3	10/21	Imix	13
	8/31	Oc	1	2/4	10/22	Ik	1
	9/1	Chuen	2	2/5	10/23	Akbal	2
	9/2	Eb	3	2/6	10/24	Kan	3
	9/3	Ben	4	2/7	10/25	Chicchan	4
	9/4	Ix	5	2/8	10/26	Cimi	5
	9/5	Men	6	2/9	10/27	Manik	6
	9/6	Cib	7	2/10	10/28	Lamat	7
	9/7	Caban	8	2/11	10/29	Muluc	8
	9/8	Etznab	9	2/12	10/30	Oc	9
	9/9	Cauac	10	2/13	10/31	Chuen	10
	9/10	Ahau	11	2/14	11/1	Eb	11
	9/11	Imix	12	2/15	11/2	Ben	12
	9/12	Ik	13	2/16	11/3	Ix	13
	9/13	Akbal	1	2/17	11/4	Men	1
	9/14	Kan	2	2/18	11/5	Cib	2
	9/15	Chiccan	3	2/19	11/6	Caban	3
	9/16	Cimi	4	2/20	11/7	Etznab	4
	9/17	Manik	5	2/21	11/8	Cauac	5
1/1	9/18	Lamat	6	2/22	11/9	Ahau	6
1/2	9/19	Muluc	7	2/23	11/10	Imix	7
1/3	9/20	Oc	8	2/24	11/11	Ik	8
1/4	9/21	Chuen	9	2/25	11/12	Akbal	9
1/5	9/22	Eb	10	2/26	11/13	Kan	10
1/6	9/23	Ben	11	2/27	11/14	Chicchan	11
1/7	9/24	Ix	12	2/28	11/15	Cimi	12
1/8	9/25	Men	13	3/1	11/16	Manik	13
1/9	9/26	Cib	1	3/2	11/17	Lamat	1
1/10	9/27	Caban	2	3/3	11/18	Muluc	2
1/11	9/28	Etznab	3	3/4	11/19	Oc	3
1/12	9/29	Cauac	4	3/5	11/20	Chuen	4
1/13	9/30	Ahau	5	3/6	11/21	Eb	5
1/14	10/1	Imix	6	3/7	11/22	Ben	6
1/15	10/2	Ik	7	3/8	11/23	Ix	7
1/16	10/3	Akbal	8	3/9	11/24	Men	8
1/17	10/4	Kan	9	3/10	11/25	Cib	9
1/18	10/5	Chiccan	10	3/11	11/26	Caban	10
1/19	10/6	Cimi	11	3/12	11/27	Etznab	11
1/20	10/7	Manik	12	3/13	11/28	Cauac	12
1/21	10/8	Lamat	13	3/14	11/29	Ahau	13

BIRTHDAY		SOLAR GLYPH	TONE	BIRTHDAY	SOLAR GLYPH	TONE	BIRTHDAY	SOLAR GLYPH	TONE
3/15	11/30	Imix	1	5/6	Ben	1	6/27	Chicchan	1
3/16	12/1	Ik	2	5/7	Ix	2	6/28	Cimi	2
3/17	12/2	Akbal	3	5/8	Men	3	6/29	Manik	3
3/18	12/3	Kan	4	5/9	Cib	4	6/30	Lamat	4
3/19	12/4	Chicchan	5	5/10	Caban	5	7/1	Muluc	5
3/20	12/5	Cimi	6	5/11	Etznab	6	7/2	Oc	6
3/21	12/6	Manik	7	5/12	Cauac	7	7/3	Chuen	7
3/22	12/7	Lamat	8	5/13	Ahau	8	7/4	Eb	8
3/23	12/8	Muluc	9	5/14	Imix	9	7/5	Ben	9
3/24	12/9	Oc	10	5/15	Ik	10	7/6	Ix	10
3/25	12/10	Chuen	11	5/16	Akbal	11	7/7	Men	11
3/26	12/11	Eb	12	5/17	Kan	12	7/8	Cib	12
3/27	12/12	Ben	13	5/18	Chicchan	13	7/9	Caban	13
3/28	12/13	Ix	1	5/19	Cimi	1	7/10	Etznab	1
3/29	12/14	Men	2	5/20	Manik	2	7/11	Cauac	2
3/30	12/15	Cib	3	5/21	Lamat	3	7/12	Ahau	3
3/31	12/16	Caban	4	5/22	Muluc	4	7/13	Imix	4
4/1	12/17	Etznab	5	5/23	Oc	5	7/14	Ik	5
4/2	12/18	Cauac	6	5/24	Chuen	6	7/15	Akbal	6
4/3	12/19	Ahau	7	5/25	Eb	7	7/16	Kan	7
4/4	12/20	Imix	8	5/26	Ben	8	7/17	Chicchan	8
4/5	12/21	Ik	9	5/27	Ix	9	7/18	Cimi	9
4/6	12/22	Akbal	10	5/28	Men	10	7/19	Manik	10
4/7	12/23	Kan	11	5/29	Cib	11	7/20	Lamat	11
4/8	12/24	Chicchan	12	5/30	Caban	12	7/21	Muluc	12
4/9	12/25	Cimi	13	5/31	Etznab	13	7/22	Oc	13
4/10	12/26	Manik	1	6/1	Cauac	1	7/23	Chuen	1
4/11	12/27	Lamat	2	6/2	Ahau	2	7/24	Eb	2
4/12	12/28	Muluc	3	6/3	Imix	3	7/25	Ben	3
4/13	12/29	Oc	4	6/4	Ik	4	7/26	Ix	4
4/14	12/30	Chuen	5	6/5	Akbal	5	7/27	Men	5
4/15	12/31	Eb	6	6/6	Kan	6	7/28	Cib	6
4/16		Ben	7	6/7	Chicchan	7	7/29	Caban	7
4/17		Ix	8	6/8	Cimi	8	7/30	Etznab	8
4/18		Men	9	6/9	Manik	9	7/31	Cauac	9
4/19		Cib	10	6/10	Lamat	10	8/1	Ahau	10
4/20		Caban	11	6/11	Muluc	11	8/2	Imix	11
4/21		Etznab	12	6/12	Oc	12	8/3	Ik	12
4/22		Cauac	13	6/13	Chuen	13	8/4	Akbal	13
4/23		Ahau	1	6/14	Eb	1	8/5	Kan	1
4/24		Imix	2	6/15	Ben	2	8/6	Chicchan	2
4/25		Ik	3	6/16	Ix	3	8/7	Cimi	3
4/26		Akbal	4	6/17	Men	4	8/8	Manik	4
4/27		Kan	5	6/18	Cib	5	8/9	Lamat	5
4/28		Chicchan	6	6/19	Caban	6	8/10	Muluc	6
4/29		Cimi	7	6/20	Etznab	7	8/11	Oc	7
4/30		Manik	8	6/21	Cauac	8	8/12	Chuen	8
5/1		Lamat	9	6/22	Ahau	9	8/13	Eb	9
5/2		Muluc	10	6/23	Imix	10	8/14	Ben	10
5/3		Oc	11	6/24	Ik	11	8/15	Ix	11
5/4		Chuen	12	6/25	Akbal	12	8/16	Men	12
5/5		Eb	13	6/26	Kan	13	8/17	Cib	13

SAMPLE				BIRTHDAY	SOLAR GLYPH	TONE		BIRTHDAY	SOLAR GLYPH	TONE
				8/17	Imix	1		1/21 · 10/8	Ben	1
BIRTHDAY	SOLAR GLYPH	TONE		8/18	Ik	2		1/22 · 10/9	Ix	2
				8/19	Akbal	3		1/23 · 10/10	Men	3
ALWAYS READ CHART FROM				8/20	Kan	4		1/24 · 10/11	Cib	4
LEFT TO RIGHT				8/21	Chicchan	5		1/25 · 10/12	Caban	5
STARTING WITH BIRTHDAY				8/22	Cimi	6		1/26 · 10/13	Etznab	6
				8/23	Manik	7		1/27 · 10/14	Cauac	7
DOUBLE LINES				8/24	Lamat	8		1/28 · 10/15	Ahau	8
SEPARATE SECTIONS				8/25	Muluc	9		1/29 · 10/16	Imix	9
				8/26	Oc	10		1/30 · 10/17	Ik	10
USE SPACE BELOW				8/27	Chuen	11		1/31 · 10/18	Akbal	11
FOR RECORDING BIRTHDAYS				8/28	Eb	12		2/1 · 10/19	Kan	12
				8/29	Ben	13		2/2 · 10/20	Chicchan	13
				8/30	Ix	1		2/3 · 10/21	Cimi	1
				8/31	Men	2		2/4 · 10/22	Manik	2
				9/1	Cib	3		2/5 · 10/23	Lamat	3
				9/2	Caban	4		2/6 · 10/24	Muluc	4
				9/3	Etznab	5		2/7 · 10/25	Oc	5
				9/4	Cauac	6		2/8 · 10/26	Chuen	6
				9/5	Ahau	7		2/9 · 10/27	Eb	7
				9/6	Imix	8		2/10 · 10/28	Ben	8
				9/7	Ik	9		2/11 · 10/29	Ix	9
				9/8	Akbal	10		2/12 · 10/30	Men	10
				9/9	Kan	11		2/13 · 10/31	Cib	11
				9/10	Chicchan	12		2/14 · 11/1	Caban	12
				9/11	Cimi	13		2/15 · 11/2	Etznab	13
				9/12	Manik	1		2/16 · 11/3	Cauac	1
				9/13	Lamat	2		2/17 · 11/4	Ahau	2
				9/14	Muluc	3		2/18 · 11/5	Imix	3
				9/15	Oc	4		2/19 · 11/6	Ik	4
				9/16	Chuen	5		2/20 · 11/7	Akbal	5
				9/17	Eb	6		2/21 · 11/8	Kan	6
			1/1	9/18	Ben	7		2/22 · 11/9	Chicchan	7
			1/2	9/19	Ix	8		2/23 · 11/10	Cimi	8
			1/3	9/20	Men	9		2/24 · 11/11	Manik	9
			1/4	9/21	Cib	10		2/25 · 11/12	Lamat	10
			1/5	9/22	Caban	11		2/26 · 11/13	Muluc	11
			1/6	9/23	Etznab	12		2/27 · 11/14	Oc	12
			1/7	9/24	Cauac	13		2/28 · 11/15	Chuen	13
			1/8	9/25	Ahau	1		3/1 · 11/16	Eb	1
			1/9	9/26	Imix	2		3/2 · 11/17	Ben	2
			1/10	9/27	Ik	3		3/3 · 11/18	Ix	3
			1/11	9/28	Akbal	4		3/4 · 11/19	Men	4
			1/12	9/29	Kan	5		3/5 · 11/20	Cib	5
			1/13	9/30	Chicchan	6		3/6 · 11/21	Caban	6
			1/14	10/1	Cimi	7		3/7 · 11/22	Etznab	7
			1/15	10/2	Manik	8		3/8 · 11/23	Cauac	8
			1/16	10/3	Lamat	9		3/9 · 11/24	Ahau	9
			1/17	10/4	Muluc	10		3/10 · 11/25	Imix	10
			1/18	10/5	Oc	11		3/11 · 11/26	Ik	11
			1/19	10/6	Chuen	12		3/12 · 11/27	Akbal	12
			1/20	10/7	Eb	13		3/13 · 11/28	Kan	13

BIRTHDAY		SOLAR GLYPH	TONE	BIRTHDAY	SOLAR GLYPH	TONE	BIRTHDAY	SOLAR GLYPH	TONE
3/14	11/29	Chicchan	1	5/5	Caban	1	6/26	Muluc	1
3/15	11/30	Cimi	2	5/6	Etznab	2	6/27	Oc	2
3/16	12/1	Manik	3	5/7	Cauac	3	6/28	Chuen	3
3/17	12/2	Lamat	4	5/8	Ahau	4	6/29	Eb	4
3/18	12/3	Muluc	5	5/9	Imix	5	6/30	Ben	5
3/19	12/4	Oc	6	5/10	Ik	6	7/1	Ix	6
3/20	12/5	Chuen	7	5/11	Akbal	7	7/2	Men	7
3/21	12/6	Eb	8	5/12	Kan	8	7/3	Cib	8
3/22	12/7	Ben	9	5/13	Chiccan	9	7/4	Caban	9
3/23	12/8	Ix	10	5/14	Cimi	10	7/5	Etznab	10
3/24	12/9	Men	11	5/15	Manik	11	7/6	Cauac	11
3/25	12/10	Cib	12	5/16	Lamat	12	7/7	Ahau	12
3/26	12/11	Caban	13	5/17	Muluc	13	7/8	Imix	13
3/27	12/12	Etznab	1	5/18	Oc	1	7/9	Ik	1
3/28	12/13	Cauac	2	5/19	Chuen	2	7/10	Akbal	2
3/29	12/14	Ahau	3	5/20	Eb	3	7/11	Kan	3
3/30	12/15	Imix	4	5/21	Ben	4	7/12	Chicchan	4
3/31	12/16	Ik	5	5/22	Ix	5	7/13	Cimi	5
4/1	12/17	Akbal	6	5/23	Men	6	7/14	Manik	6
4/2	12/18	Kan	7	5/24	Cib	7	7/15	Lamat	7
4/3	12/19	Chicchan	8	5/25	Caban	8	7/16	Muluc	8
4/4	12/20	Cimi	9	5/26	Etznab	9	7/17	Oc	9
4/5	12/21	Manik	10	5/27	Cauac	10	7/18	Chuen	10
4/6	12/22	Lamat	11	5/28	Ahau	11	7/19	Eb	11
4/7	12/23	Muluc	12	5/29	Imix	12	7/20	Ben	12
4/8	12/24	Oc	13	5/30	Ik	13	7/21	Ix	13
4/9	12/25	Chuen	1	5/31	Akbal	1	7/22	Men	1
4/10	12/26	Eb	2	6/1	Kan	2	7/23	Cib	2
4/11	12/27	Ben	3	6/2	Chicchan	3	7/24	Caban	3
4/12	12/28	Ix	4	6/3	Cimi	4	7/25	Etznab	4
4/13	12/29	Men	5	6/4	Manik	5	7/26	Cauac	5
4/14	12/30	Cib	6	6/5	Lamat	6	7/27	Ahau	6
4/15	12/31	Caban	7	6/6	Muluc	7	7/28	Imix	7
4/16		Etznab	8	6/7	Oc	8	7/29	Ik	8
4/17		Cauac	9	6/8	Chuen	9	7/30	Akbal	9
4/18		Ahau	10	6/9	Eb	10	7/31	Kan	10
4/19		Imix	11	6/10	Ben	11	8/1	Chicchan	11
4/20		Ik	12	6/11	Ix	12	8/2	Cimi	12
4/21		Akbal	13	6/12	Men	13	8/3	Manik	13
4/22		Kan	1	6/13	Cib	1	8/4	Lamat	1
4/23		Chicchan	2	6/14	Caban	2	8/5	Muluc	2
4/24		Cimi	3	6/15	Etznab	3	8/6	Oc	3
4/25		Manik	4	6/16	Cauac	4	8/7	Chuen	4
4/26		Lamat	5	6/17	Ahau	5	8/8	Eb	5
4/27		Muluc	6	6/18	Imix	6	8/9	Ben	6
4/28		Oc	7	6/19	Ik	7	8/10	Ix	7
4/29		Chuen	8	6/20	Akbal	8	8/11	Men	8
4/30		Eb	9	6/21	Kan	9	8/12	Cib	9
5/1		Ben	10	6/22	Chicchan	10	8/13	Caban	10
5/2		Ix	11	6/23	Cimi	11	8/14	Etznab	11
5/3		Men	12	6/24	Manik	12	8/15	Cauac	12
5/4		Cib	13	6/25	Lamat	13	8/16	Ahau	13

SAMPLE			BIRTHDAY	SOLAR GLYPH	TONE	BIRTHDAY		SOLAR GLYPH	TONE
			8/16	Chicchan	1	1/20	10/7	Caban	1
BIRTHDAY	SOLAR GLYPH	TONE	8/17	Cimi	2	1/21	10/8	Etznab	2
			8/18	Manik	3	1/22	10/9	Cauac	3
ALWAYS READ CHART FROM			8/19	Lamat	4	1/23	10/10	Ahau	4
LEFT TO RIGHT			8/20	Muluc	5	1/24	10/11	Imix	5
STARTING WITH BIRTHDAY			8/21	Oc	6	1/25	10/12	Ik	6
			8/22	Chuen	7	1/26	10/13	Akbal	7
DOUBLE LINES			8/23	Eb	8	1/27	10/14	Kan	8
SEPARATE SECTIONS			8/24	Ben	9	1/28	10/15	Chiccan	9
			8/25	Ix	10	1/29	10/16	Cimi	10
USE SPACE BELOW			8/26	Men	11	1/30	10/17	Manik	11
FOR RECORDING BIRTHDAYS			8/27	Cib	12	1/31	10/18	Lamat	12
			8/28	Caban	13	2/1	10/19	Muluc	13
			8/29	Etznab	1	2/2	10/20	Oc	1
			8/30	Cauac	2	2/3	10/21	Chuen	2
			8/31	Ahau	3	2/4	10/22	Eb	3
			9/1	Imix	4	2/5	10/23	Ben	4
			9/2	Ik	5	2/6	10/24	Ix	5
			9/3	Akbal	6	2/7	10/25	Men	6
			9/4	Kan	7	2/8	10/26	Cib	7
			9/5	Chicchan	8	2/9	10/27	Caban	8
			9/6	Cimi	9	2/10	10/28	Etznab	9
			9/7	Manik	10	2/11	10/29	Cauac	10
			9/8	Lamat	11	2/12	10/30	Ahau	11
			9/9	Muluc	12	2/13	10/31	Imix	12
			9/10	Oc	13	2/14	11/1	Ik	13
			9/11	Chuen	1	2/15	11/2	Akbal	1
			9/12	Eb	2	2/16	11/3	Kan	2
			9/13	Ben	3	2/17	11/4	Chicchan	3
			9/14	Ix	4	2/18	11/5	Cimi	4
			9/15	Men	5	2/19	11/6	Manik	5
			9/16	Cib	6	2/20	11/7	Lamat	6
			9/17	Caban	7	2/21	11/8	Muluc	7
	1/1	9/18	Etznab	8	2/22	11/9	Oc	8
	1/2	9/19	Cauac	9	2/23	11/10	Chuen	9
	1/3	9/20	Ahau	10	2/24	11/11	Eb	10
	1/4	9/21	Imix	11	2/25	11/12	Ben	11
	1/5	9/22	Ik	12	2/26	11/13	Ix	12
	1/6	9/23	Akbal	13	2/27	11/14	Men	13
	1/7	9/24	Kan	1	2/28	11/15	Cib	1
	1/8	9/25	Chicchan	2	3/1	11/16	Caban	2
	1/9	9/26	Cimi	3	3/2	11/17	Etznab	3
	1/10	9/27	Manik	4	3/3	11/18	Cauac	4
	1/11	9/28	Lamat	5	3/4	11/19	Ahau	5
	1/12	9/29	Muluc	6	3/5	11/20	Imix	6
	1/13	9/30	Oc	7	3/6	11/21	Ik	7
	1/14	10/1	Chuen	8	3/7	11/22	Akbal	8
	1/15	10/2	Eb	9	3/8	11/23	Kan	9
	1/16	10/3	Ben	10	3/9	11/24	Chicchan	10
	1/17	10/4	Ix	11	3/10	11/25	Cimi	11
	1/18	10/5	Men	12	3/11	11/26	Manik	12
	1/19	10/6	Cib	13	3/12	11/27	Lamat	13

BIRTHDAY		SOLAR GLYPH	TONE	BIRTHDAY	SOLAR GLYPH	TONE	BIRTHDAY	SOLAR GLYPH	TONE
3/13	11/28	Muluc	1	5/4	Imix	1	6/25	Ben	1
3/14	11/29	Oc	2	5/5	Ik	2	6/26	Ix	2
3/15	11/30	Chuen	3	5/6	Akbal	3	6/27	Men	3
3/16	12/1	Eb	4	5/7	Kan	4	6/28	Cib	4
3/17	12/2	Ben	5	5/8	Chicchan	5	6/29	Caban	5
3/18	12/3	Ix	6	5/9	Cimi	6	6/30	Etznab	6
3/19	12/4	Men	7	5/10	Manik	7	7/1	Cauac	7
3/20	12/5	Cib	8	5/11	Lamat	8	7/2	Ahau	8
3/21	12/6	Caban	9	5/12	Muluc	9	7/3	Imix	9
3/22	12/7	Etznab	10	5/13	Oc	10	7/4	Ik	10
3/23	12/8	Cauac	11	5/14	Chuen	11	7/5	Akbal	11
3/24	12/9	Ahau	12	5/15	Eb	12	7/6	Kan	12
3/25	12/10	Imix	13	5/16	Ben	13	7/7	Chicchan	13
3/26	12/11	Ik	1	5/17	Ix	1	7/8	Cimi	1
3/27	12/12	Akbal	2	5/18	Men	2	7/9	Manik	2
3/28	12/13	Kan	3	5/19	Cib	3	7/10	Lamat	3
3/29	12/14	Chicchan	4	5/20	Caban	4	7/11	Muluc	4
3/30	12/15	Cimi	5	5/21	Etznab	5	7/12	Oc	5
3/31	12/16	Manik	6	5/22	Cauac	6	7/13	Chuen	6
4/1	12/17	Lamat	7	5/23	Ahau	7	7/14	Eb	7
4/2	12/18	Muluc	8	5/24	Imix	8	7/15	Ben	8
4/3	12/19	Oc	9	5/25	Ik	9	7/16	Ix	9
4/4	12/20	Chuen	10	5/26	Akbal	10	7/17	Men	10
4/5	12/21	Eb	11	5/27	Kan	11	7/18	Cib	11
4/6	12/22	Ben	12	5/28	Chicchan	12	7/19	Caban	12
4/7	12/23	Ix	13	5/29	Cimi	13	7/20	Etznab	13
4/8	12/24	Men	1	5/30	Manik	1	7/21	Cauac	1
4/9	12/25	Cib	2	5/31	Lamat	2	7/22	Ahau	2
4/10	12/26	Caban	3	6/1	Muluc	3	7/23	Imix	3
4/11	12/27	Etznab	4	6/2	Oc	4	7/24	Ik	4
4/12	12/28	Cauac	5	6/3	Chuen	5	7/25	Akbal	5
4/13	12/29	Ahau	6	6/4	Eb	6	7/26	Kan	6
4/14	12/30	Imix	7	6/5	Ben	7	7/27	Chicchan	7
4/15	12/31	Ik	8	6/6	Ix	8	7/28	Cimi	8
4/16		Akbal	9	6/7	Men	9	7/29	Manik	9
4/17		Kan	10	6/8	Cib	10	7/30	Lamat	10
4/18		Chicchan	11	6/9	Caban	11	7/31	Muluc	11
4/19		Cimi	12	6/10	Etznab	12	8/1	Oc	12
4/20		Manik	13	6/11	Cauac	13	8/2	Chuen	13
4/21		Lamat	1	6/12	Ahau	1	8/3	Eb	1
4/22		Muluc	2	6/13	Imix	2	8/4	Ben	2
4/23		Oc	3	6/14	Ik	3	8/5	Ix	3
4/24		Chuen	4	6/15	Akbal	4	8/6	Men	4
4/25		Eb	5	6/16	Kan	5	8/7	Cib	5
4/26		Ben	6	6/17	Chicchan	6	8/8	Caban	6
4/27		Ix	7	6/18	Cimi	7	8/9	Etznab	7
4/28		Men	8	6/19	Manik	8	8/10	Cauac	8
4/29		Cib	9	6/20	Lamat	9	8/11	Ahau	9
4/30		Caban	10	6/21	Muluc	10	8/12	Imix	10
5/1		Etznab	11	6/22	Oc	11	8/13	Ik	11
5/2		Cauac	12	6/23	Chuen	12	8/14	Akbal	12
5/3		Ahau	13	6/24	Eb	13	8/15	Kan	13

SAMPLE			BIRTHDAY	SOLAR GLYPH	TONE	BIRTHDAY	SOLAR GLYPH	TONE
			8/15	Muluc	1	1/19	10/6	Imix	1
BIRTHDAY	SOLAR GLYPH	TONE	8/16	Oc	2	1/20	10/7	Ik	2
			8/17	Chuen	3	1/21	10/8	Akbal	3
ALWAYS READ CHART FROM			8/18	Eb	4	1/22	10/9	Kan	4
LEFT TO RIGHT			8/19	Ben	5	1/23	10/10	Chicchan	5
STARTING WITH BIRTHDAY			8/20	Ix	6	1/24	10/11	Cimi	6
			8/21	Men	7	1/25	10/12	Manik	7
DOUBLE LINES			8/22	Cib	8	1/26	10/13	Lamat	8
SEPARATE SECTIONS			8/23	Caban	9	1/27	10/14	Muluc	9
			8/24	Etznab	10	1/28	10/15	Oc	10
USE SPACE BELOW			8/25	Cauac	11	1/29	10/16	Chuen	11
FOR RECORDING BIRTHDAYS			8/26	Ahau	12	1/30	10/17	Eb	12
			8/27	Imix	13	1/31	10/18	Ben	13
			8/28	Ik	1	2/1	10/19	Ix	1
			8/29	Akbal	2	2/2	10/20	Men	2
			8/30	Kan	3	2/3	10/21	Cib	3
			8/31	Chicchan	4	2/4	10/22	Caban	4
			9/1	Cimi	5	2/5	10/23	Etznab	5
			9/2	Manik	6	2/6	10/24	Cauac	6
			9/3	Lamat	7	2/7	10/25	Ahau	7
			9/4	Muluc	8	2/8	10/26	Imix	8
			9/5	Oc	9	2/9	10/27	Ik	9
			9/6	Chuen	10	2/10	10/28	Akbal	10
			9/7	Eb	11	2/11	10/29	Kan	11
			9/8	Ben	12	2/12	10/30	Chicchan	12
			9/9	Ix	13	2/13	10/31	Cimi	13
			9/10	Men	1	2/14	11/1	Manik	1
			9/11	Cib	2	2/15	11/2	Lamat	2
			9/12	Caban	3	2/16	11/3	Muluc	3
			9/13	Etznab	4	2/17	11/4	Oc	4
			9/14	Cauac	5	2/18	11/5	Chuen	5
			9/15	Ahau	6	2/19	11/6	Eb	6
			9/16	Imix	7	2/20	11/7	Ben	7
			9/17	Ik	8	2/21	11/8	Ix	8
		1/1	9/18	Akbal	9	2/22	11/9	Men	9
		1/2	9/19	Kan	10	2/23	11/10	Cib	10
		1/3	9/20	Chicchan	11	2/24	11/11	Caban	11
		1/4	9/21	Cimi	12	2/25	11/12	Etznab	12
		1/5	9/22	Manik	13	2/26	11/13	Cauac	13
		1/6	9/23	Lamat	1	2/27	11/14	Ahau	1
		1/7	9/24	Muluc	2	2/28	11/15	Imix	2
		1/8	9/25	Oc	3	3/1	11/16	Ik	3
		1/9	9/26	Chuen	4	3/2	11/17	Akbal	4
		1/10	9/27	Eb	5	3/3	11/18	Kan	5
		1/11	9/28	Ben	6	3/4	11/19	Chicchan	6
		1/12	9/29	Ix	7	3/5	11/20	Cimi	7
		1/13	9/30	Men	8	3/6	11/21	Manik	8
		1/14	10/1	Cib	9	3/7	11/22	Lamat	9
		1/15	10/2	Caban	10	3/8	11/23.	Muluc	10
		1/16	10/3	Etznab	11	3/9	11/24	Oc	11
		1/17	10/4	Cauac	12	3/10	11/25	Chuen	12
		1/18	10/5	Ahau	13	3/11	11/26	Eb	13

104

BIRTHDAY		SOLAR GLYPH	TONE	BIRTHDAY	SOLAR GLYPH	TONE	BIRTHDAY	SOLAR GLYPH	TONE
3/12	11/27	Ben	1	5/3	Chicchan	1	6/24	Caban	1
3/13	11/28	Ix	2	5/4	Cimi	2	6/25	Etznab	2
3/14	11/29	Men	3	5/5	Manik	3	6/26	Cauac	3
3/15	11/30	Cib	4	5/6	Lamat	4	6/27	Ahau	4
3/16	12/1	Caban	5	5/7	Muluc	5	6/28	Imix	5
3/17	12/2	Etznab	6	5/8	Oc	6	6/29	Ik	6
3/18	12/3	Cauac	7	5/9	Chuen	7	6/30	Akbal	7
3/19	12/4	Ahau	8	5/10	Eb	8	7/1	Kan	8
3/20	12/5	Imix	9	5/11	Ben	9	7/2	Chiccan	9
3/21	12/6	Ik	10	5/12	Ix	10	7/3	Cimi	10
3/22	12/7	Akbal	11	5/13	Men	11	7/4	Manik	11
3/23	12/8	Kan	12	5/14	Cib	12	7/5	Lamat	12
3/24	12/9	Chicchan	13	5/15	Caban	13	7/6	Muluc	13
3/25	12/10	Cimi	1	5/16	Etznab	1	7/7	Oc	1
3/26	12/11	Manik	2	5/17	Cauac	2	7/8	Chuen	2
3/27	12/12	Lamat	3	5/18	Ahau	3	7/9	Eb	3
3/28	12/13	Muluc	4	5/19	Imix	4	7/10	Ben	4
3/29	12/14	Oc	5	5/20	Ik	5	7/11	Ix	5
3/30	12/15	Chuen	6	5/21	Akbal	6	7/12	Men	6
3/31	12/16	Eb	7	5/22	Kan	7	7/13	Cib	7
4/1	12/17	Ben	8	5/23	Chicchan	8	7/14	Caban	8
4/2	12/18	Ix	9	5/24	Cimi	9	7/15	Etznab	9
4/3	12/19	Men	10	5/25	Manik	10	7/16	Cauac	10
4/4	12/20	Cib	11	5/26	Lamat	11	7/17	Ahau	11
4/5	12/21	Caban	12	5/27	Muluc	12	7/18	Imix	12
4/6	12/22	Etznab	13	5/28	Oc	13	7/19	Ik	13
4/7	12/23	Cauac	1	5/29	Chuen	1	7/20	Akbal	1
4/8	12/24	Ahau	2	5/30	Eb	2	7/21	Kan	2
4/9	12/25	Imix	3	5/31	Ben	3	7/22	Chicchan	3
4/10	12/26	Ik	4	6/1	Ix	4	7/23	Cimi	4
4/11	12/27	Akbal	5	6/2	Men	5	7/24	Manik	5
4/12	12/28	Kan	6	6/3	Cib	6	7/25	Lamat	6
4/13	12/29	Chicchan	7	6/4	Caban	7	7/26	Muluc	7
4/14	12/30	Cimi	8	6/5	Etznab	8	7/27	Oc	8
4/15	12/31	Manik	9	6/6	Cauac	9	7/28	Chuen	9
4/16		Lamat	10	6/7	Ahau	10	7/29	Eb	10
4/17		Muluc	11	6/8	Imix	11	7/30	Ben	11
4/18		Oc	12	6/9	Ik	12	7/31	Ix	12
4/19		Chuen	13	6/10	Akbal	13	8/1	Men	13
4/20		Eb	1	6/11	Kan	1	8/2	Cib	1
4/21		Ben	2	6/12	Chicchan	2	8/3	Caban	2
4/22		Ix	3	6/13	Cimi	3	8/4	Etznab	3
4/23		Men	4	6/14	Manik	4	8/5	Cauac	4
4/24		Cib	5	6/15	Lamat	5	8/6	Ahau	5
4/25		Caban	6	6/16	Muluc	6	8/7	Imix	6
4/26		Etznab	7	6/17	Oc	7	8/8	Ik	7
4/27		Cauac	8	6/18	Chuen	8	8/9	Akbal	8
4/28		Ahau	9	6/19	Eb	9	8/10	Kan	9
4/29		Imix	10	6/20	Ben	10	8/11	Chicchan	10
4/30		Ik	11	6/21	Ix	11	8/12	Cimi	11
5/1		Akbal	12	6/22	Men	12	8/13	Manik	12
5/2		Kan	13	6/23	Cib	13	8/14	Lamat	13

SAMPLE

BIRTHDAY	SOLAR GLYPH	TONE

ALWAYS READ CHART FROM
LEFT TO RIGHT
STARTING WITH BIRTHDAY

DOUBLE LINES
SEPARATE SECTIONS

USE SPACE BELOW
FOR RECORDING BIRTHDAYS

Record	BIRTHDAY	SOLAR GLYPH	TONE	BIRTHDAY		SOLAR GLYPH	TONE
	8/14	Ben	1	1/18	10/5	Chicchan	1
	8/15	Ix	2	1/19	10/6	Cimi	2
	8/16	Men	3	1/20	10/7	Manik	3
	8/17	Cib	4	1/21	10/8	Lamat	4
	8/18	Caban	5	1/22	10/9	Muluc	5
	8/19	Etznab	6	1/23	10/10	Oc	6
	8/20	Cauac	7	1/24	10/11	Chuen	7
	8/21	Ahau	8	1/25	10/12	Eb	8
	8/22	Imix	9	1/26	10/13	Ben	9
	8/23	Ik	10	1/27	10/14	Ix	10
	8/24	Akbal	11	1/28	10/15	Men	11
	8/25	Kan	12	1/29	10/16	Cib	12
	8/26	Chicchan	13	1/30	10/17	Caban	13
	8/27	Cimi	1	1/31	10/18	Etznab	1
	8/28	Manik	2	2/1	10/19	Cauac	2
	8/29	Lamat	3	2/2	10/20	Ahau	3
	8/30	Muluc	4	2/3	10/21	Imix	4
	8/31	Oc	5	2/4	10/22	Ik	5
	9/1	Chuen	6	2/5	10/23	Akbal	6
	9/2	Eb	7	2/6	10/24	Kan	7
	9/3	Ben	8	2/7	10/25	Chicchan	8
	9/4	Ix	9	2/8	10/26	Cimi	9
	9/5	Men	10	2/9	10/27	Manik	10
	9/6	Cib	11	2/10	10/28	Lamat	11
	9/7	Caban	12	2/11	10/29	Muluc	12
	9/8	Etznab	13	2/12	10/30	Oc	13
	9/9	Cauac	1	2/13	10/31	Chuen	1
	9/10	Ahau	2	2/14	11/1	Eb	2
	9/11	Imix	3	2/15	11/2	Ben	3
	9/12	Ik	4	2/16	11/3	Ix	4
	9/13	Akbal	5	2/17	11/4	Men	5
	9/14	Kan	6	2/18	11/5	Cib	6
	9/15	Chicchan	7	2/19	11/6	Caban	7
	9/16	Cimi	8	2/20	11/7	Etznab	8
	9/17	Manik	9	2/21	11/8	Cauac	9
1/1	9/18	Lamat	10	2/22	11/9	Ahau	10
1/2	9/19	Muluc	11	2/23	11/10	Imix	11
1/3	9/20	Oc	12	2/24	11/11	Ik	12
1/4	9/21	Chuen	13	2/25	11/12	Akbal	13
1/5	9/22	Eb	1	2/26	11/13	Kan	1
1/6	9/23	Ben	2	2/27	11/14	Chicchan	2
1/7	9/24	Ix	3	2/28	11/15	Cimi	3
1/8	9/25	Men	4	3/1	11/16	Manik	4
1/9	9/26	Cib	5	3/2	11/17	Lamat	5
1/10	9/27	Caban	6	3/3	11/18	Muluc	6
1/11	9/28	Etznab	7	3/4	11/19	Oc	7
1/12	9/29	Cauac	8	3/5	11/20	Chuen	8
1/13	9/30	Ahau	9	3/6	11/21	Eb	9
1/14	10/1	Imix	10	3/7	11/22	Ben	10
1/15	10/2	Ik	11	3/8	11/23	Ix	11
1/16	10/3	Akbal	12	3/9	11/24	Men	12
1/17	10/4	Kan	13	3/10	11/25	Cib	13

BIRTHDAY		SOLAR GLYPH	TONE	BIRTHDAY	SOLAR GLYPH	TONE	BIRTHDAY	SOLAR GLYPH	TONE
3/11	11/26	Caban	1	5/2	Muluc	1	6/23	Imix	1
3/12	11/27	Etznab	2	5/3	Oc	2	6/24	Ik	2
3/13	11/28	Cauac	3	5/4	Chuen	3	6/25	Akbal	3
3/14	11/29	Ahau	4	5/5	Eb	4	6/26	Kan	4
3/15	11/30	Imix	5	5/6	Ben	5	6/27	Chicchan	5
3/16	12/1	Ik	6	5/7	Ix	6	6/28	Cimi	6
3/17	12/2	Akbal	7	5/8	Men	7	6/29	Manik	7
3/18	12/3	Kan	8	5/9	Cib	8	6/30	Lamat	8
3/19	12/4	Chiccan	9	5/10	Caban	9	7/1	Muluc	9
3/20	12/5	Cimi	10	5/11	Etznab	10	7/2	Oc	10
3/21	12/6	Manik	11	5/12	Cauac	11	7/3	Chuen	11
3/22	12/7	Lamat	12	5/13	Ahau	12	7/4	Eb	12
3/23	12/8	Muluc	13	5/14	Imix	13	7/5	Ben	13
3/24	12/9	Oc	1	5/15	Ik	1	7/6	Ix	1
3/25	12/10	Chuen	2	5/16	Akbal	2	7/7	Men	2
3/26	12/11	Eb	3	5/17	Kan	3	7/8	Cib	3
3/27	12/12	Ben	4	5/18	Chicchan	4	7/9	Caban	4
3/28	12/13	Ix	5	5/19	Cimi	5	7/10	Etznab	5
3/29	12/14	Men	6	5/20	Manik	6	7/11	Cauac	6
3/30	12/15	Cib	7	5/21	Lamat	7	7/12	Ahau	7
3/31	12/16	Caban	8	5/22	Muluc	8	7/13	Imix	8
4/1	12/17	Etznab	9	5/23	Oc	9	7/14	Ik	9
4/2	12/18	Cauac	10	5/24	Chuen	10	7/15	Akbal	10
4/3	12/19	Ahau	11	5/25	Eb	11	7/16	Kan	11
4/4	12/20	Imix	12	5/26	Ben	12	7/17	Chicchan	12
4/5	12/21	Ik	13	5/27	Ix	13	7/18	Cimi	13
4/6	12/22	Akbal	1	5/28	Men	1	7/19	Manik	1
4/7	12/23	Kan	2	5/29	Cib	2	7/20	Lamat	2
4/8	12/24	Chicchan	3	5/30	Caban	3	7/21	Muluc	3
4/9	12/25	Cimi	4	5/31	Etznab	4	7/22	Oc	4
4/10	12/26	Manik	5	6/1	Cauac	5	7/23	Chuen	5
4/11	12/27	Lamat	6	6/2	Ahau	6	7/24	Eb	6
4/12	12/28	Muluc	7	6/3	Imix	7	7/25	Ben	7
4/13	12/29	Oc	8	6/4	Ik	8	7/26	Ix	8
4/14	12/30	Chuen	9	6/5	Akbal	9	7/27	Men	9
4/15	12/31	Eb	10	6/6	Kan	10	7/28	Cib	10
4/16		Ben	11	6/7	Chicchan	11	7/29	Caban	11
4/17		Ix	12	6/8	Cimi	12	7/30	Etznab	12
4/18		Men	13	6/9	Manik	13	7/31	Cauac	13
4/19		Cib	1	6/10	Lamat	1	8/1	Ahau	1
4/20		Caban	2	6/11	Muluc	2	8/2	Imix	2
4/21		Etznab	3	6/12	Oc	3	8/3	Ik	3
4/22		Cauac	4	6/13	Chuen	4	8/4	Akbal	4
4/23		Ahau	5	6/14	Eb	5	8/5	Kan	5
4/24		Imix	6	6/15	Ben	6	8/6	Chicchan	6
4/25		Ik	7	6/16	Ix	7	8/7	Cimi	7
4/26		Akbal	8	6/17	Men	8	8/8	Manik	8
4/27		Kan	9	6/18	Cib	9	8/9	Lamat	9
4/28		Chicchan	10	6/19	Caban	10	8/10	Muluc	10
4/29		Cimi	11	6/20	Etznab	11	8/11	Oc	11
4/30		Manik	12	6/21	Cauac	12	8/12	Chuen	12
5/1		Lamat	13	6/22	Ahau	13	8/13	Eb	13

SAMPLE			BIRTHDAY		SOLAR GLYPH	TONE	BIRTHDAY		SOLAR GLYPH	TONE
				8/13	Caban	1	1/17	10/4	Muluc	1
BIRTHDAY	SOLAR GLYPH	TONE		8/14	Etznab	2	1/18	10/5	Oc	2
				8/15	Cauac	3	1/19	10/6	Chuen	3
ALWAYS READ CHART FROM				8/16	Ahau	4	1/20	10/7	Eb	4
LEFT TO RIGHT				8/17	Imix	5	1/21	10/8	Ben	5
STARTING WITH BIRTHDAY				8/18	Ik	6	1/22	10/9	Ix	6
				8/19	Akbal	7	1/23	10/10	Men	7
DOUBLE LINES				8/20	Kan	8	1/24	10/11	Cib	8
SEPARATE SECTIONS				8/21	Chiccan	9	1/25	10/12	Caban	9
				8/22	Cimi	10	1/26	10/13	Etznab	10
USE SPACE BELOW				8/23	Manik	11	1/27	10/14	Cauac	11
FOR RECORDING BIRTHDAYS				8/24	Lamat	12	1/28	10/15	Ahau	12
				8/25	Muluc	13	1/29	10/16	Imix	13
				8/26	Oc	1	1/30	10/17	Ik	1
				8/27	Chuen	2	1/31	10/18	Akbal	2
				8/28	Eb	3	2/1	10/19	Kan	3
				8/29	Ben	4	2/2	10/20	Chicchan	4
				8/30	Ix	5	2/3	10/21	Cimi	5
				8/31	Men	6	2/4	10/22	Manik	6
				9/1	Cib	7	2/5	10/23	Lamat	7
				9/2	Caban	8	2/6	10/24	Muluc	8
				9/3	Etznab	9	2/7	10/25	Oc	9
				9/4	Cauac	10	2/8	10/26	Chuen	10
				9/5	Ahau	11	2/9	10/27	Eb	11
				9/6	Imix	12	2/10	10/28	Ben	12
				9/7	Ik	13	2/11	10/29	Ix	13
				9/8	Akbal	1	2/12	10/30	Men	1
				9/9	Kan	2	2/13	10/31	Cib	2
				9/10	Chicchan	3	2/14	11/1	Caban	3
				9/11	Cimi	4	2/15	11/2	Etznab	4
				9/12	Manik	5	2/16	11/3	Cauac	5
				9/13	Lamat	6	2/17	11/4	Ahau	6
				9/14	Muluc	7	2/18	11/5	Imix	7
				9/15	Oc	8	2/19	11/6	Ik	8
				9/16	Chuen	9	2/20	11/7	Akbal	9
				9/17	Eb	10	2/21	11/8	Kan	10
			1/1	9/18	Ben	11	2/22	11/9	Chicchan	11
			1/2	9/19	Ix	12	2/23	11/10	Cimi	12
			1/3	9/20	Men	13	2/24	11/11	Manik	13
			1/4	9/21	Cib	1	2/25	11/12	Lamat	1
			1/5	9/22	Caban	2	2/26	11/13	Muluc	2
			1/6	9/23	Etznab	3	2/27	11/14	Oc	3
			1/7	9/24	Cauac	4	2/28	11/15	Chuen	4
			1/8	9/25	Ahau	5	3/1	11/16	Eb	5
			1/9	9/26	Imix	6	3/2	11/17	Ben	6
			1/10	9/27	Ik	7	3/3	11/18	Ix	7
			1/11	9/28	Akbal	8	3/4	11/19	Men	8
			1/12	9/29	Kan	9	3/5	11/20	Cib	9
			1/13	9/30	Chicchan	10	3/6	11/21	Caban	10
			1/14	10/1	Cimi	11	3/7	11/22	Etznab	11
			1/15	10/2	Manik	12	3/8	11/23	Cauac	12
			1/16	10/3	Lamat	13	3/9	11/24	Ahau	13

BIRTHDAY		SOLAR GLYPH	TONE	BIRTHDAY	SOLAR GLYPH	TONE	BIRTHDAY	SOLAR GLYPH	TONE
3/10	11/25	Imix	1	5/1	Ben	1	6/22	Chicchan	1
3/11	11/26	Ik	2	5/2	Ix	2	6/23	Cimi	2
3/12	11/27	Akbal	3	5/3	Men	3	6/24	Manik	3
3/13	11/28	Kan	4	5/4	Cib	4	6/25	Lamat	4
3/14	11/29	Chiccan	5	5/5	Caban	5	6/26	Muluc	5
3/15	11/30	Cimi	6	5/6	Etznab	6	6/27	Oc	6
3/16	12/1	Manik	7	5/7	Cauac	7	6/28	Chuen	7
3/17	12/2	Lamat	8	5/8	Ahau	8	6/29	Eb	8
3/18	12/3	Muluc	9	5/9	Imix	9	6/30	Ben	9
3/19	12/4	Oc	10	5/10	Ik	10	7/1	Ix	10
3/20	12/5	Chuen	11	5/11	Akbal	11	7/2	Men	11
3/21	12/6	Eb	12	5/12	Kan	12	7/3	Cib	12
3/22	12/7	Ben	13	5/13	Chicchan	13	7/4	Caban	13
3/23	12/8	Ix	1	5/14	Cimi	1	7/5	Etznab	1
3/24	12/9	Men	2	5/15	Manik	2	7/6	Cauac	2
3/25	12/10	Cib	3	5/16	Lamat	3	7/7	Ahau	3
3/26	12/11	Caban	4	5/17	Muluc	4	7/8	Imix	4
3/27	12/12	Etznab	5	5/18	Oc	5	7/9	Ik	5
3/28	12/13	Cauac	6	5/19	Chuen	6	7/10	Akbal	6
3/29	12/14	Ahau	7	5/20	Eb	7	7/11	Kan	7
3/30	12/15	Imix	8	5/21	Ben	8	7/12	Chicchan	8
3/31	12/16	Ik	9	5/22	Ix	9	7/13	Cimi	9
4/1	12/17	Akbal	10	5/23	Men	10	7/14	Manik	10
4/2	12/18	Kan	11	5/24	Cib	11	7/15	Lamat	11
4/3	12/19	Chicchan	12	5/25	Caban	12	7/16	Muluc	12
4/4	12/20	Cimi	13	5/26	Etznab	13	7/17	Oc	13
4/5	12/21	Manik	1	5/27	Cauac	1	7/18	Chuen	1
4/6	12/22	Lamat	2	5/28	Ahau	2	7/19	Eb	2
4/7	12/23	Muluc	3	5/29	Imix	3	7/20	Ben	3
4/8	12/24	Oc	4	5/30	Ik	4	7/21	Ix	4
4/9	12/25	Chuen	5	5/31	Akbal	5	7/22	Men	5
4/10	12/26	Eb	6	6/1	Kan	6	7/23	Cib	6
4/11	12/27	Ben	7	6/2	Chicchan	7	7/24	Caban	7
4/12	12/28	Ix	8	6/3	Cimi	8	7/25	Etznab	8
4/13	12/29	Men	9	6/4	Manik	9	7/26	Cauac	9
4/14	12/30	Cib	10	6/5	Lamat	10	7/27	Ahau	10
4/15	12/31	Caban	11	6/6	Muluc	11	7/28	Imix	11
4/16		Etznab	12	6/7	Oc	12	7/29	Ik	12
4/17		Cauac	13	6/8	Chuen	13	7/30	Akbal	13
4/18		Ahau	1	6/9	Eb	1	7/31	Kan	1
4/19		Imix	2	6/10	Ben	2	8/1	Chicchan	2
4/20		Ik	3	6/11	Ix	3	8/2	Cimi	3
4/21		Akbal	4	6/12	Men	4	8/3	Manik	4
4/22		Kan	5	6/13	Cib	5	8/4	Lamat	5
4/23		Chicchan	6	6/14	Caban	6	8/5	Muluc	6
4/24		Cimi	7	6/15	Etznab	7	8/6	Oc	7
4/25		Manik	8	6/16	Cauac	8	8/7	Chuen	8
4/26		Lamat	9	6/17	Ahau	9	8/8	Eb	9
4/27		Muluc	10	6/18	Imix	10	8/9	Ben	10
4/28		Oc	11	6/19	Ik	11	8/10	Ix	11
4/29		Chuen	12	6/20	Akbal	12	8/11	Men	12
4/30		Eb	13	6/21	Kan	13	8/12	Cib	13

SAMPLE			BIRTHDAY	SOLAR GLYPH	TONE	BIRTHDAY	SOLAR GLYPH	TONE
			8/12	Imix	1	1/16	10/3	Ben	1
BIRTHDAY	SOLAR GLYPH	TONE	8/13	Ik	2	1/17	10/4	Ix	2
			8/14	Akbal	3	1/18	10/5	Men	3
ALWAYS READ CHART FROM			8/15	Kan	4	1/19	10/6	Cib	4
LEFT TO RIGHT			8/16	Chicchan	5	1/20	10/7	Caban	5
STARTING WITH BIRTHDAY			8/17	Cimi	6	1/21	10/8	Etznab	6
			8/18	Manik	7	1/22	10/9	Cauac	7
DOUBLE LINES			8/19	Lamat	8	1/23	10/10	Ahau	8
SEPARATE SECTIONS			8/20	Muluc	9	1/24	10/11	Imix	9
			8/21	Oc	10	1/25	10/12	Ik	10
USE SPACE BELOW			8/22	Chuen	11	1/26	10/13	Akbal	11
FOR RECORDING BIRTHDAYS			8/23	Eb	12	1/27	10/14	Kan	12
			8/24	Ben	13	1/28	10/15	Chicchan	13
			8/25	Ix	1	1/29	10/16	Cimi	1
			8/26	Men	2	1/30	10/17	Manik	2
			8/27	Cib	3	1/31	10/18	Lamat	3
			8/28	Caban	4	2/1	10/19	Muluc	4
			8/29	Etznab	5	2/2	10/20	Oc	5
			8/30	Cauac	6	2/3	10/21	Chuen	6
			8/31	Ahau	7	2/4	10/22	Eb	7
			9/1	Imix	8	2/5	10/23	Ben	8
			9/2	Ik	9	2/6	10/24	Ix	9
			9/3	Akbal	10	2/7	10/25	Men	10
			9/4	Kan	11	2/8	10/26	Cib	11
			9/5	Chicchan	12	2/9	10/27	Caban	12
			9/6	Cimi	13	2/10	10/28	Etznab	13
			9/7	Manik	1	2/11	10/29	Cauac	1
			9/8	Lamat	2	2/12	10/30	Ahau	2
			9/9	Muluc	3	2/13	10/31	Imix	3
			9/10	Oc	4	2/14	11/1	Ik	4
			9/11	Chuen	5	2/15	11/2	Akbal	5
			9/12	Eb	6	2/16	11/3	Kan	6
			9/13	Ben	7	2/17	11/4	Chicchan	7
			9/14	Ix	8	2/18	11/5	Cimi	8
			9/15	Men	9	2/19	11/6	Manik	9
			9/16	Cib	10	2/20	11/7	Lamat	10
			9/17	Caban	11	2/21	11/8	Muluc	11
		1/1	9/18	Etznab	12	2/22	11/9	Oc	12
		1/2	9/19	Cauac	13	2/23	11/10	Chuen	13
		1/3	9/20	Ahau	1	2/24	11/11	Eb	1
		1/4	9/21	Imix	2	2/25	11/12	Ben	2
		1/5	9/22	Ik	3	2/26	11/13	Ix	3
		1/6	9/23	Akbal	4	2/27	11/14	Men	4
		1/7	9/24	Kan	5	2/28	11/15	Cib	5
		1/8	9/25	Chicchan	6	3/1	11/16	Caban	6
		1/9	9/26	Cimi	7	3/2	11/17	Etznab	7
		1/10	9/27	Manik	8	3/3	11/18	Cauac	8
		1/11	9/28	Lamat	9	3/4	11/19	Ahau	9
		1/12	9/29	Muluc	10	3/5	11/20	Imix	10
		1/13	9/30	Oc	11	3/6	11/21	Ik	11
		1/14	10/1	Chuen	12	3/7	11/22	Akbal	12
		1/15	10/2	Eb	13	3/8	11/23	Kan	13

BIRTHDAY		SOLAR GLYPH	TONE	BIRTHDAY	SOLAR GLYPH	TONE	BIRTHDAY	SOLAR GLYPH	TONE
3/9	11/24	Chicchan	1	4/30	Caban	1	6/21	Muluc	1
3/10	11/25	Cimi	2	5/1	Etznab	2	6/22	Oc	2
3/11	11/26	Manik	3	5/2	Cauac	3	6/23	Chuen	3
3/12	11/27	Lamat	4	5/3	Ahau	4	6/24	Eb	4
3/13	11/28	Muluc	5	5/4	Imix	5	6/25	Ben	5
3/14	11/29	Oc	6	5/5	Ik	6	6/26	Ix	6
3/15	11/30	Chuen	7	5/6	Akbal	7	6/27	Men	7
3/16	12/1	Eb	8	5/7	Kan	8	6/28	Cib	8
3/17	12/2	Ben	9	5/8	Chiccan	9	6/29	Caban	9
3/18	12/3	Ix	10	5/9	Cimi	10	6/30	Etznab	10
3/19	12/4	Men	11	5/10	Manik	11	7/1	Cauac	11
3/20	12/5	Cib	12	5/11	Lamat	12	7/2	Ahau	12
3/21	12/6	Caban	13	5/12	Muluc	13	7/3	Imix	13
3/22	12/7	Etznab	1	5/13	Oc	1	7/4	Ik	1
3/23	12/8	Cauac	2	5/14	Chuen	2	7/5	Akbal	2
3/24	12/9	Ahau	3	5/15	Eb	3	7/6	Kan	3
3/25	12/10	Imix	4	5/16	Ben	4	7/7	Chicchan	4
3/26	12/11	Ik	5	5/17	Ix	5	7/8	Cimi	5
3/27	12/12	Akbal	6	5/18	Men	6	7/9	Manik	6
3/28	12/13	Kan	7	5/19	Cib	7	7/10	Lamat	7
3/29	12/14	Chicchan	8	5/20	Caban	8	7/11	Muluc	8
3/30	12/15	Cimi	9	5/21	Etznab	9	7/12	Oc	9
3/31	12/16	Manik	10	5/22	Cauac	10	7/13	Chuen	10
4/1	12/17	Lamat	11	5/23	Ahau	11	7/14	Eb	11
4/2	12/18	Muluc	12	5/24	Imix	12	7/15	Ben	12
4/3	12/19	Oc	13	5/25	Ik	13	7/16	Ix	13
4/4	12/20	Chuen	1	5/26	Akbal	1	7/17	Men	1
4/5	12/21	Eb	2	5/27	Kan	2	7/18	Cib	2
4/6	12/22	Ben	3	5/28	Chicchan	3	7/19	Caban	3
4/7	12/23	Ix	4	5/29	Cimi	4	7/20	Etznab	4
4/8	12/24	Men	5	5/30	Manik	5	7/21	Cauac	5
4/9	12/25	Cib	6	5/31	Lamat	6	7/22	Ahau	6
4/10	12/26	Caban	7	6/1	Muluc	7	7/23	Imix	7
4/11	12/27	Etznab	8	6/2	Oc	8	7/24	Ik	8
4/12	12/28	Cauac	9	6/3	Chuen	9	7/25	Akbal	9
4/13	12/29	Ahau	10	6/4	Eb	10	7/26	Kan	10
4/14	12/30	Imix	11	6/5	Ben	11	7/27	Chicchan	11
4/15	12/31	Ik	12	6/6	Ix	12	7/28	Cimi	12
4/16		Akbal	13	6/7	Men	13	7/29	Manik	13
4/17		Kan	1	6/8	Cib	1	7/30	Lamat	1
4/18		Chicchan	2	6/9	Caban	2	7/31	Muluc	2
4/19		Cimi	3	6/10	Etznab	3	8/1	Oc	3
4/20		Manik	4	6/11	Cauac	4	8/2	Chuen	4
4/21		Lamat	5	6/12	Ahau	5	8/3	Eb	5
4/22		Muluc	6	6/13	Imix	6	8/4	Ben	6
4/23		Oc	7	6/14	Ik	7	8/5	Ix	7
4/24		Chuen	8	6/15	Akbal	8	8/6	Men	8
4/25		Eb	9	6/16	Kan	9	8/7	Cib	9
4/26		Ben	10	6/17	Chicchan	10	8/8	Caban	10
4/27		Ix	11	6/18	Cimi	11	8/9	Etznab	11
4/28		Men	12	6/19	Manik	12	8/10	Cauac	12
4/29		Cib	13	6/20	Lamat	13	8/11	Ahau	13

SAMPLE				BIRTHDAY	SOLAR GLYPH	TONE	BIRTHDAY		SOLAR GLYPH	TONE
BIRTHDAY	SOLAR GLYPH	TONE		8/11	Chicchan	1	1/15	10/2	Caban	1
				8/12	Cimi	2	1/16	10/3	Etznab	2
ALWAYS READ CHART FROM				8/13	Manik	3	1/17	10/4	Cauac	3
LEFT TO RIGHT				8/14	Lamat	4	1/18	10/5	Ahau	4
STARTING WITH BIRTHDAY				8/15	Muluc	5	1/19	10/6	Imix	5
				8/16	Oc	6	1/20	10/7	Ik	6
DOUBLE LINES				8/17	Chuen	7	1/21	10/8	Akbal	7
SEPARATE SECTIONS				8/18	Eb	8	1/22	10/9	Kan	8
				8/19	Ben	9	1/23	10/10	Chiccan	9
USE SPACE BELOW				8/20	Ix	10	1/24	10/11	Cimi	10
FOR RECORDING BIRTHDAYS				8/21	Men	11	1/25	10/12	Manik	11
				8/22	Cib	12	1/26	10/13	Lamat	12
				8/23	Caban	13	1/27	10/14	Muluc	13
				8/24	Etznab	1	1/28	10/15	Oc	1
				8/25	Cauac	2	1/29	10/16	Chuen	2
				8/26	Ahau	3	1/30	10/17	Eb	3
				8/27	Imix	4	1/31	10/18	Ben	4
				8/28	Ik	5	2/1	10/19	Ix	5
				8/29	Akbal	6	2/2	10/20	Men	6
				8/30	Kan	7	2/3	10/21	Cib	7
				8/31	Chicchan	8	2/4	10/22	Caban	8
				9/1	Cimi	9	2/5	10/23	Etznab	9
				9/2	Manik	10	2/6	10/24	Cauac	10
				9/3	Lamat	11	2/7	10/25	Ahau	11
				9/4	Muluc	12	2/8	10/26	Imix	12
				9/5	Oc	13	2/9	10/27	Ik	13
				9/6	Chuen	1	2/10	10/28	Akbal	1
				9/7	Eb	2	2/11	10/29	Kan	2
				9/8	Ben	3	2/12	10/30	Chicchan	3
				9/9	Ix	4	2/13	10/31	Cimi	4
				9/10	Men	5	2/14	11/1	Manik	5
				9/11	Cib	6	2/15	11/2	Lamat	6
				9/12	Caban	7	2/16	11/3	Muluc	7
				9/13	Etznab	8	2/17	11/4	Oc	8
				9/14	Cauac	9	2/18	11/5	Chuen	9
				9/15	Ahau	10	2/19	11/6	Eb	10
				9/16	Imix	11	2/20	11/7	Ben	11
				9/17	Ik	12	2/21	11/8	Ix	12
			1/1	9/18	Akbal	13	2/22	11/9	Men	13
			1/2	9/19	Kan	1	2/23	11/10	Cib	1
			1/3	9/20	Chicchan	2	2/24	11/11	Caban	2
			1/4	9/21	Cimi	3	2/25	11/12	Etznab	3
			1/5	9/22	Manik	4	2/26	11/13	Cauac	4
			1/6	9/23	Lamat	5	2/27	11/14	Ahau	5
			1/7	9/24	Muluc	6	2/28	11/15	Imix	6
			1/8	9/25	Oc	7	3/1	11/16	Ik	7
			1/9	9/26	Chuen	8	3/2	11/17	Akbal	8
			1/10	9/27	Eb	9	3/3	11/18	Kan	9
			1/11	9/28	Ben	10	3/4	11/19	Chicchan	10
			1/12	9/29	Ix	11	3/5	11/20	Cimi	11
			1/13	9/30	Men	12	3/6	11/21	Manik	12
			1/14	10/1	Cib	13	3/7	11/22	Lamat	13

BIRTHDAY		SOLAR GLYPH	TONE	BIRTHDAY	SOLAR GLYPH	TONE	BIRTHDAY	SOLAR GLYPH	TONE
3/8	11/23	Muluc	1	4/29	Imix	1	6/20	Ben	1
3/9	11/24	Oc	2	4/30	Ik	2	6/21	Ix	2
3/10	11/25	Chuen	3	5/1	Akbal	3	6/22	Men	3
3/11	11/26	Eb	4	5/2	Kan	4	6/23	Cib	4
3/12	11/27	Ben	5	5/3	Chicchan	5	6/24	Caban	5
3/13	11/28	Ix	6	5/4	Cimi	6	6/25	Etznab	6
3/14	11/29	Men	7	5/5	Manik	7	6/26	Cauac	7
3/15	11/30	Cib	8	5/6	Lamat	8	6/27	Ahau	8
3/16	12/1	Caban	9	5/7	Muluc	9	6/28	Imix	9
3/17	12/2	Etznab	10	5/8	Oc	10	6/29	Ik	10
3/18	12/3	Cauac	11	5/9	Chuen	11	6/30	Akbal	11
3/19	12/4	Ahau	12	5/10	Eb	12	7/1	Kan	12
3/20	12/5	Imix	13	5/11	Ben	13	7/2	Chicchan	13
3/21	12/6	Ik	1	5/12	Ix	1	7/3	Cimi	1
3/22	12/7	Akbal	2	5/13	Men	2	7/4	Manik	2
3/23	12/8	Kan	3	5/14	Cib	3	7/5	Lamat	3
3/24	12/9	Chicchan	4	5/15	Caban	4	7/6	Muluc	4
3/25	12/10	Cimi	5	5/16	Etznab	5	7/7	Oc	5
3/26	12/11	Manik	6	5/17	Cauac	6	7/8	Chuen	6
3/27	12/12	Lamat	7	5/18	Ahau	7	7/9	Eb	7
3/28	12/13	Muluc	8	5/19	Imix	8	7/10	Ben	8
3/29	12/14	Oc	9	5/20	Ik	9	7/11	Ix	9
3/30	12/15	Chuen	10	5/21	Akbal	10	7/12	Men	10
3/31	12/16	Eb	11	5/22	Kan	11	7/13	Cib	11
4/1	12/17	Ben	12	5/23	Chicchan	12	7/14	Caban	12
4/2	12/18	Ix	13	5/24	Cimi	13	7/15	Etznab	13
4/3	12/19	Men	1	5/25	Manik	1	7/16	Cauac	1
4/4	12/20	Cib	2	5/26	Lamat	2	7/17	Ahau	2
4/5	12/21	Caban	3	5/27	Muluc	3	7/18	Imix	3
4/6	12/22	Etznab	4	5/28	Oc	4	7/19	Ik	4
4/7	12/23	Cauac	5	5/29	Chuen	5	7/20	Akbal	5
4/8	12/24	Ahau	6	5/30	Eb	6	7/21	Kan	6
4/9	12/25	Imix	7	5/31	Ben	7	7/22	Chicchan	7
4/10	12/26	Ik	8	6/1	Ix	8	7/23	Cimi	8
4/11	12/27	Akbal	9	6/2	Men	9	7/24	Manik	9
4/12	12/28	Kan	10	6/3	Cib	10	7/25	Lamat	10
4/13	12/29	Chicchan	11	6/4	Caban	11	7/26	Muluc	11
4/14	12/30	Cimi	12	6/5	Etznab	12	7/27	Oc	12
4/15	12/31	Manik	13	6/6	Cauac	13	7/28	Chuen	13
4/16		Lamat	1	6/7	Ahau	1	7/29	Eb	1
4/17		Muluc	2	6/8	Imix	2	7/30	Ben	2
4/18		Oc	3	6/9	Ik	3	7/31	Ix	3
4/19		Chuen	4	6/10	Akbal	4	8/1	Men	4
4/20		Eb	5	6/11	Kan	5	8/2	Cib	5
4/21		Ben	6	6/12	Chicchan	6	8/3	Caban	6
4/22		Ix	7	6/13	Cimi	7	8/4	Etznab	7
4/23		Men	8	6/14	Manik	8	8/5	Cauac	8
4/24		Cib	9	6/15	Lamat	9	8/6	Ahau	9
4/25		Caban	10	6/16	Muluc	10	8/7	Imix	10
4/26		Etznab	11	6/17	Oc	11	8/8	Ik	11
4/27		Cauac	12	6/18	Chuen	12	8/9	Akbal	12
4/28		Ahau	13	6/19	Eb	13	8/10	Kan	13

SAMPLE			BIRTHDAY		SOLAR GLYPH	TONE	BIRTHDAY		SOLAR GLYPH	TONE
				8/10	Muluc	1	1/14	10/1	Imix	1
BIRTHDAY	SOLAR GLYPH	TONE		8/11	Oc	2	1/15	10/2	Ik	2
				8/12	Chuen	3	1/16	10/3	Akbal	3
ALWAYS READ CHART FROM				8/13	Eb	4	1/17	10/4	Kan	4
LEFT TO RIGHT				8/14	Ben	5	1/18	10/5	Chicchan	5
STARTING WITH BIRTHDAY				8/15	Ix	6	1/19	10/6	Cimi	6
				8/16	Men	7	1/20	10/7	Manik	7
DOUBLE LINES				8/17	Cib	8	1/21	10/8	Lamat	8
SEPARATE SECTIONS				8/18	Caban	9	1/22	10/9	Muluc	9
				8/19	Etznab	10	1/23	10/10	Oc	10
USE SPACE BELOW				8/20	Cauac	11	1/24	10/11	Chuen	11
FOR RECORDING BIRTHDAYS				8/21	Ahau	12	1/25	10/12	Eb	12
				8/22	Imix	13	1/26	10/13	Ben	13
				8/23	Ik	1	1/27	10/14	Ix	1
				8/24	Akbal	2	1/28	10/15	Men	2
				8/25	Kan	3	1/29	10/16	Cib	3
				8/26	Chicchan	4	1/30	10/17	Caban	4
				8/27	Cimi	5	1/31	10/18	Etznab	5
				8/28	Manik	6	2/1	10/19	Cauac	6
				8/29	Lamat	7	2/2	10/20	Ahau	7
				8/30	Muluc	8	2/3	10/21	Imix	8
				8/31	Oc	9	2/4	10/22	Ik	9
				9/1	Chuen	10	2/5	10/23	Akbal	10
				9/2	Eb	11	2/6	10/24	Kan	11
				9/3	Ben	12	2/7	10/25	Chicchan	12
				9/4	Ix	13	2/8	10/26	Cimi	13
				9/5	Men	1	2/9	10/27	Manik	1
				9/6	Cib	2	2/10	10/28	Lamat	2
				9/7	Caban	3	2/11	10/29	Muluc	3
				9/8	Etznab	4	2/12	10/30	Oc	4
				9/9	Cauac	5	2/13	10/31	Chuen	5
				9/10	Ahau	6	2/14	11/1	Eb	6
				9/11	Imix	7	2/15	11/2	Ben	7
				9/12	Ik	8	2/16	11/3	Ix	8
				9/13	Akbal	9	2/17	11/4	Men	9
				9/14	Kan	10	2/18	11/5	Cib	10
				9/15	Chicchan	11	2/19	11/6	Caban	11
				9/16	Cimi	12	2/20	11/7	Etznab	12
				9/17	Manik	13	2/21	11/8	Cauac	13
			1/1	9/18	Lamat	1	2/22	11/9	Ahau	1
			1/2	9/19	Muluc	2	2/23	11/10	Imix	2
			1/3	9/20	Oc	3	2/24	11/11	Ik	3
			1/4	9/21	Chuen	4	2/25	11/12	Akbal	4
			1/5	9/22	Eb	5	2/26	11/13	Kan	5
			1/6	9/23	Ben	6	2/27	11/14	Chicchan	6
			1/7	9/24	Ix	7	2/28	11/15	Cimi	7
			1/8	9/25	Men	8	3/1	11/16	Manik	8
			1/9	9/26	Cib	9	3/2	11/17	Lamat	9
			1/10	9/27	Caban	10	3/3	11/18	Muluc	10
			1/11	9/28	Etznab	11	3/4	11/19	Oc	11
			1/12	9/29	Cauac	12	3/5	11/20	Chuen	12
			1/13	9/30	Ahau	13	3/6	11/21	Eb	13

BIRTHDAY		SOLAR GLYPH	TONE	BIRTHDAY	SOLAR GLYPH	TONE	BIRTHDAY	SOLAR GLYPH	TONE
3/7	11/22	Ben	1	4/28	Chicchan	1	6/19	Caban	1
3/8	11/23	Ix	2	4/29	Cimi	2	6/20	Etznab	2
3/9	11/24	Men	3	4/30	Manik	3	6/21	Cauac	3
3/10	11/25	Cib	4	5/1	Lamat	4	6/22	Ahau	4
3/11	11/26	Caban	5	5/2	Muluc	5	6/23	Imix	5
3/12	11/27	Etznab	6	5/3	Oc	6	6/24	Ik	6
3/13	11/28	Cauac	7	5/4	Chuen	7	6/25	Akbal	7
3/14	11/29	Ahau	8	5/5	Eb	8	6/26	Kan	8
3/15	11/30	Imix	9	5/6	Ben	9	6/27	Chiccan	9
3/16	12/1	Ik	10	5/7	Ix	10	6/28	Cimi	10
3/17	12/2	Akbal	11	5/8	Men	11	6/29	Manik	11
3/18	12/3	Kan	12	5/9	Cib	12	6/30	Lamat	12
3/19	12/4	Chicchan	13	5/10	Caban	13	7/1	Muluc	13
3/20	12/5	Cimi	1	5/11	Etznab	1	7/2	Oc	1
3/21	12/6	Manik	2	5/12	Cauac	2	7/3	Chuen	2
3/22	12/7	Lamat	3	5/13	Ahau	3	7/4	Eb	3
3/23	12/8	Muluc	4	5/14	Imix	4	7/5	Ben	4
3/24	12/9	Oc	5	5/15	Ik	5	7/6	Ix	5
3/25	12/10	Chuen	6	5/16	Akbal	6	7/7	Men	6
3/26	12/11	Eb	7	5/17	Kan	7	7/8	Cib	7
3/27	12/12	Ben	8	5/18	Chicchan	8	7/9	Caban	8
3/28	12/13	Ix	9	5/19	Cimi	9	7/10	Etznab	9
3/29	12/14	Men	10	5/20	Manik	10	7/11	Cauac	10
3/30	12/15	Cib	11	5/21	Lamat	11	7/12	Ahau	11
3/31	12/16	Caban	12	5/22	Muluc	12	7/13	Imix	12
4/1	12/17	Etznab	13	5/23	Oc	13	7/14	Ik	13
4/2	12/18	Cauac	1	5/24	Chuen	1	7/15	Akbal	1
4/3	12/19	Ahau	2	5/25	Eb	2	7/16	Kan	2
4/4	12/20	Imix	3	5/26	Ben	3	7/17	Chicchan	3
4/5	12/21	Ik	4	5/27	Ix	4	7/18	Cimi	4
4/6	12/22	Akbal	5	5/28	Men	5	7/19	Manik	5
4/7	12/23	Kan	6	5/29	Cib	6	7/20	Lamat	6
4/8	12/24	Chicchan	7	5/30	Caban	7	7/21	Muluc	7
4/9	12/25	Cimi	8	5/31	Etznab	8	7/22	Oc	8
4/10	12/26	Manik	9	6/1	Cauac	9	7/23	Chuen	9
4/11	12/27	Lamat	10	6/2	Ahau	10	7/24	Eb	10
4/12	12/28	Muluc	11	6/3	Imix	11	7/25	Ben	11
4/13	12/29	Oc	12	6/4	Ik	12	7/26	Ix	12
4/14	12/30	Chuen	13	6/5	Akbal	13	7/27	Men	13
4/15	12/31	Eb	1	6/6	Kan	1	7/28	Cib	1
4/16		Ben	2	6/7	Chicchan	2	7/29	Caban	2
4/17		Ix	3	6/8	Cimi	3	7/30	Etznab	3
4/18		Men	4	6/9	Manik	4	7/31	Cauac	4
4/19		Cib	5	6/10	Lamat	5	8/1	Ahau	5
4/20		Caban	6	6/11	Muluc	6	8/2	Imix	6
4/21		Etznab	7	6/12	Oc	7	8/3	Ik	7
4/22		Cauac	8	6/13	Chuen	8	8/4	Akbal	8
4/23		Ahau	9	6/14	Eb	9	8/5	Kan	9
4/24		Imix	10	6/15	Ben	10	8/6	Chicchan	10
4/25		Ik	11	6/16	Ix	11	8/7	Cimi	11
4/26		Akbal	12	6/17	Men	12	8/8	Manik	12
4/27		Kan	13	6/18	Cib	13	8/9	Lamat	13

SAMPLE

BIRTHDAY	SOLAR GLYPH	TONE

ALWAYS READ CHART FROM
LEFT TO RIGHT
STARTING WITH BIRTHDAY

DOUBLE LINES
SEPARATE SECTIONS

USE SPACE BELOW
FOR RECORDING BIRTHDAYS

BIRTHDAY		SOLAR GLYPH	TONE	BIRTHDAY		SOLAR GLYPH	TONE
	8/9	Ben	1	1/13	9/30	Chicchan	1
	8/10	Ix	2	1/14	10/1	Cimi	2
	8/11	Men	3	1/15	10/2	Manik	3
	8/12	Cib	4	1/16	10/3	Lamat	4
	8/13	Caban	5	1/17	10/4	Muluc	5
	8/14	Etznab	6	1/18	10/5	Oc	6
	8/15	Cauac	7	1/19	10/6	Chuen	7
	8/16	Ahau	8	1/20	10/7	Eb	8
	8/17	Imix	9	1/21	10/8	Ben	9
	8/18	Ik	10	1/22	10/9	Ix	10
	8/19	Akbal	11	1/23	10/10	Men	11
	8/20	Kan	12	1/24	10/11	Cib	12
	8/21	Chicchan	13	1/25	10/12	Caban	13
	8/22	Cimi	1	1/26	10/13	Etznab	1
	8/23	Manik	2	1/27	10/14	Cauac	2
	8/24	Lamat	3	1/28	10/15	Ahau	3
	8/25	Muluc	4	1/29	10/16	Imix	4
	8/26	Oc	5	1/30	10/17	Ik	5
	8/27	Chuen	6	1/31	10/18	Akbal	6
	8/28	Eb	7	2/1	10/19	Kan	7
	8/29	Ben	8	2/2	10/20	Chicchan	8
	8/30	Ix	9	2/3	10/21	Cimi	9
	8/31	Men	10	2/4	10/22	Manik	10
	9/1	Cib	11	2/5	10/23	Lamat	11
	9/2	Caban	12	2/6	10/24	Muluc	12
	9/3	Etznab	13	2/7	10/25	Oc	13
	9/4	Cauac	1	2/8	10/26	Chuen	1
	9/5	Ahau	2	2/9	10/27	Eb	2
	9/6	Imix	3	2/10	10/28	Ben	3
	9/7	Ik	4	2/11	10/29	Ix	4
	9/8	Akbal	5	2/12	10/30	Men	5
	9/9	Kan	6	2/13	10/31	Cib	6
	9/10	Chicchan	7	2/14	11/1	Caban	7
	9/11	Cimi	8	2/15	11/2	Etznab	8
	9/12	Manik	9	2/16	11/3	Cauac	9
	9/13	Lamat	10	2/17	11/4	Ahau	10
	9/14	Muluc	11	2/18	11/5	Imix	11
	9/15	Oc	12	2/19	11/6	Ik	12
	9/16	Chuen	13	2/20	11/7	Akbal	13
	9/17	Eb	1	2/21	11/8	Kan	1
1/1	9/18	Ben	2	2/22	11/9	Chicchan	2
1/2	9/19	Ix	3	2/23	11/10	Cimi	3
1/3	9/20	Men	4	2/24	11/11	Manik	4
1/4	9/21	Cib	5	2/25	11/12	Lamat	5
1/5	9/22	Caban	6	2/26	11/13	Muluc	6
1/6	9/23	Etznab	7	2/27	11/14	Oc	7
1/7	9/24	Cauac	8	2/28	11/15	Chuen	8
1/8	9/25	Ahau	9	3/1	11/16	Eb	9
1/9	9/26	Imix	10	3/2	11/17	Ben	10
1/10	9/27	Ik	11	3/3	11/18	Ix	11
1/11	9/28	Akbal	12	3/4	11/19	Men	12
1/12	9/29	Kan	13	3/5	11/20	Cib	13

BIRTHDAY		SOLAR GLYPH	TONE	BIRTHDAY	SOLAR GLYPH	TONE	BIRTHDAY	SOLAR GLYPH	TONE
3/6	11/21	Caban	1	4/27	Muluc	1	6/18	Imix	1
3/7	11/22	Etznab	2	4/28	Oc	2	6/19	Ik	2
3/8	11/23	Cauac	3	4/29	Chuen	3	6/20	Akbal	3
3/9	11/24	Ahau	4	4/30	Eb	4	6/21	Kan	4
3/10	11/25	Imix	5	5/1	Ben	5	6/22	Chicchan	5
3/11	11/26	Ik	6	5/2	Ix	6	6/23	Cimi	6
3/12	11/27	Akbal	7	5/3	Men	7	6/24	Manik	7
3/13	11/28	Kan	8	5/4	Cib	8	6/25	Lamat	8
3/14	11/29	Chiccan	9	5/5	Caban	9	6/26	Muluc	9
3/15	11/30	Cimi	10	5/6	Etznab	10	6/27	Oc	10
3/16	12/1	Manik	11	5/7	Cauac	11	6/28	Chuen	11
3/17	12/2	Lamat	12	5/8	Ahau	12	6/29	Eb	12
3/18	12/3	Muluc	13	5/9	Imix	13	6/30	Ben	13
3/19	12/4	Oc	1	5/10	Ik	1	7/1	Ix	1
3/20	12/5	Chuen	2	5/11	Akbal	2	7/2	Men	2
3/21	12/6	Eb	3	5/12	Kan	3	7/3	Cib	3
3/22	12/7	Ben	4	5/13	Chicchan	4	7/4	Caban	4
3/23	12/8	Ix	5	5/14	Cimi	5	7/5	Etznab	5
3/24	12/9	Men	6	5/15	Manik	6	7/6	Cauac	6
3/25	12/10	Cib	7	5/16	Lamat	7	7/7	Ahau	7
3/26	12/11	Caban	8	5/17	Muluc	8	7/8	Imix	8
3/27	12/12	Etznab	9	5/18	Oc	9	7/9	Ik	9
3/28	12/13	Cauac	10	5/19	Chuen	10	7/10	Akbal	10
3/29	12/14	Ahau	11	5/20	Eb	11	7/11	Kan	11
3/30	12/15	Imix	12	5/21	Ben	12	7/12	Chicchan	12
3/31	12/16	Ik	13	5/22	Ix	13	7/13	Cimi	13
4/1	12/17	Akbal	1	5/23	Men	1	7/14	Manik	1
4/2	12/18	Kan	2	5/24	Cib	2	7/15	Lamat	2
4/3	12/19	Chicchan	3	5/25	Caban	3	7/16	Muluc	3
4/4	12/20	Cimi	4	5/26	Etznab	4	7/17	Oc	4
4/5	12/21	Manik	5	5/27	Cauac	5	7/18	Chuen	5
4/6	12/22	Lamat	6	5/28	Ahau	6	7/19	Eb	6
4/7	12/23	Muluc	7	5/29	Imix	7	7/20	Ben	7
4/8	12/24	Oc	8	5/30	Ik	8	7/21	Ix	8
4/9	12/25	Chuen	9	5/31	Akbal	9	7/22	Men	9
4/10	12/26	Eb	10	6/1	Kan	10	7/23	Cib	10
4/11	12/27	Ben	11	6/2	Chicchan	11	7/24	Caban	11
4/12	12/28	Ix	12	6/3	Cimi	12	7/25	Etznab	12
4/13	12/29	Men	13	6/4	Manik	13	7/26	Cauac	13
4/14	12/30	Cib	1	6/5	Lamat	1	7/27	Ahau	1
4/15	12/31	Caban	2	6/6	Muluc	2	7/28	Imix	2
4/16		Etznab	3	6/7	Oc	3	7/29	Ik	3
4/17		Cauac	4	6/8	Chuen	4	7/30	Akbal	4
4/18		Ahau	5	6/9	Eb	5	7/31	Kan	5
4/19		Imix	6	6/10	Ben	6	8/1	Chicchan	6
4/20		Ik	7	6/11	Ix	7	8/2	Cimi	7
4/21		Akbal	8	6/12	Men	8	8/3	Manik	8
4/22		Kan	9	6/13	Cib	9	8/4	Lamat	9
4/23		Chicchan	10	6/14	Caban	10	8/5	Muluc	10
4/24		Cimi	11	6/15	Etznab	11	8/6	Oc	11
4/25		Manik	12	6/16	Cauac	12	8/7	Chuen	12
4/26		Lamat	13	6/17	Ahau	13	8/8	Eb	13

SAMPLE			BIRTHDAY	SOLAR GLYPH	TONE	BIRTHDAY		SOLAR GLYPH	TONE
			8/8	Caban	1	1/12	9/29	Muluc	1
BIRTHDAY	SOLAR GLYPH	TONE	8/9	Etznab	2	1/13	9/30	Oc	2
			8/10	Cauac	3	1/14	10/1	Chuen	3
ALWAYS READ CHART FROM			8/11	Ahau	4	1/15	10/2	Eb	4
LEFT TO RIGHT			8/12	Imix	5	1/16	10/3	Ben	5
STARTING WITH BIRTHDAY			8/13	Ik	6	1/17	10/4	Ix	6
			8/14	Akbal	7	1/18	10/5	Men	7
DOUBLE LINES			8/15	Kan	8	1/19	10/6	Cib	8
SEPARATE SECTIONS			8/16	Chiccan	9	1/20	10/7	Caban	9
			8/17	Cimi	10	1/21	10/8	Etznab	10
USE SPACE BELOW			8/18	Manik	11	1/22	10/9	Cauac	11
FOR RECORDING BIRTHDAYS			8/19	Lamat	12	1/23	10/10	Ahau	12
			8/20	Muluc	13	1/24	10/11	Imix	13
			8/21	Oc	1	1/25	10/12	Ik	1
			8/22	Chuen	2	1/26	10/13	Akbal	2
			8/23	Eb	3	1/27	10/14	Kan	3
			8/24	Ben	4	1/28	10/15	Chiccan	4
			8/25	Ix	5	1/29	10/16	Cimi	5
			8/26	Men	6	1/30	10/17	Manik	6
			8/27	Cib	7	1/31	10/18	Lamat	7
			8/28	Caban	8	2/1	10/19	Muluc	8
			8/29	Etznab	9	2/2	10/20	Oc	9
			8/30	Cauac	10	2/3	10/21	Chuen	10
			8/31	Ahau	11	2/4	10/22	Eb	11
			9/1	Imix	12	2/5	10/23	Ben	12
			9/2	Ik	13	2/6	10/24	Ix	13
			9/3	Akbal	1	2/7	10/25	Men	1
			9/4	Kan	2	2/8	10/26	Cib	2
			9/5	Chiccan	3	2/9	10/27	Caban	3
			9/6	Cimi	4	2/10	10/28	Etznab	4
			9/7	Manik	5	2/11	10/29	Cauac	5
			9/8	Lamat	6	2/12	10/30	Ahau	6
			9/9	Muluc	7	2/13	10/31	Imix	7
			9/10	Oc	8	2/14	11/1	Ik	8
			9/11	Chuen	9	2/15	11/2	Akbal	9
			9/12	Eb	10	2/16	11/3	Kan	10
			9/13	Ben	11	2/17	11/4	Chiccan	11
			9/14	Ix	12	2/18	11/5	Cimi	12
			9/15	Men	13	2/19	11/6	Manik	13
			9/16	Cib	1	2/20	11/7	Lamat	1
			9/17	Caban	2	2/21	11/8	Muluc	2
		1/1	9/18	Etznab	3	2/22	11/9	Oc	3
		1/2	9/19	Cauac	4	2/23	11/10	Chuen	4
		1/3	9/20	Ahau	5	2/24	11/11	Eb	5
		1/4	9/21	Imix	6	2/25	11/12	Ben	6
		1/5	9/22	Ik	7	2/26	11/13	Ix	7
		1/6	9/23	Akbal	8	2/27	11/14	Men	8
		1/7	9/24	Kan	9	2/28	11/15	Cib	9
		1/8	9/25	Chiccan	10	3/1	11/16	Caban	10
		1/9	9/26	Cimi	11	3/2	11/17	Etznab	11
		1/10	9/27	Manik	12	3/3	11/18	Cauac	12
		1/11	9/28	Lamat	13	3/4	11/19	Ahau	13

BIRTHDAY		SOLAR GLYPH	TONE	BIRTHDAY	SOLAR GLYPH	TONE	BIRTHDAY	SOLAR GLYPH	TONE
3/5	11/20	Imix	1	4/26	Ben	1	6/17	Chicchan	1
3/6	11/21	Ik	2	4/27	Ix	2	6/18	Cimi	2
3/7	11/22	Akbal	3	4/28	Men	3	6/19	Manik	3
3/8	11/23	Kan	4	4/29	Cib	4	6/20	Lamat	4
3/9	11/24	Chicchan	5	4/30	Caban	5	6/21	Muluc	5
3/10	11/25	Cimi	6	5/1	Etznab	6	6/22	Oc	6
3/11	11/26	Manik	7	5/2	Cauac	7	6/23	Chuen	7
3/12	11/27	Lamat	8	5/3	Ahau	8	6/24	Eb	8
3/13	11/28	Muluc	9	5/4	Imix	9	6/25	Ben	9
3/14	11/29	Oc	10	5/5	Ik	10	6/26	Ix	10
3/15	11/30	Chuen	11	5/6	Akbal	11	6/27	Men	11
3/16	12/1	Eb	12	5/7	Kan	12	6/28	Cib	12
3/17	12/2	Ben	13	5/8	Chicchan	13	6/29	Caban	13
3/18	12/3	Ix	1	5/9	Cimi	1	6/30	Etznab	1
3/19	12/4	Men	2	5/10	Manik	2	7/1	Cauac	2
3/20	12/5	Cib	3	5/11	Lamat	3	7/2	Ahau	3
3/21	12/6	Caban	4	5/12	Muluc	4	7/3	Imix	4
3/22	12/7	Etznab	5	5/13	Oc	5	7/4	Ik	5
3/23	12/8	Cauac	6	5/14	Chuen	6	7/5	Akbal	6
3/24	12/9	Ahau	7	5/15	Eb	7	7/6	Kan	7
3/25	12/10	Imix	8	5/16	Ben	8	7/7	Chicchan	8
3/26	12/11	Ik	9	5/17	Ix	9	7/8	Cimi	9
3/27	12/12	Akbal	10	5/18	Men	10	7/9	Manik	10
3/28	12/13	Kan	11	5/19	Cib	11	7/10	Lamat	11
3/29	12/14	Chicchan	12	5/20	Caban	12	7/11	Muluc	12
3/30	12/15	Cimi	13	5/21	Etznab	13	7/12	Oc	13
3/31	12/16	Manik	1	5/22	Cauac	1	7/13	Chuen	1
4/1	12/17	Lamat	2	5/23	Ahau	2	7/14	Eb	2
4/2	12/18	Muluc	3	5/24	Imix	3	7/15	Ben	3
4/3	12/19	Oc	4	5/25	Ik	4	7/16	Ix	4
4/4	12/20	Chuen	5	5/26	Akbal	5	7/17	Men	5
4/5	12/21	Eb	6	5/27	Kan	6	7/18	Cib	6
4/6	12/22	Ben	7	5/28	Chicchan	7	7/19	Caban	7
4/7	12/23	Ix	8	5/29	Cimi	8	7/20	Etznab	8
4/8	12/24	Men	9	5/30	Manik	9	7/21	Cauac	9
4/9	12/25	Cib	10	5/31	Lamat	10	7/22	Ahau	10
4/10	12/26	Caban	11	6/1	Muluc	11	7/23	Imix	11
4/11	12/27	Etznab	12	6/2	Oc	12	7/24	Ik	12
4/12	12/28	Cauac	13	6/3	Chuen	13	7/25	Akbal	13
4/13	12/29	Ahau	1	6/4	Eb	1	7/26	Kan	1
4/14	12/30	Imix	2	6/5	Ben	2	7/27	Chicchan	2
4/15	12/31	Ik	3	6/6	Ix	3	7/28	Cimi	3
4/16		Akbal	4	6/7	Men	4	7/29	Manik	4
4/17		Kan	5	6/8	Cib	5	7/30	Lamat	5
4/18		Chicchan	6	6/9	Caban	6	7/31	Muluc	6
4/19		Cimi	7	6/10	Etznab	7	8/1	Oc	7
4/20		Manik	8	6/11	Cauac	8	8/2	Chuen	8
4/21		Lamat	9	6/12	Ahau	9	8/3	Eb	9
4/22		Muluc	10	6/13	Imix	10	8/4	Ben	10
4/23		Oc	11	6/14	Ik	11	8/5	Ix	11
4/24		Chuen	12	6/15	Akbal	12	8/6	Men	12
4/25		Eb	13	6/16	Kan	13	8/7	Cib	13

SAMPLE

BIRTHDAY	SOLAR GLYPH	TONE

ALWAYS READ CHART FROM
LEFT TO RIGHT
STARTING WITH BIRTHDAY

DOUBLE LINES
SEPARATE SECTIONS

USE SPACE BELOW
FOR RECORDING BIRTHDAYS

	BIRTHDAY	SOLAR GLYPH	TONE		BIRTHDAY	BIRTHDAY	SOLAR GLYPH	TONE
	8/7	Imix	1		1/11	9/28	Ben	1
	8/8	Ik	2		1/12	9/29	Ix	2
	8/9	Akbal	3		1/13	9/30	Men	3
	8/10	Kan	4		1/14	10/1	Cib	4
	8/11	Chicchan	5		1/15	10/2	Caban	5
	8/12	Cimi	6		1/16	10/3	Etznab	6
	8/13	Manik	7		1/17	10/4	Cauac	7
	8/14	Lamat	8		1/18	10/5	Ahau	8
	8/15	Muluc	9		1/19	10/6	Imix	9
	8/16	Oc	10		1/20	10/7	Ik	10
	8/17	Chuen	11		1/21	10/8	Akbal	11
	8/18	Eb	12		1/22	10/9	Kan	12
	8/19	Ben	13		1/23	10/10	Chicchan	13
	8/20	Ix	1		1/24	10/11	Cimi	1
	8/21	Men	2		1/25	10/12	Manik	2
	8/22	Cib	3		1/26	10/13	Lamat	3
	8/23	Caban	4		1/27	10/14	Muluc	4
	8/24	Etznab	5		1/28	10/15	Oc	5
	8/25	Cauac	6		1/29	10/16	Chuen	6
	8/26	Ahau	7		1/30	10/17	Eb	7
	8/27	Imix	8		1/31	10/18	Ben	8
	8/28	Ik	9		2/1	10/19	Ix	9
	8/29	Akbal	10		2/2	10/20	Men	10
	8/30	Kan	11		2/3	10/21	Cib	11
	8/31	Chicchan	12		2/4	10/22	Caban	12
	9/1	Cimi	13		2/5	10/23	Etznab	13
	9/2	Manik	1		2/6	10/24	Cauac	1
	9/3	Lamat	2		2/7	10/25	Ahau	2
	9/4	Muluc	3		2/8	10/26	Imix	3
	9/5	Oc	4		2/9	10/27	Ik	4
	9/6	Chuen	5		2/10	10/28	Akbal	5
	9/7	Eb	6		2/11	10/29	Kan	6
	9/8	Ben	7		2/12	10/30	Chicchan	7
	9/9	Ix	8		2/13	10/31	Cimi	8
	9/10	Men	9		2/14	11/1	Manik	9
	9/11	Cib	10		2/15	11/2	Lamat	10
	9/12	Caban	11		2/16	11/3	Muluc	11
	9/13	Etznab	12		2/17	11/4	Oc	12
	9/14	Cauac	13		2/18	11/5	Chuen	13
	9/15	Ahau	1		2/19	11/6	Eb	1
	9/16	Imix	2		2/20	11/7	Ben	2
	9/17	Ik	3		2/21	11/8	Ix	3
1/1	9/18	Akbal	4		2/22	11/9	Men	4
1/2	9/19	Kan	5		2/23	11/10	Cib	5
1/3	9/20	Chicchan	6		2/24	11/11	Caban	6
1/4	9/21	Cimi	7		2/25	11/12	Etznab	7
1/5	9/22	Manik	8		2/26	11/13	Cauac	8
1/6	9/23	Lamat	9		2/27	11/14	Ahau	9
1/7	9/24	Muluc	10		2/28	11/15	Imix	10
1/8	9/25	Oc	11		3/1	11/16	Ik	11
1/9	9/26	Chuen	12		3/2	11/17	Akbal	12
1/10	9/27	Eb	13		3/3	11/18	Kan	13

BIRTHDAY		SOLAR GLYPH	TONE	BIRTHDAY	SOLAR GLYPH	TONE	BIRTHDAY	SOLAR GLYPH	TONE
3/4	11/19	Chicchan	1	4/25	Caban	1	6/16	Muluc	1
3/5	11/20	Cimi	2	4/26	Etznab	2	6/17	Oc	2
3/6	11/21	Manik	3	4/27	Cauac	3	6/18	Chuen	3
3/7	11/22	Lamat	4	4/28	Ahau	4	6/19	Eb	4
3/8	11/23	Muluc	5	4/29	Imix	5	6/20	Ben	5
3/9	11/24	Oc	6	4/30	Ik	6	6/21	Ix	6
3/10	11/25	Chuen	7	5/1	Akbal	7	6/22	Men	7
3/11	11/26	Eb	8	5/2	Kan	8	6/23	Cib	8
3/12	11/27	Ben	9	5/3	Chiccan	9	6/24	Caban	9
3/13	11/28	Ix	10	5/4	Cimi	10	6/25	Etznab	10
3/14	11/29	Men	11	5/5	Manik	11	6/26	Cauac	11
3/15	11/30	Cib	12	5/6	Lamat	12	6/27	Ahau	12
3/16	12/1	Caban	13	5/7	Muluc	13	6/28	Imix	13
3/17	12/2	Etznab	1	5/8	Oc	1	6/29	Ik	1
3/18	12/3	Cauac	2	5/9	Chuen	2	6/30	Akbal	2
3/19	12/4	Ahau	3	5/10	Eb	3	7/1	Kan	3
3/20	12/5	Imix	4	5/11	Ben	4	7/2	Chicchan	4
3/21	12/6	Ik	5	5/12	Ix	5	7/3	Cimi	5
3/22	12/7	Akbal	6	5/13	Men	6	7/4	Manik	6
3/23	12/8	Kan	7	5/14	Cib	7	7/5	Lamat	7
3/24	12/9	Chicchan	8	5/15	Caban	8	7/6	Muluc	8
3/25	12/10	Cimi	9	5/16	Etznab	9	7/7	Oc	9
3/26	12/11	Manik	10	5/17	Cauac	10	7/8	Chuen	10
3/27	12/12	Lamat	11	5/18	Ahau	11	7/9	Eb	11
3/28	12/13	Muluc	12	5/19	Imix	12	7/10	Ben	12
3/29	12/14	Oc	13	5/20	Ik	13	7/11	Ix	13
3/30	12/15	Chuen	1	5/21	Akbal	1	7/12	Men	1
3/31	12/16	Eb	2	5/22	Kan	2	7/13	Cib	2
4/1	12/17	Ben	3	5/23	Chicchan	3	7/14	Caban	3
4/2	12/18	Ix	4	5/24	Cimi	4	7/15	Etznab	4
4/3	12/19	Men	5	5/25	Manik	5	7/16	Cauac	5
4/4	12/20	Cib	6	5/26	Lamat	6	7/17	Ahau	6
4/5	12/21	Caban	7	5/27	Muluc	7	7/18	Imix	7
4/6	12/22	Etznab	8	5/28	Oc	8	7/19	Ik	8
4/7	12/23	Cauac	9	5/29	Chuen	9	7/20	Akbal	9
4/8	12/24	Ahau	10	5/30	Eb	10	7/21	Kan	10
4/9	12/25	Imix	11	5/31	Ben	11	7/22	Chicchan	11
4/10	12/26	Ik	12	6/1	Ix	12	7/23	Cimi	12
4/11	12/27	Akbal	13	6/2	Men	13	7/24	Manik	13
4/12	12/28	Kan	1	6/3	Cib	1	7/25	Lamat	1
4/13	12/29	Chicchan	2	6/4	Caban	2	7/26	Muluc	2
4/14	12/30	Cimi	3	6/5	Etznab	3	7/27	Oc	3
4/15	12/31	Manik	4	6/6	Cauac	4	7/28	Chuen	4
4/16		Lamat	5	6/7	Ahau	5	7/29	Eb	5
4/17		Muluc	6	6/8	Imix	6	7/30	Ben	6
4/18		Oc	7	6/9	Ik	7	7/31	Ix	7
4/19		Chuen	8	6/10	Akbal	8	8/1	Men	8
4/20		Eb	9	6/11	Kan	9	8/2	Cib	9
4/21		Ben	10	6/12	Chicchan	10	8/3	Caban	10
4/22		Ix	11	6/13	Cimi	11	8/4	Etznab	11
4/23		Men	12	6/14	Manik	12	8/5	Cauac	12
4/24		Cib	13	6/15	Lamat	13	8/6	Ahau	13

1943, 1995, 2047

SAMPLE

BIRTHDAY	SOLAR GLYPH	TONE
ALWAYS READ CHART FROM		
LEFT TO RIGHT		
STARTING WITH BIRTHDAY		
DOUBLE LINES		
SEPARATE SECTIONS		
USE SPACE BELOW		
FOR RECORDING BIRTHDAYS		

	BIRTHDAY	SOLAR GLYPH	TONE		BIRTHDAY	SOLAR GLYPH	TONE
	8/6	Chicchan	1	1/10	9/27	Caban	1
	8/7	Cimi	2	1/11	9/28	Etznab	2
	8/8	Manik	3	1/12	9/29	Cauac	3
	8/9	Lamat	4	1/13	9/30	Ahau	4
	8/10	Muluc	5	1/14	10/1	Imix	5
	8/11	Oc	6	1/15	10/2	Ik	6
	8/12	Chuen	7	1/16	10/3	Akbal	7
	8/13	Eb	8	1/17	10/4	Kan	8
	8/14	Ben	9	1/18	10/5	Chiccan	9
	8/15	Ix	10	1/19	10/6	Cimi	10
	8/16	Men	11	1/20	10/7	Manik	11
	8/17	Cib	12	1/21	10/8	Lamat	12
	8/18	Caban	13	1/22	10/9	Muluc	13
	8/19	Etznab	1	1/23	10/10	Oc	1
	8/20	Cauac	2	1/24	10/11	Chuen	2
	8/21	Ahau	3	1/25	10/12	Eb	3
	8/22	Imix	4	1/26	10/13	Ben	4
	8/23	Ik	5	1/27	10/14	Ix	5
	8/24	Akbal	6	1/28	10/15	Men	6
	8/25	Kan	7	1/29	10/16	Cib	7
	8/26	Chicchan	8	1/30	10/17	Caban	8
	8/27	Cimi	9	1/31	10/18	Etznab	9
	8/28	Manik	10	2/1	10/19	Cauac	10
	8/29	Lamat	11	2/2	10/20	Ahau	11
	8/30	Muluc	12	2/3	10/21	Imix	12
	8/31	Oc	13	2/4	10/22	Ik	13
	9/1	Chuen	1	2/5	10/23	Akbal	1
	9/2	Eb	2	2/6	10/24	Kan	2
	9/3	Ben	3	2/7	10/25	Chicchan	3
	9/4	Ix	4	2/8	10/26	Cimi	4
	9/5	Men	5	2/9	10/27	Manik	5
	9/6	Cib	6	2/10	10/28	Lamat	6
	9/7	Caban	7	2/11	10/29	Muluc	7
	9/8	Etznab	8	2/12	10/30	Oc	8
	9/9	Cauac	9	2/13	10/31	Chuen	9
	9/10	Ahau	10	2/14	11/1	Eb	10
	9/11	Imix	11	2/15	11/2	Ben	11
	9/12	Ik	12	2/16	11/3	Ix	12
	9/13	Akbal	13	2/17	11/4	Men	13
	9/14	Kan	1	2/18	11/5	Cib	1
	9/15	Chicchan	2	2/19	11/6	Caban	2
	9/16	Cimi	3	2/20	11/7	Etznab	3
	9/17	Manik	4	2/21	11/8	Cauac	4
1/1	9/18	Lamat	5	2/22	11/9	Ahau	5
1/2	9/19	Muluc	6	2/23	11/10	Imix	6
1/3	9/20	Oc	7	2/24	11/11	Ik	7
1/4	9/21	Chuen	8	2/25	11/12	Akbal	8
1/5	9/22	Eb	9	2/26	11/13	Kan	9
1/6	9/23	Ben	10	2/27	11/14	Chicchan	10
1/7	9/24	Ix	11	2/28	11/15	Cimi	11
1/8	9/25	Men	12	3/1	11/16	Manik	12
1/9	9/26	Cib	13	3/2	11/17	Lamat	13

BIRTHDAY		SOLAR GLYPH	TONE	BIRTHDAY	SOLAR GLYPH	TONE	BIRTHDAY	SOLAR GLYPH	TONE
3/3	11/18	Muluc	1	4/24	Imix	1	6/15	Ben	1
3/4	11/19	Oc	2	4/25	Ik	2	6/16	Ix	2
3/5	11/20	Chuen	3	4/26	Akbal	3	6/17	Men	3
3/6	11/21	Eb	4	4/27	Kan	4	6/18	Cib	4
3/7	11/22	Ben	5	4/28	Chicchan	5	6/19	Caban	5
3/8	11/23	Ix	6	4/29	Cimi	6	6/20	Etznab	6
3/9	11/24	Men	7	4/30	Manik	7	6/21	Cauac	7
3/10	11/25	Cib	8	5/1	Lamat	8	6/22	Ahau	8
3/11	11/26	Caban	9	5/2	Muluc	9	6/23	Imix	9
3/12	11/27	Etznab	10	5/3	Oc	10	6/24	Ik	10
3/13	11/28	Cauac	11	5/4	Chuen	11	6/25	Akbal	11
3/14	11/29	Ahau	12	5/5	Eb	12	6/26	Kan	12
3/15	11/30	Imix	13	5/6	Ben	13	6/27	Chicchan	13
3/16	12/1	Ik	1	5/7	Ix	1	6/28	Cimi	1
3/17	12/2	Akbal	2	5/8	Men	2	6/29	Manik	2
3/18	12/3	Kan	3	5/9	Cib	3	6/30	Lamat	3
3/19	12/4	Chicchan	4	5/10	Caban	4	7/1	Muluc	4
3/20	12/5	Cimi	5	5/11	Etznab	5	7/2	Oc	5
3/21	12/6	Manik	6	5/12	Cauac	6	7/3	Chuen	6
3/22	12/7	Lamat	7	5/13	Ahau	7	7/4	Eb	7
3/23	12/8	Muluc	8	5/14	Imix	8	7/5	Ben	8
3/24	12/9	Oc	9	5/15	Ik	9	7/6	Ix	9
3/25	12/10	Chuen	10	5/16	Akbal	10	7/7	Men	10
3/26	12/11	Eb	11	5/17	Kan	11	7/8	Cib	11
3/27	12/12	Ben	12	5/18	Chicchan	12	7/9	Caban	12
3/28	12/13	Ix	13	5/19	Cimi	13	7/10	Etznab	13
3/29	12/14	Men	1	5/20	Manik	1	7/11	Cauac	1
3/30	12/15	Cib	2	5/21	Lamat	2	7/12	Ahau	2
3/31	12/16	Caban	3	5/22	Muluc	3	7/13	Imix	3
4/1	12/17	Etznab	4	5/23	Oc	4	7/14	Ik	4
4/2	12/18	Cauac	5	5/24	Chuen	5	7/15	Akbal	5
4/3	12/19	Ahau	6	5/25	Eb	6	7/16	Kan	6
4/4	12/20	Imix	7	5/26	Ben	7	7/17	Chicchan	7
4/5	12/21	Ik	8	5/27	Ix	8	7/18	Cimi	8
4/6	12/22	Akbal	9	5/28	Men	9	7/19	Manik	9
4/7	12/23	Kan	10	5/29	Cib	10	7/20	Lamat	10
4/8	12/24	Chicchan	11	5/30	Caban	11	7/21	Muluc	11
4/9	12/25	Cimi	12	5/31	Etznab	12	7/22	Oc	12
4/10	12/26	Manik	13	6/1	Cauac	13	7/23	Chuen	13
4/11	12/27	Lamat	1	6/2	Ahau	1	7/24	Eb	1
4/12	12/28	Muluc	2	6/3	Imix	2	7/25	Ben	2
4/13	12/29	Oc	3	6/4	Ik	3	7/26	Ix	3
4/14	12/30	Chuen	4	6/5	Akbal	4	7/27	Men	4
4/15	12/31	Eb	5	6/6	Kan	5	7/28	Cib	5
4/16		Ben	6	6/7	Chicchan	6	7/29	Caban	6
4/17		Ix	7	6/8	Cimi	7	7/30	Etznab	7
4/18		Men	8	6/9	Manik	8	7/31	Cauac	8
4/19		Cib	9	6/10	Lamat	9	8/1	Ahau	9
4/20		Caban	10	6/11	Muluc	10	8/2	Imix	10
4/21		Etznab	11	6/12	Oc	11	8/3	Ik	11
4/22		Cauac	12	6/13	Chuen	12	8/4	Akbal	12
4/23		Ahau	13	6/14	Eb	13	8/5	Kan	13

SAMPLE			BIRTHDAY		SOLAR GLYPH	TONE	BIRTHDAY		SOLAR GLYPH	TONE
				8/5	Muluc	1	1/9	9/26	Imix	1
BIRTHDAY	SOLAR GLYPH	TONE		8/6	Oc	2	1/10	9/27	Ik	2
				8/7	Chuen	3	1/11	9/28	Akbal	3
ALWAYS READ CHART FROM				8/8	Eb	4	1/12	9/29	Kan	4
LEFT TO RIGHT				8/9	Ben	5	1/13	9/30	Chicchan	5
STARTING WITH BIRTHDAY				8/10	Ix	6	1/14	10/1	Cimi	6
				8/11	Men	7	1/15	10/2	Manik	7
DOUBLE LINES				8/12	Cib	8	1/16	10/3	Lamat	8
SEPARATE SECTIONS				8/13	Caban	9	1/17	10/4	Muluc	9
				8/14	Etznab	10	1/18	10/5	Oc	10
USE SPACE BELOW				8/15	Cauac	11	1/19	10/6	Chuen	11
FOR RECORDING BIRTHDAYS				8/16	Ahau	12	1/20	10/7	Eb	12
				8/17	Imix	13	1/21	10/8	Ben	13
				8/18	Ik	1	1/22	10/9	Ix	1
				8/19	Akbal	2	1/23	10/10	Men	2
				8/20	Kan	3	1/24	10/11	Cib	3
				8/21	Chicchan	4	1/25	10/12	Caban	4
				8/22	Cimi	5	1/26	10/13	Etznab	5
				8/23	Manik	6	1/27	10/14	Cauac	6
				8/24	Lamat	7	1/28	10/15	Ahau	7
				8/25	Muluc	8	1/29	10/16	Imix	8
				8/26	Oc	9	1/30	10/17	Ik	9
				8/27	Chuen	10	1/31	10/18	Akbal	10
				8/28	Eb	11	2/1	10/19	Kan	11
				8/29	Ben	12	2/2	10/20	Chicchan	12
				8/30	Ix	13	2/3	10/21	Cimi	13
				8/31	Men	1	2/4	10/22	Manik	1
				9/1	Cib	2	2/5	10/23	Lamat	2
				9/2	Caban	3	2/6	10/24	Muluc	3
				9/3	Etznab	4	2/7	10/25	Oc	4
				9/4	Cauac	5	2/8	10/26	Chuen	5
				9/5	Ahau	6	2/9	10/27	Eb	6
				9/6	Imix	7	2/10	10/28	Ben	7
				9/7	Ik	8	2/11	10/29	Ix	8
				9/8	Akbal	9	2/12	10/30	Men	9
				9/9	Kan	10	2/13	10/31	Cib	10
				9/10	Chicchan	11	2/14	11/1	Caban	11
				9/11	Cimi	12	2/15	11/2	Etznab	12
				9/12	Manik	13	2/16	11/3	Cauac	13
				9/13	Lamat	1	2/17	11/4	Ahau	1
				9/14	Muluc	2	2/18	11/5	Imix	2
				9/15	Oc	3	2/19	11/6	Ik	3
				9/16	Chuen	4	2/20	11/7	Akbal	4
				9/17	Eb	5	2/21	11/8	Kan	5
			1/1	9/18	Ben	6	2/22	11/9	Chicchan	6
			1/2	9/19	Ix	7	2/23	11/10	Cimi	7
			1/3	9/20	Men	8	2/24	11/11	Manik	8
			1/4	9/21	Cib	9	2/25	11/12	Lamat	9
			1/5	9/22	Caban	10	2/26	11/13	Muluc	10
			1/6	9/23	Etznab	11	2/27	11/14	Oc	11
			1/7	9/24	Cauac	12	2/28	11/15	Chuen	12
			1/8	9/25	Ahau	13	3/1	11/16	Eb	13

BIRTHDAY		SOLAR GLYPH	TONE	BIRTHDAY	SOLAR GLYPH	TONE	BIRTHDAY	SOLAR GLYPH	TONE
3/2	11/17	Ben	1	4/23	Chicchan	1	6/14	Caban	1
3/3	11/18	Ix	2	4/24	Cimi	2	6/15	Etznab	2
3/4	11/19	Men	3	4/25	Manik	3	6/16	Cauac	3
3/5	11/20	Cib	4	4/26	Lamat	4	6/17	Ahau	4
3/6	11/21	Caban	5	4/27	Muluc	5	6/18	Imix	5
3/7	11/22	Etznab	6	4/28	Oc	6	6/19	Ik	6
3/8	11/23	Cauac	7	4/29	Chuen	7	6/20	Akbal	7
3/9	11/24	Ahau	8	4/30	Eb	8	6/21	Kan	8
3/10	11/25	Imix	9	5/1	Ben	9	6/22	Chiccan	9
3/11	11/26	Ik	10	5/2	Ix	10	6/23	Cimi	10
3/12	11/27	Akbal	11	5/3	Men	11	6/24	Manik	11
3/13	11/28	Kan	12	5/4	Cib	12	6/25	Lamat	12
3/14	11/29	Chicchan	13	5/5	Caban	13	6/26	Muluc	13
3/15	11/30	Cimi	1	5/6	Etznab	1	6/27	Oc	1
3/16	12/1	Manik	2	5/7	Cauac	2	6/28	Chuen	2
3/17	12/2	Lamat	3	5/8	Ahau	3	6/29	Eb	3
3/18	12/3	Muluc	4	5/9	Imix	4	6/30	Ben	4
3/19	12/4	Oc	5	5/10	Ik	5	7/1	Ix	5
3/20	12/5	Chuen	6	5/11	Akbal	6	7/2	Men	6
3/21	12/6	Eb	7	5/12	Kan	7	7/3	Cib	7
3/22	12/7	Ben	8	5/13	Chicchan	8	7/4	Caban	8
3/23	12/8	Ix	9	5/14	Cimi	9	7/5	Etznab	9
3/24	12/9	Men	10	5/15	Manik	10	7/6	Cauac	10
3/25	12/10	Cib	11	5/16	Lamat	11	7/7	Ahau	11
3/26	12/11	Caban	12	5/17	Muluc	12	7/8	Imix	12
3/27	12/12	Etznab	13	5/18	Oc	13	7/9	Ik	13
3/28	12/13	Cauac	1	5/19	Chuen	1	7/10	Akbal	1
3/29	12/14	Ahau	2	5/20	Eb	2	7/11	Kan	2
3/30	12/15	Imix	3	5/21	Ben	3	7/12	Chicchan	3
3/31	12/16	Ik	4	5/22	Ix	4	7/13	Cimi	4
4/1	12/17	Akbal	5	5/23	Men	5	7/14	Manik	5
4/2	12/18	Kan	6	5/24	Cib	6	7/15	Lamat	6
4/3	12/19	Chicchan	7	5/25	Caban	7	7/16	Muluc	7
4/4	12/20	Cimi	8	5/26	Etznab	8	7/17	Oc	8
4/5	12/21	Manik	9	5/27	Cauac	9	7/18	Chuen	9
4/6	12/22	Lamat	10	5/28	Ahau	10	7/19	Eb	10
4/7	12/23	Muluc	11	5/29	Imix	11	7/20	Ben	11
4/8	12/24	Oc	12	5/30	Ik	12	7/21	Ix	12
4/9	12/25	Chuen	13	5/31	Akbal	13	7/22	Men	13
4/10	12/26	Eb	1	6/1	Kan	1	7/23	Cib	1
4/11	12/27	Ben	2	6/2	Chicchan	2	7/24	Caban	2
4/12	12/28	Ix	3	6/3	Cimi	3	7/25	Etznab	3
4/13	12/29	Men	4	6/4	Manik	4	7/26	Cauac	4
4/14	12/30	Cib	5	6/5	Lamat	5	7/27	Ahau	5
4/15	12/31	Caban	6	6/6	Muluc	6	7/28	Imix	6
4/16		Etznab	7	6/7	Oc	7	7/29	Ik	7
4/17		Cauac	8	6/8	Chuen	8	7/30	Akbal	8
4/18		Ahau	9	6/9	Eb	9	7/31	Kan	9
4/19		Imix	10	6/10	Ben	10	8/1	Chicchan	10
4/20		Ik	11	6/11	Ix	11	8/2	Cimi	11
4/21		Akbal	12	6/12	Men	12	8/3	Manik	12
4/22		Kan	13	6/13	Cib	13	8/4	Lamat	13

SAMPLE			BIRTHDAY	SOLAR GLYPH	TONE	BIRTHDAY		SOLAR GLYPH	TONE
			8/4	Ben	1	1/8	9/25	Chicchan	1
BIRTHDAY	SOLAR GLYPH	TONE	8/5	Ix	2	1/9	9/26	Cimi	2
			8/6	Men	3	1/10	9/27	Manik	3
ALWAYS READ CHART FROM			8/7	Cib	4	1/11	9/28	Lamat	4
LEFT TO RIGHT			8/8	Caban	5	1/12	9/29	Muluc	5
STARTING WITH BIRTHDAY			8/9	Etznab	6	1/13	9/30	Oc	6
			8/10	Cauac	7	1/14	10/1	Chuen	7
DOUBLE LINES			8/11	Ahau	8	1/15	10/2	Eb	8
SEPARATE SECTIONS			8/12	Imix	9	1/16	10/3	Ben	9
			8/13	Ik	10	1/17	10/4	Ix	10
USE SPACE BELOW			8/14	Akbal	11	1/18	10/5	Men	11
FOR RECORDING BIRTHDAYS			8/15	Kan	12	1/19	10/6	Cib	12
			8/16	Chicchan	13	1/20	10/7	Caban	13
			8/17	Cimi	1	1/21	10/8	Etznab	1
			8/18	Manik	2	1/22	10/9	Cauac	2
			8/19	Lamat	3	1/23	10/10	Ahau	3
			8/20	Muluc	4	1/24	10/11	Imix	4
			8/21	Oc	5	1/25	10/12	Ik	5
			8/22	Chuen	6	1/26	10/13	Akbal	6
			8/23	Eb	7	1/27	10/14	Kan	7
			8/24	Ben	8	1/28	10/15	Chicchan	8
			8/25	Ix	9	1/29	10/16	Cimi	9
			8/26	Men	10	1/30	10/17	Manik	10
			8/27	Cib	11	1/31	10/18	Lamat	11
			8/28	Caban	12	2/1	10/19	Muluc	12
			8/29	Etznab	13	2/2	10/20	Oc	13
			8/30	Cauac	1	2/3	10/21	Chuen	1
			8/31	Ahau	2	2/4	10/22	Eb	2
			9/1	Imix	3	2/5	10/23	Ben	3
			9/2	Ik	4	2/6	10/24	Ix	4
			9/3	Akbal	5	2/7	10/25	Men	5
			9/4	Kan	6	2/8	10/26	Cib	6
			9/5	Chicchan	7	2/9	10/27	Caban	7
			9/6	Cimi	8	2/10	10/28	Etznab	8
			9/7	Manik	9	2/11	10/29	Cauac	9
			9/8	Lamat	10	2/12	10/30	Ahau	10
			9/9	Muluc	11	2/13	10/31	Imix	11
			9/10	Oc	12	2/14	11/1	Ik	12
			9/11	Chuen	13	2/15	11/2	Akbal	13
			9/12	Eb	1	2/16	11/3	Kan	1
			9/13	Ben	2	2/17	11/4	Chicchan	2
			9/14	Ix	3	2/18	11/5	Cimi	3
			9/15	Men	4	2/19	11/6	Manik	4
			9/16	Cib	5	2/20	11/7	Lamat	5
			9/17	Caban	6	2/21	11/8	Muluc	6
		1/1	9/18	Etznab	7	2/22	11/9	Oc	7
		1/2	9/19	Cauac	8	2/23	11/10	Chuen	8
		1/3	9/20	Ahau	9	2/24	11/11	Eb	9
		1/4	9/21	Imix	10	2/25	11/12	Ben	10
		1/5	9/22	Ik	11	2/26	11/13	Ix	11
		1/6	9/23	Akbal	12	2/27	11/14	Men	12
		1/7	9/24	Kan	13	2/28	11/15	Cib	13

BIRTHDAY		SOLAR GLYPH	TONE	BIRTHDAY	SOLAR GLYPH	TONE	BIRTHDAY	SOLAR GLYPH	TONE
3/1	11/16	Caban	1	4/22	Muluc	1	6/13	Imix	1
3/2	11/17	Etznab	2	4/23	Oc	2	6/14	Ik	2
3/3	11/18	Cauac	3	4/24	Chuen	3	6/15	Akbal	3
3/4	11/19	Ahau	4	4/25	Eb	4	6/16	Kan	4
3/5	11/20	Imix	5	4/26	Ben	5	6/17	Chicchan	5
3/6	11/21	Ik	6	4/27	Ix	6	6/18	Cimi	6
3/7	11/22	Akbal	7	4/28	Men	7	6/19	Manik	7
3/8	11/23	Kan	8	4/29	Cib	8	6/20	Lamat	8
3/9	11/24	Chiccan	9	4/30	Caban	9	6/21	Muluc	9
3/10	11/25	Cimi	10	5/1	Etznab	10	6/22	Oc	10
3/11	11/26	Manik	11	5/2	Cauac	11	6/23	Chuen	11
3/12	11/27	Lamat	12	5/3	Ahau	12	6/24	Eb	12
3/13	11/28	Muluc	13	5/4	Imix	13	6/25	Ben	13
3/14	11/29	Oc	1	5/5	Ik	1	6/26	Ix	1
3/15	11/30	Chuen	2	5/6	Akbal	2	6/27	Men	2
3/16	12/1	Eb	3	5/7	Kan	3	6/28	Cib	3
3/17	12/2	Ben	4	5/8	Chicchan	4	6/29	Caban	4
3/18	12/3	Ix	5	5/9	Cimi	5	6/30	Etznab	5
3/19	12/4	Men	6	5/10	Manik	6	7/1	Cauac	6
3/20	12/5	Cib	7	5/11	Lamat	7	7/2	Ahau	7
3/21	12/6	Caban	8	5/12	Muluc	8	7/3	Imix	8
3/22	12/7	Etznab	9	5/13	Oc	9	7/4	Ik	9
3/23	12/8	Cauac	10	5/14	Chuen	10	7/5	Akbal	10
3/24	12/9	Ahau	11	5/15	Eb	11	7/6	Kan	11
3/25	12/10	Imix	12	5/16	Ben	12	7/7	Chicchan	12
3/26	12/11	Ik	13	5/17	Ix	13	7/8	Cimi	13
3/27	12/12	Akbal	1	5/18	Men	1	7/9	Manik	1
3/28	12/13	Kan	2	5/19	Cib	2	7/10	Lamat	2
3/29	12/14	Chicchan	3	5/20	Caban	3	7/11	Muluc	3
3/30	12/15	Cimi	4	5/21	Etznab	4	7/12	Oc	4
3/31	12/16	Manik	5	5/22	Cauac	5	7/13	Chuen	5
4/1	12/17	Lamat	6	5/23	Ahau	6	7/14	Eb	6
4/2	12/18	Muluc	7	5/24	Imix	7	7/15	Ben	7
4/3	12/19	Oc	8	5/25	Ik	8	7/16	Ix	8
4/4	12/20	Chuen	9	5/26	Akbal	9	7/17	Men	9
4/5	12/21	Eb	10	5/27	Kan	10	7/18	Cib	10
4/6	12/22	Ben	11	5/28	Chicchan	11	7/19	Caban	11
4/7	12/23	Ix	12	5/29	Cimi	12	7/20	Etznab	12
4/8	12/24	Men	13	5/30	Manik	13	7/21	Cauac	13
4/9	12/25	Cib	1	5/31	Lamat	1	7/22	Ahau	1
4/10	12/26	Caban	2	6/1	Muluc	2	7/23	Imix	2
4/11	12/27	Etznab	3	6/2	Oc	3	7/24	Ik	3
4/12	12/28	Cauac	4	6/3	Chuen	4	7/25	Akbal	4
4/13	12/29	Ahau	5	6/4	Eb	5	7/26	Kan	5
4/14	12/30	Imix	6	6/5	Ben	6	7/27	Chicchan	6
4/15	12/31	Ik	7	6/6	Ix	7	7/28	Cimi	7
4/16		Akbal	8	6/7	Men	8	7/29	Manik	8
4/17		Kan	9	6/8	Cib	9	7/30	Lamat	9
4/18		Chicchan	10	6/9	Caban	10	7/31	Muluc	10
4/19		Cimi	11	6/10	Etznab	11	8/1	Oc	11
4/20		Manik	12	6/11	Cauac	12	8/2	Chuen	12
4/21		Lamat	13	6/12	Ahau	13	8/3	Eb	13

SAMPLE			BIRTHDAY	SOLAR GLYPH	TONE	BIRTHDAY	SOLAR GLYPH	TONE
			8/3	Caban	1	1/7	9/24	Muluc	1
BIRTHDAY	SOLAR GLYPH	TONE	8/4	Etznab	2	1/8	9/25	Oc	2
			8/5	Cauac	3	1/9	9/26	Chuen	3
ALWAYS READ CHART FROM			8/6	Ahau	4	1/10	9/27	Eb	4
LEFT TO RIGHT			8/7	Imix	5	1/11	9/28	Ben	5
STARTING WITH BIRTHDAY			8/8	Ik	6	1/12	9/29	Ix	6
			8/9	Akbal	7	1/13	9/30	Men	7
DOUBLE LINES			8/10	Kan	8	1/14	10/1	Cib	8
SEPARATE SECTIONS			8/11	Chiccan	9	1/15	10/2	Caban	9
			8/12	Cimi	10	1/16	10/3	Etznab	10
USE SPACE BELOW			8/13	Manik	11	1/17	10/4	Cauac	11
FOR RECORDING BIRTHDAYS			8/14	Lamat	12	1/18	10/5	Ahau	12
			8/15	Muluc	13	1/19	10/6	Imix	13
			8/16	Oc	1	1/20	10/7	Ik	1
			8/17	Chuen	2	1/21	10/8	Akbal	2
			8/18	Eb	3	1/22	10/9	Kan	3
			8/19	Ben	4	1/23	10/10	Chicchan	4
			8/20	Ix	5	1/24	10/11	Cimi	5
			8/21	Men	6	1/25	10/12	Manik	6
			8/22	Cib	7	1/26	10/13	Lamat	7
			8/23	Caban	8	1/27	10/14	Muluc	8
			8/24	Etznab	9	1/28	10/15	Oc	9
			8/25	Cauac	10	1/29	10/16	Chuen	10
			8/26	Ahau	11	1/30	10/17	Eb	11
			8/27	Imix	12	1/31	10/18	Ben	12
			8/28	Ik	13	2/1	10/19	Ix	13
			8/29	Akbal	1	2/2	10/20	Men	1
			8/30	Kan	2	2/3	10/21	Cib	2
			8/31	Chicchan	3	2/4	10/22	Caban	3
			9/1	Cimi	4	2/5	10/23	Etznab	4
			9/2	Manik	5	2/6	10/24	Cauac	5
			9/3	Lamat	6	2/7	10/25	Ahau	6
			9/4	Muluc	7	2/8	10/26	Imix	7
			9/5	Oc	8	2/9	10/27	Ik	8
			9/6	Chuen	9	2/10	10/28	Akbal	9
			9/7	Eb	10	2/11	10/29	Kan	10
			9/8	Ben	11	2/12	10/30	Chicchan	11
			9/9	Ix	12	2/13	10/31	Cimi	12
			9/10	Men	13	2/14	11/1	Manik	13
			9/11	Cib	1	2/15	11/2	Lamat	1
			9/12	Caban	2	2/16	11/3	Muluc	2
			9/13	Etznab	3	2/17	11/4	Oc	3
			9/14	Cauac	4	2/18	11/5	Chuen	4
			9/15	Ahau	5	2/19	11/6	Eb	5
			9/16	Imix	6	2/20	11/7	Ben	6
			9/17	Ik	7	2/21	11/8	Ix	7
	1/1	9/18	Akbal	8	2/22	11/9	Men	8
	1/2	9/19	Kan	9	2/23	11/10	Cib	9
	1/3	9/20	Chicchan	10	2/24	11/11	Caban	10
	1/4	9/21	Cimi	11	2/25	11/12	Etznab	11
	1/5	9/22	Manik	12	2/26	11/13	Cauac	12
	1/6	9/23	Lamat	13	2/27	11/14	Ahau	13

BIRTHDAY		SOLAR GLYPH	TONE	BIRTHDAY	SOLAR GLYPH	TONE	BIRTHDAY	SOLAR GLYPH	TONE
2/28	11/5	Imix	1	4/21	Ben	1	6/12	Chicchan	1
3/1	11/16	Ik	2	4/22	Ix	2	6/13	Cimi	2
3/2	11/17	Akbal	3	4/23	Men	3	6/14	Manik	3
3/3	11/18	Kan	4	4/24	Cib	4	6/15	Lamat	4
3/4	11/19	Chicchan	5	4/25	Caban	5	6/16	Muluc	5
3/5	11/20	Cimi	6	4/26	Etznab	6	6/17	Oc	6
3/6	11/21	Manik	7	4/27	Cauac	7	6/18	Chuen	7
3/7	11/22	Lamat	8	4/28	Ahau	8	6/19	Eb	8
3/8	11/23	Muluc	9	4/29	Imix	9	6/20	Ben	9
3/9	11/24	Oc	10	4/30	Ik	10	6/21	Ix	10
3/10	11/25	Chuen	11	5/1	Akbal	11	6/22	Men	11
3/11	11/26	Eb	12	5/2	Kan	12	6/23	Cib	12
3/12	11/27	Ben	13	5/3	Chicchan	13	6/24	Caban	13
3/13	11/28	Ix	1	5/4	Cimi	1	6/25	Etznab	1
3/14	11/29	Men	2	5/5	Manik	2	6/26	Cauac	2
3/15	11/30	Cib	3	5/6	Lamat	3	6/27	Ahau	3
3/16	12/1	Caban	4	5/7	Muluc	4	6/28	Imix	4
3/17	12/2	Etznab	5	5/8	Oc	5	6/29	Ik	5
3/18	12/3	Cauac	6	5/9	Chuen	6	6/30	Akbal	6
3/19	12/4	Ahau	7	5/10	Eb	7	7/1	Kan	7
3/20	12/5	Imix	8	5/11	Ben	8	7/2	Chicchan	8
3/21	12/6	Ik	9	5/12	Ix	9	7/3	Cimi	9
3/22	12/7	Akbal	10	5/13	Men	10	7/4	Manik	10
3/23	12/8	Kan	11	5/14	Cib	11	7/5	Lamat	11
3/24	12/9	Chicchan	12	5/15	Caban	12	7/6	Muluc	12
3/25	12/10	Cimi	13	5/16	Etznab	13	7/7	Oc	13
3/26	12/11	Manik	1	5/17	Cauac	1	7/8	Chuen	1
3/27	12/12	Lamat	2	5/18	Ahau	2	7/9	Eb	2
3/28	12/13	Muluc	3	5/19	Imix	3	7/10	Ben	3
3/29	12/14	Oc	4	5/20	Ik	4	7/11	Ix	4
3/30	12/15	Chuen	5	5/21	Akbal	5	7/12	Men	5
3/31	12/16	Eb	6	5/22	Kan	6	7/13	Cib	6
4/1	12/17	Ben	7	5/23	Chicchan	7	7/14	Caban	7
4/2	12/18	Ix	8	5/24	Cimi	8	7/15	Etznab	8
4/3	12/19	Men	9	5/25	Manik	9	7/16	Cauac	9
4/4	12/20	Cib	10	5/26	Lamat	10	7/17	Ahau	10
4/5	12/21	Caban	11	5/27	Muluc	11	7/18	Imix	11
4/6	12/22	Etznab	12	5/28	Oc	12	7/19	Ik	12
4/7	12/23	Cauac	13	5/29	Chuen	13	7/20	Akbal	13
4/8	12/24	Ahau	1	5/30	Eb	1	7/21	Kan	1
4/9	12/25	Imix	2	5/31	Ben	2	7/22	Chicchan	2
4/10	12/26	Ik	3	6/1	Ix	3	7/23	Cimi	3
4/11	12/27	Akbal	4	6/2	Men	4	7/24	Manik	4
4/12	12/28	Kan	5	6/3	Cib	5	7/25	Lamat	5
4/13	12/29	Chicchan	6	6/4	Caban	6	7/26	Muluc	6
4/14	12/30	Cimi	7	6/5	Etznab	7	7/27	Oc	7
4/15	12/31	Manik	8	6/6	Cauac	8	7/28	Chuen	8
4/16		Lamat	9	6/7	Ahau	9	7/29	Eb	9
4/17		Muluc	10	6/8	Imix	10	7/30	Ben	10
4/18		Oc	11	6/9	Ik	11	7/31	Ix	11
4/19		Chuen	12	6/10	Akbal	12	8/1	Men	12
4/20		Eb	13	6/11	Kan	13	8/2	Cib	13

SAMPLE			BIRTHDAY		SOLAR GLYPH	TONE	BIRTHDAY		SOLAR GLYPH	TONE
				8/2	Imix	1	1/6	9/23	Ben	1
BIRTHDAY	SOLAR GLYPH	TONE		8/3	Ik	2	1/7	9/24	Ix	2
				8/4	Akbal	3	1/8	9/25	Men	3
ALWAYS READ CHART FROM				8/5	Kan	4	1/9	9/26	Cib	4
LEFT TO RIGHT				8/6	Chicchan	5	1/10	9/27	Caban	5
STARTING WITH BIRTHDAY				8/7	Cimi	6	1/11	9/28	Etznab	6
				8/8	Manik	7	1/12	9/29	Cauac	7
DOUBLE LINES				8/9	Lamat	8	1/13	9/30	Ahau	8
SEPARATE SECTIONS				8/10	Muluc	9	1/14	10/1	Imix	9
				8/11	Oc	10	1/15	10/2	Ik	10
USE SPACE BELOW				8/12	Chuen	11	1/16	10/3	Akbal	11
FOR RECORDING BIRTHDAYS				8/13	Eb	12	1/17	10/4	Kan	12
				8/14	Ben	13	1/18	10/5	Chicchan	13
				8/15	Ix	1	1/19	10/6	Cimi	1
				8/16	Men	2	1/20	10/7	Manik	2
				8/17	Cib	3	1/21	10/8	Lamat	3
				8/18	Caban	4	1/22	10/9	Muluc	4
				8/19	Etznab	5	1/23	10/10	Oc	5
				8/20	Cauac	6	1/24	10/11	Chuen	6
				8/21	Ahau	7	1/25	10/12	Eb	7
				8/22	Imix	8	1/26	10/13	Ben	8
				8/23	Ik	9	1/27	10/14	Ix	9
				8/24	Akbal	10	1/28	10/15	Men	10
				8/25	Kan	11	1/29	10/16	Cib	11
				8/26	Chicchan	12	1/30	10/17	Caban	12
				8/27	Cimi	13	1/31	10/18	Etznab	13
				8/28	Manik	1	2/1	10/19	Cauac	1
				8/29	Lamat	2	2/2	10/20	Ahau	2
				8/30	Muluc	3	2/3	10/21	Imix	3
				8/31	Oc	4	2/4	10/22	Ik	4
				9/1	Chuen	5	2/5	10/23	Akbal	5
				9/2	Eb	6	2/6	10/24	Kan	6
				9/3	Ben	7	2/7	10/25	Chicchan	7
				9/4	Ix	8	2/8	10/26	Cimi	8
				9/5	Men	9	2/9	10/27	Manik	9
				9/6	Cib	10	2/10	10/28	Lamat	10
				9/7	Caban	11	2/11	10/29	Muluc	11
				9/8	Etznab	12	2/12	10/30	Oc	12
				9/9	Cauac	13	2/13	10/31	Chuen	13
				9/10	Ahau	1	2/14	11/1	Eb	1
				9/11	Imix	2	2/15	11/2	Ben	2
				9/12	Ik	3	2/16	11/3	Ix	3
				9/13	Akbal	4	2/17	11/4	Men	4
				9/14	Kan	5	2/18	11/5	Cib	5
				9/15	Chicchan	6	2/19	11/6	Caban	6
				9/16	Cimi	7	2/20	11/7	Etznab	7
				9/17	Manik	8	2/21	11/8	Cauac	8
			1/1	9/18	Lamat	9	2/22	11/9	Ahau	9
			1/2	9/19	Muluc	10	2/23	11/10	Imix	10
			1/3	9/20	Oc	11	2/24	11/11	Ik	11
			1/4	9/21	Chuen	12	2/25	11/12	Akbal	12
			1/5	9/22	Eb	13	2/26	11/13	Kan	13

BIRTHDAY		SOLAR GLYPH	TONE	BIRTHDAY	SOLAR GLYPH	TONE	BIRTHDAY	SOLAR GLYPH	TONE
2/27	11/14	Chicchan	1	4/20	Caban	1	6/11	Muluc	1
2/28	11/5	Cimi	2	4/21	Etznab	2	6/12	Oc	2
3/1	11/16	Manik	3	4/22	Cauac	3	6/13	Chuen	3
3/2	11/17	Lamat	4	4/23	Ahau	4	6/14	Eb	4
3/3	11/18	Muluc	5	4/24	Imix	5	6/15	Ben	5
3/4	11/19	Oc	6	4/25	Ik	6	6/16	Ix	6
3/5	11/20	Chuen	7	4/26	Akbal	7	6/17	Men	7
3/6	11/21	Eb	8	4/27	Kan	8	6/18	Cib	8
3/7	11/22	Ben	9	4/28	Chiccan	9	6/19	Caban	9
3/8	11/23	Ix	10	4/29	Cimi	10	6/20	Etznab	10
3/9	11/24	Men	11	4/30	Manik	11	6/21	Cauac	11
3/10	11/25	Cib	12	5/1	Lamat	12	6/22	Ahau	12
3/11	11/26	Caban	13	5/2	Muluc	13	6/23	Imix	13
3/12	11/27	Etznab	1	5/3	Oc	1	6/24	Ik	1
3/13	11/28	Cauac	2	5/4	Chuen	2	6/25	Akbal	2
3/14	11/29	Ahau	3	5/5	Eb	3	6/26	Kan	3
3/15	11/30	Imix	4	5/6	Ben	4	6/27	Chicchan	4
3/16	12/1	Ik	5	5/7	Ix	5	6/28	Cimi	5
3/17	12/2	Akbal	6	5/8	Men	6	6/29	Manik	6
3/18	12/3	Kan	7	5/9	Cib	7	6/30	Lamat	7
3/19	12/4	Chicchan	8	5/10	Caban	8	7/1	Muluc	8
3/20	12/5	Cimi	9	5/11	Etznab	9	7/2	Oc	9
3/21	12/6	Manik	10	5/12	Cauac	10	7/3	Chuen	10
3/22	12/7	Lamat	11	5/13	Ahau	11	7/4	Eb	11
3/23	12/8	Muluc	12	5/14	Imix	12	7/5	Ben	12
3/24	12/9	Oc	13	5/15	Ik	13	7/6	Ix	13
3/25	12/10	Chuen	1	5/16	Akbal	1	7/7	Men	1
3/26	12/11	Eb	2	5/17	Kan	2	7/8	Cib	2
3/27	12/12	Ben	3	5/18	Chicchan	3	7/9	Caban	3
3/28	12/13	Ix	4	5/19	Cimi	4	7/10	Etznab	4
3/29	12/14	Men	5	5/20	Manik	5	7/11	Cauac	5
3/30	12/15	Cib	6	5/21	Lamat	6	7/12	Ahau	6
3/31	12/16	Caban	7	5/22	Muluc	7	7/13	Imix	7
4/1	12/17	Etznab	8	5/23	Oc	8	7/14	Ik	8
4/2	12/18	Cauac	9	5/24	Chuen	9	7/15	Akbal	9
4/3	12/19	Ahau	10	5/25	Eb	10	7/16	Kan	10
4/4	12/20	Imix	11	5/26	Ben	11	7/17	Chicchan	11
4/5	12/21	Ik	12	5/27	Ix	12	7/18	Cimi	12
4/6	12/22	Akbal	13	5/28	Men	13	7/19	Manik	13
4/7	12/23	Kan	1	5/29	Cib	1	7/20	Lamat	1
4/8	12/24	Chicchan	2	5/30	Caban	2	7/21	Muluc	2
4/9	12/25	Cimi	3	5/31	Etznab	3	7/22	Oc	3
4/10	12/26	Manik	4	6/1	Cauac	4	7/23	Chuen	4
4/11	12/27	Lamat	5	6/2	Ahau	5	7/24	Eb	5
4/12	12/28	Muluc	6	6/3	Imix	6	7/25	Ben	6
4/13	12/29	Oc	7	6/4	Ik	7	7/26	Ix	7
4/14	12/30	Chuen	8	6/5	Akbal	8	7/27	Men	8
4/15	12/31	Eb	9	6/6	Kan	9	7/28	Cib	9
4/16		Ben	10	6/7	Chicchan	10	7/29	Caban	10
4/17		Ix	11	6/8	Cimi	11	7/30	Etznab	11
4/18		Men	12	6/9	Manik	12	7/31	Cauac	12
4/19		Cib	13	6/10	Lamat	13	8/1	Ahau	13

SAMPLE

BIRTHDAY	SOLAR GLYPH	TONE

ALWAYS READ CHART FROM
LEFT TO RIGHT
STARTING WITH BIRTHDAY

DOUBLE LINES
SEPARATE SECTIONS

USE SPACE BELOW
FOR RECORDING BIRTHDAYS

Alt	BIRTHDAY	SOLAR GLYPH	TONE	BIRTHDAY		SOLAR GLYPH	TONE
	8/1	Chicchan	1	1/5	9/22	Caban	1
	8/2	Cimi	2	1/6	9/23	Etznab	2
	8/3	Manik	3	1/7	9/24	Cauac	3
	8/4	Lamat	4	1/8	9/25	Ahau	4
	8/5	Muluc	5	1/9	9/26	Imix	5
	8/6	Oc	6	1/10	9/27	Ik	6
	8/7	Chuen	7	1/11	9/28	Akbal	7
	8/8	Eb	8	1/12	9/29	Kan	8
	8/9	Ben	9	1/13	9/30	Chiccan	9
	8/10	Ix	10	1/14	10/1	Cimi	10
	8/11	Men	11	1/15	10/2	Manik	11
	8/12	Cib	12	1/16	10/3	Lamat	12
	8/13	Caban	13	1/17	10/4	Muluc	13
	8/14	Etznab	1	1/18	10/5	Oc	1
	8/15	Cauac	2	1/19	10/6	Chuen	2
	8/16	Ahau	3	1/20	10/7	Eb	3
	8/17	Imix	4	1/21	10/8	Ben	4
	8/18	Ik	5	1/22	10/9	Ix	5
	8/19	Akbal	6	1/23	10/10	Men	6
	8/20	Kan	7	1/24	10/11	Cib	7
	8/21	Chicchan	8	1/25	10/12	Caban	8
	8/22	Cimi	9	1/26	10/13	Etznab	9
	8/23	Manik	10	1/27	10/14	Cauac	10
	8/24	Lamat	11	1/28	10/15	Ahau	11
	8/25	Muluc	12	1/29	10/16	Imix	12
	8/26	Oc	13	1/30	10/17	Ik	13
	8/27	Chuen	1	1/31	10/18	Akbal	1
	8/28	Eb	2	2/1	10/19	Kan	2
	8/29	Ben	3	2/2	10/20	Chicchan	3
	8/30	Ix	4	2/3	10/21	Cimi	4
	8/31	Men	5	2/4	10/22	Manik	5
	9/1	Cib	6	2/5	10/23	Lamat	6
	9/2	Caban	7	2/6	10/24	Muluc	7
	9/3	Etznab	8	2/7	10/25	Oc	8
	9/4	Cauac	9	2/8	10/26	Chuen	9
	9/5	Ahau	10	2/9	10/27	Eb	10
	9/6	Imix	11	2/10	10/28	Ben	11
	9/7	Ik	12	2/11	10/29	Ix	12
	9/8	Akbal	13	2/12	10/30	Men	13
	9/9	Kan	1	2/13	10/31	Cib	1
	9/10	Chicchan	2	2/14	11/1	Caban	2
	9/11	Cimi	3	2/15	11/2	Etznab	3
	9/12	Manik	4	2/16	11/3	Cauac	4
	9/13	Lamat	5	2/17	11/4	Ahau	5
	9/14	Muluc	6	2/18	11/5	Imix	6
	9/15	Oc	7	2/19	11/6	Ik	7
	9/16	Chuen	8	2/20	11/7	Akbal	8
	9/17	Eb	9	2/21	11/8	Kan	9
1/1	9/18	Ben	10	2/22	11/9	Chicchan	10
1/2	9/19	Ix	11	2/23	11/10	Cimi	11
1/3	9/20	Men	12	2/24	11/11	Manik	12
1/4	9/21	Cib	13	2/25	11/12	Lamat	13

BIRTHDAY		SOLAR GLYPH	TONE	BIRTHDAY	SOLAR GLYPH	TONE	BIRTHDAY	SOLAR GLYPH	TONE
2/26	11/13	Muluc	1	4/19	Imix	1	6/10	Ben	1
2/27	11/14	Oc	2	4/20	Ik	2	6/11	Ix	2
2/28	11/5	Chuen	3	4/21	Akbal	3	6/12	Men	3
3/1	11/16	Eb	4	4/22	Kan	4	6/13	Cib	4
3/2	11/17	Ben	5	4/23	Chicchan	5	6/14	Caban	5
3/3	11/18	Ix	6	4/24	Cimi	6	6/15	Etznab	6
3/4	11/19	Men	7	4/25	Manik	7	6/16	Cauac	7
3/5	11/20	Cib	8	4/26	Lamat	8	6/17	Ahau	8
3/6	11/21	Caban	9	4/27	Muluc	9	6/18	Imix	9
3/7	11/22	Etznab	10	4/28	Oc	10	6/19	Ik	10
3/8	11/23	Cauac	11	4/29	Chuen	11	6/20	Akbal	11
3/9	11/24	Ahau	12	4/30	Eb	12	6/21	Kan	12
3/10	11/25	Imix	13	5/1	Ben	13	6/22	Chicchan	13
3/11	11/26	Ik	1	5/2	Ix	1	6/23	Cimi	1
3/12	11/27	Akbal	2	5/3	Men	2	6/24	Manik	2
3/13	11/28	Kan	3	5/4	Cib	3	6/25	Lamat	3
3/14	11/29	Chicchan	4	5/5	Caban	4	6/26	Muluc	4
3/15	11/30	Cimi	5	5/6	Etznab	5	6/27	Oc	5
3/16	12/1	Manik	6	5/7	Cauac	6	6/28	Chuen	6
3/17	12/2	Lamat	7	5/8	Ahau	7	6/29	Eb	7
3/18	12/3	Muluc	8	5/9	Imix	8	6/30	Ben	8
3/19	12/4	Oc	9	5/10	Ik	9	7/1	Ix	9
3/20	12/5	Chuen	10	5/11	Akbal	10	7/2	Men	10
3/21	12/6	Eb	11	5/12	Kan	11	7/3	Cib	11
3/22	12/7	Ben	12	5/13	Chicchan	12	7/4	Caban	12
3/23	12/8	Ix	13	5/14	Cimi	13	7/5	Etznab	13
3/24	12/9	Men	1	5/15	Manik	1	7/6	Cauac	1
3/25	12/10	Cib	2	5/16	Lamat	2	7/7	Ahau	2
3/26	12/11	Caban	3	5/17	Muluc	3	7/8	Imix	3
3/27	12/12	Etznab	4	5/18	Oc	4	7/9	Ik	4
3/28	12/13	Cauac	5	5/19	Chuen	5	7/10	Akbal	5
3/29	12/14	Ahau	6	5/20	Eb	6	7/11	Kan	6
3/30	12/15	Imix	7	5/21	Ben	7	7/12	Chicchan	7
3/31	12/16	Ik	8	5/22	Ix	8	7/13	Cimi	8
4/1	12/17	Akbal	9	5/23	Men	9	7/14	Manik	9
4/2	12/18	Kan	10	5/24	Cib	10	7/15	Lamat	10
4/3	12/19	Chicchan	11	5/25	Caban	11	7/16	Muluc	11
4/4	12/20	Cimi	12	5/26	Etznab	12	7/17	Oc	12
4/5	12/21	Manik	13	5/27	Cauac	13	7/18	Chuen	13
4/6	12/22	Lamat	1	5/28	Ahau	1	7/19	Eb	1
4/7	12/23	Muluc	2	5/29	Imix	2	7/20	Ben	2
4/8	12/24	Oc	3	5/30	Ik	3	7/21	Ix	3
4/9	12/25	Chuen	4	5/31	Akbal	4	7/22	Men	4
4/10	12/26	Eb	5	6/1	Kan	5	7/23	Cib	5
4/11	12/27	Ben	6	6/2	Chicchan	6	7/24	Caban	6
4/12	12/28	Ix	7	6/3	Cimi	7	7/25	Etznab	7
4/13	12/29	Men	8	6/4	Manik	8	7/26	Cauac	8
4/14	12/30	Cib	9	6/5	Lamat	9	7/27	Ahau	9
4/15	12/31	Caban	10	6/6	Muluc	10	7/28	Imix	10
4/16		Etznab	11	6/7	Oc	11	7/29	Ik	11
4/17		Cauac	12	6/8	Chuen	12	7/30	Akbal	12
4/18		Ahau	13	6/9	Eb	13	7/31	Kan	13

SAMPLE			BIRTHDAY	SOLAR GLYPH	TONE	BIRTHDAY		SOLAR GLYPH	TONE
			7/31	Muluc	1	1/4	9/21	Imix	1
BIRTHDAY	SOLAR GLYPH	TONE	8/1	Oc	2	1/5	9/22	Ik	2
			8/2	Chuen	3	1/6	9/23	Akbal	3
ALWAYS READ CHART FROM			8/3	Eb	4	1/7	9/24	Kan	4
LEFT TO RIGHT			8/4	Ben	5	1/8	9/25	Chicchan	5
STARTING WITH BIRTHDAY			8/5	Ix	6	1/9	9/26	Cimi	6
			8/6	Men	7	1/10	9/27	Manik	7
DOUBLE LINES			8/7	Cib	8	1/11	9/28	Lamat	8
SEPARATE SECTIONS			8/8	Caban	9	1/12	9/29	Muluc	9
			8/9	Etznab	10	1/13	9/30	Oc	10
USE SPACE BELOW			8/10	Cauac	11	1/14	10/1	Chuen	11
FOR RECORDING BIRTHDAYS			8/11	Ahau	12	1/15	10/2	Eb	12
			8/12	Imix	13	1/16	10/3	Ben	13
			8/13	Ik	1	1/17	10/4	Ix	1
			8/14	Akbal	2	1/18	10/5	Men	2
			8/15	Kan	3	1/19	10/6	Cib	3
			8/16	Chicchan	4	1/20	10/7	Caban	4
			8/17	Cimi	5	1/21	10/8	Etznab	5
			8/18	Manik	6	1/22	10/9	Cauac	6
			8/19	Lamat	7	1/23	10/10	Ahau	7
			8/20	Muluc	8	1/24	10/11	Imix	8
			8/21	Oc	9	1/25	10/12	Ik	9
			8/22	Chuen	10	1/26	10/13	Akbal	10
			8/23	Eb	11	1/27	10/14	Kan	11
			8/24	Ben	12	1/28	10/15	Chicchan	12
			8/25	Ix	13	1/29	10/16	Cimi	13
			8/26	Men	1	1/30	10/17	Manik	1
			8/27	Cib	2	1/31	10/18	Lamat	2
			8/28	Caban	3	2/1	10/19	Muluc	3
			8/29	Etznab	4	2/2	10/20	Oc	4
			8/30	Cauac	5	2/3	10/21	Chuen	5
			8/31	Ahau	6	2/4	10/22	Eb	6
			9/1	Imix	7	2/5	10/23	Ben	7
			9/2	Ik	8	2/6	10/24	Ix	8
			9/3	Akbal	9	2/7	10/25	Men	9
			9/4	Kan	10	2/8	10/26	Cib	10
			9/5	Chicchan	11	2/9	10/27	Caban	11
			9/6	Cimi	12	2/10	10/28	Etznab	12
			9/7	Manik	13	2/11	10/29	Cauac	13
			9/8	Lamat	1	2/12	10/30	Ahau	1
			9/9	Muluc	2	2/13	10/31	Imix	2
			9/10	Oc	3	2/14	11/1	Ik	3
			9/11	Chuen	4	2/15	11/2	Akbal	4
			9/12	Eb	5	2/16	11/3	Kan	5
			9/13	Ben	6	2/17	11/4	Chicchan	6
			9/14	Ix	7	2/18	11/5	Cimi	7
			9/15	Men	8	2/19	11/6	Manik	8
			9/16	Cib	9	2/20	11/7	Lamat	9
			9/17	Caban	10	2/21	11/8	Muluc	10
		1/1	9/18	Etznab	11	2/22	11/9	Oc	11
		1/2	9/19	Cauac	12	2/23	11/10	Chuen	12
		1/3	9/20	Ahau	13	2/24	11/11	Eb	13

BIRTHDAY		SOLAR GLYPH	TONE
2/25	11/12	Ben	1
2/26	11/13	Ix	2
2/27	11/14	Men	3
2/28	11/5	Cib	4
3/1	11/16	Caban	5
3/2	11/17	Etznab	6
3/3	11/18	Cauac	7
3/4	11/19	Ahau	8
3/5	11/20	Imix	9
3/6	11/21	Ik	10
3/7	11/22	Akbal	11
3/8	11/23	Kan	12
3/9	11/24	Chicchan	13
3/10	11/25	Cimi	1
3/11	11/26	Manik	2
3/12	11/27	Lamat	3
3/13	11/28	Muluc	4
3/14	11/29	Oc	5
3/15	11/30	Chuen	6
3/16	12/1	Eb	7
3/17	12/2	Ben	8
3/18	12/3	Ix	9
3/19	12/4	Men	10
3/20	12/5	Cib	11
3/21	12/6	Caban	12
3/22	12/7	Etznab	13
3/23	12/8	Cauac	1
3/24	12/9	Ahau	2
3/25	12/10	Imix	3
3/26	12/11	Ik	4
3/27	12/12	Akbal	5
3/28	12/13	Kan	6
3/29	12/14	Chicchan	7
3/30	12/15	Cimi	8
3/31	12/16	Manik	9
4/1	12/17	Lamat	10
4/2	12/18	Muluc	11
4/3	12/19	Oc	12
4/4	12/20	Chuen	13
4/5	12/21	Eb	1
4/6	12/22	Ben	2
4/7	12/23	Ix	3
4/8	12/24	Men	4
4/9	12/25	Cib	5
4/10	12/26	Caban	6
4/11	12/27	Etznab	7
4/12	12/28	Cauac	8
4/13	12/29	Ahau	9
4/14	12/30	Imix	10
4/15	12/31	Ik	11
4/16		Akbal	12
4/17		Kan	13

BIRTHDAY	SOLAR GLYPH	TONE
4/18	Chicchan	1
4/19	Cimi	2
4/20	Manik	3
4/21	Lamat	4
4/22	Muluc	5
4/23	Oc	6
4/24	Chuen	7
4/25	Eb	8
4/26	Ben	9
4/27	Ix	10
4/28	Men	11
4/29	Cib	12
4/30	Caban	13
5/1	Etznab	1
5/2	Cauac	2
5/3	Ahau	3
5/4	Imix	4
5/5	Ik	5
5/6	Akbal	6
5/7	Kan	7
5/8	Chicchan	8
5/9	Cimi	9
5/10	Manik	10
5/11	Lamat	11
5/12	Muluc	12
5/13	Oc	13
5/14	Chuen	1
5/15	Eb	2
5/16	Ben	3
5/17	Ix	4
5/18	Men	5
5/19	Cib	6
5/20	Caban	7
5/21	Etznab	8
5/22	Cauac	9
5/23	Ahau	10
5/24	Imix	11
5/25	Ik	12
5/26	Akbal	13
5/27	Kan	1
5/28	Chicchan	2
5/29	Cimi	3
5/30	Manik	4
5/31	Lamat	5
6/1	Muluc	6
6/2	Oc	7
6/3	Chuen	8
6/4	Eb	9
6/5	Ben	10
6/6	Ix	11
6/7	Men	12
6/8	Cib	13

BIRTHDAY	SOLAR GLYPH	TONE
6/9	Caban	1
6/10	Etznab	2
6/11	Cauac	3
6/12	Ahau	4
6/13	Imix	5
6/14	Ik	6
6/15	Akbal	7
6/16	Kan	8
6/17	Chiccan	9
6/18	Cimi	10
6/19	Manik	11
6/20	Lamat	12
6/21	Muluc	13
6/22	Oc	1
6/23	Chuen	2
6/24	Eb	3
6/25	Ben	4
6/26	Ix	5
6/27	Men	6
6/28	Cib	7
6/29	Caban	8
6/30	Etznab	9
7/1	Cauac	10
7/2	Ahau	11
7/3	Imix	12
7/4	Ik	13
7/5	Akbal	1
7/6	Kan	2
7/7	Chicchan	3
7/8	Cimi	4
7/9	Manik	5
7/10	Lamat	6
7/11	Muluc	7
7/12	Oc	8
7/13	Chuen	9
7/14	Eb	10
7/15	Ben	11
7/16	Ix	12
7/17	Men	13
7/18	Cib	1
7/19	Caban	2
7/20	Etznab	3
7/21	Cauac	4
7/22	Ahau	5
7/23	Imix	6
7/24	Ik	7
7/25	Akbal	8
7/26	Kan	9
7/27	Chicchan	10
7/28	Cimi	11
7/29	Manik	12
7/30	Lamat	13

SAMPLE			BIRTHDAY	SOLAR GLYPH	TONE	BIRTHDAY		SOLAR GLYPH	TONE
			7/30	Ben	1	1/3	9/20	Chicchan	1
BIRTHDAY	SOLAR GLYPH	TONE	7/31	Ix	2	1/4	9/21	Cimi	2
			8/1	Men	3	1/5	9/22	Manik	3
ALWAYS READ CHART FROM			8/2	Cib	4	1/6	9/23	Lamat	4
LEFT TO RIGHT			8/3	Caban	5	1/7	9/24	Muluc	5
STARTING WITH BIRTHDAY			8/4	Etznab	6	1/8	9/25	Oc	6
			8/5	Cauac	7	1/9	9/26	Chuen	7
DOUBLE LINES			8/6	Ahau	8	1/10	9/27	Eb	8
SEPARATE SECTIONS			8/7	Imix	9	1/11	9/28	Ben	9
			8/8	Ik	10	1/12	9/29	Ix	10
USE SPACE BELOW			8/9	Akbal	11	1/13	9/30	Men	11
FOR RECORDING BIRTHDAYS			8/10	Kan	12	1/14	10/1	Cib	12
			8/11	Chicchan	13	1/15	10/2	Caban	13
			8/12	Cimi	1	1/16	10/3	Etznab	1
			8/13	Manik	2	1/17	10/4	Cauac	2
			8/14	Lamat	3	1/18	10/5	Ahau	3
			8/15	Muluc	4	1/19	10/6	Imix	4
			8/16	Oc	5	1/20	10/7	Ik	5
			8/17	Chuen	6	1/21	10/8	Akbal	6
			8/18	Eb	7	1/22	10/9	Kan	7
			8/19	Ben	8	1/23	10/10	Chicchan	8
			8/20	Ix	9	1/24	10/11	Cimi	9
			8/21	Men	10	1/25	10/12	Manik	10
			8/22	Cib	11	1/26	10/13	Lamat	11
			8/23	Caban	12	1/27	10/14	Muluc	12
			8/24	Etznab	13	1/28	10/15	Oc	13
			8/25	Cauac	1	1/29	10/16	Chuen	1
			8/26	Ahau	2	1/30	10/17	Eb	2
			8/27	Imix	3	1/31	10/18	Ben	3
			8/28	Ik	4	2/1	10/19	Ix	4
			8/29	Akbal	5	2/2	10/20	Men	5
			8/30	Kan	6	2/3	10/21	Cib	6
			8/31	Chicchan	7	2/4	10/22	Caban	7
			9/1	Cimi	8	2/5	10/23	Etznab	8
			9/2	Manik	9	2/6	10/24	Cauac	9
			9/3	Lamat	10	2/7	10/25	Ahau	10
			9/4	Muluc	11	2/8	10/26	Imix	11
			9/5	Oc	12	2/9	10/27	Ik	12
			9/6	Chuen	13	2/10	10/28	Akbal	13
			9/7	Eb	1	2/11	10/29	Kan	1
			9/8	Ben	2	2/12	10/30	Chicchan	2
			9/9	Ix	3	2/13	10/31	Cimi	3
			9/10	Men	4	2/14	11/1	Manik	4
			9/11	Cib	5	2/15	11/2	Lamat	5
			9/12	Caban	6	2/16	11/3	Muluc	6
			9/13	Etznab	7	2/17	11/4	Oc	7
			9/14	Cauac	8	2/18	11/5	Chuen	8
			9/15	Ahau	9	2/19	11/6	Eb	9
			9/16	Imix	10	2/20	11/7	Ben	10
			9/17	Ik	11	2/21	11/8	Ix	11
		1/1	9/18	Akbal	12	2/22	11/9	Men	12
		1/2	9/19	Kan	13	2/23	11/10	Cib	13

BIRTHDAY		SOLAR GLYPH	TONE	BIRTHDAY		SOLAR GLYPH	TONE	BIRTHDAY		SOLAR GLYPH	TONE
2/24	11/11	Caban	1	4/17		Muluc	1	6/8		Imix	1
2/25	11/12	Etznab	2	4/18		Oc	2	6/9		Ik	2
2/26	11/13	Cauac	3	4/19		Chuen	3	6/10		Akbal	3
2/27	11/14	Ahau	4	4/20		Eb	4	6/11		Kan	4
2/28	11/5	Imix	5	4/21		Ben	5	6/12		Chicchan	5
3/1	11/16	Ik	6	4/22		Ix	6	6/13		Cimi	6
3/2	11/17	Akbal	7	4/23		Men	7	6/14		Manik	7
3/3	11/18	Kan	8	4/24		Cib	8	6/15		Lamat	8
3/4	11/19	Chiccan	9	4/25		Caban	9	6/16		Muluc	9
3/5	11/20	Cimi	10	4/26		Etznab	10	6/17		Oc	10
3/6	11/21	Manik	11	4/27		Cauac	11	6/18		Chuen	11
3/7	11/22	Lamat	12	4/28		Ahau	12	6/19		Eb	12
3/8	11/23	Muluc	13	4/29		Imix	13	6/20		Ben	13
3/9	11/24	Oc	1	4/30		Ik	1	6/21		Ix	1
3/10	11/25	Chuen	2	5/1		Akbal	2	6/22		Men	2
3/11	11/26	Eb	3	5/2		Kan	3	6/23		Cib	3
3/12	11/27	Ben	4	5/3		Chicchan	4	6/24		Caban	4
3/13	11/28	Ix	5	5/4		Cimi	5	6/25		Etznab	5
3/14	11/29	Men	6	5/5		Manik	6	6/26		Cauac	6
3/15	11/30	Cib	7	5/6		Lamat	7	6/27		Ahau	7
3/16	12/1	Caban	8	5/7		Muluc	8	6/28		Imix	8
3/17	12/2	Etznab	9	5/8		Oc	9	6/29		Ik	9
3/18	12/3	Cauac	10	5/9		Chuen	10	6/30		Akbal	10
3/19	12/4	Ahau	11	5/10		Eb	11	7/1		Kan	11
3/20	12/5	Imix	12	5/11		Ben	12	7/2		Chicchan	12
3/21	12/6	Ik	13	5/12		Ix	13	7/3		Cimi	13
3/22	12/7	Akbal	1	5/13		Men	1	7/4		Manik	1
3/23	12/8	Kan	2	5/14		Cib	2	7/5		Lamat	2
3/24	12/9	Chicchan	3	5/15		Caban	3	7/6		Muluc	3
3/25	12/10	Cimi	4	5/16		Etznab	4	7/7		Oc	4
3/26	12/11	Manik	5	5/17		Cauac	5	7/8		Chuen	5
3/27	12/12	Lamat	6	5/18		Ahau	6	7/9		Eb	6
3/28	12/13	Muluc	7	5/19		Imix	7	7/10		Ben	7
3/29	12/14	Oc	8	5/20		Ik	8	7/11		Ix	8
3/30	12/15	Chuen	9	5/21		Akbal	9	7/12		Men	9
3/31	12/16	Eb	10	5/22		Kan	10	7/13		Cib	10
4/1	12/17	Ben	11	5/23		Chicchan	11	7/14		Caban	11
4/2	12/18	Ix	12	5/24		Cimi	12	7/15		Etznab	12
4/3	12/19	Men	13	5/25		Manik	13	7/16		Cauac	13
4/4	12/20	Cib	1	5/26		Lamat	1	7/17		Ahau	1
4/5	12/21	Caban	2	5/27		Muluc	2	7/18		Imix	2
4/6	12/22	Etznab	3	5/28		Oc	3	7/19		Ik	3
4/7	12/23	Cauac	4	5/29		Chuen	4	7/20		Akbal	4
4/8	12/24	Ahau	5	5/30		Eb	5	7/21		Kan	5
4/9	12/25	Imix	6	5/31		Ben	6	7/22		Chicchan	6
4/10	12/26	Ik	7	6/1		Ix	7	7/23		Cimi	7
4/11	12/27	Akbal	8	6/2		Men	8	7/24		Manik	8
4/12	12/28	Kan	9	6/3		Cib	9	7/25		Lamat	9
4/13	12/29	Chicchan	10	6/4		Caban	10	7/26		Muluc	10
4/14	12/30	Cimi	11	6/5		Etznab	11	7/27		Oc	11
4/15	12/31	Manik	12	6/6		Cauac	12	7/28		Chuen	12
4/16		Lamat	13	6/7		Ahau	13	7/29		Eb	13

SAMPLE

BIRTHDAY	SOLAR GLYPH	TONE
ALWAYS READ CHART FROM		
LEFT TO RIGHT		
STARTING WITH BIRTHDAY		
DOUBLE LINES		
SEPARATE SECTIONS		
USE SPACE BELOW		
FOR RECORDING BIRTHDAYS		

BIRTHDAY	SOLAR GLYPH	TONE
7/29	Caban	1
7/30	Etznab	2
7/31	Cauac	3
8/1	Ahau	4
8/2	Imix	5
8/3	Ik	6
8/4	Akbal	7
8/5	Kan	8
8/6	Chiccan	9
8/7	Cimi	10
8/8	Manik	11
8/9	Lamat	12
8/10	Muluc	13
8/11	Oc	1
8/12	Chuen	2
8/13	Eb	3
8/14	Ben	4
8/15	Ix	5
8/16	Men	6
8/17	Cib	7
8/18	Caban	8
8/19	Etznab	9
8/20	Cauac	10
8/21	Ahau	11
8/22	Imix	12
8/23	Ik	13
8/24	Akbal	1
8/25	Kan	2
8/26	Chicchan	3
8/27	Cimi	4
8/28	Manik	5
8/29	Lamat	6
8/30	Muluc	7
8/31	Oc	8
9/1	Chuen	9
9/2	Eb	10
9/3	Ben	11
9/4	Ix	12
9/5	Men	13
9/6	Cib	1
9/7	Caban	2
9/8	Etznab	3
9/9	Cauac	4
9/10	Ahau	5
9/11	Imix	6
9/12	Ik	7
9/13	Akbal	8
9/14	Kan	9
9/15	Chicchan	10
9/16	Cimi	11
9/17	Manik	12
1/1	9/18 Lamat	13

BIRTHDAY	BIRTHDAY	SOLAR GLYPH	TONE
1/2	9/19	Muluc	1
1/3	9/20	Oc	2
1/4	9/21	Chuen	3
1/5	9/22	Eb	4
1/6	9/23	Ben	5
1/7	9/24	Ix	6
1/8	9/25	Men	7
1/9	9/26	Cib	8
1/10	9/27	Caban	9
1/11	9/28	Etznab	10
1/12	9/29	Cauac	11
1/13	9/30	Ahau	12
1/14	10/1	Imix	13
1/15	10/2	Ik	1
1/16	10/3	Akbal	2
1/17	10/4	Kan	3
1/18	10/5	Chicchan	4
1/19	10/6	Cimi	5
1/20	10/7	Manik	6
1/21	10/8	Lamat	7
1/22	10/9	Muluc	8
1/23	10/10	Oc	9
1/24	10/11	Chuen	10
1/25	10/12	Eb	11
1/26	10/13	Ben	12
1/27	10/14	Ix	13
1/28	10/15	Men	1
1/29	10/16	Cib	2
1/30	10/17	Caban	3
1/31	10/18	Etznab	4
2/1	10/19	Cauac	5
2/2	10/20	Ahau	6
2/3	10/21	Imix	7
2/4	10/22	Ik	8
2/5	10/23	Akbal	9
2/6	10/24	Kan	10
2/7	10/25	Chicchan	11
2/8	10/26	Cimi	12
2/9	10/27	Manik	13
2/10	10/28	Lamat	1
2/11	10/29	Muluc	2
2/12	10/30	Oc	3
2/13	10/31	Chuen	4
2/14	11/1	Eb	5
2/15	11/2	Ben	6
2/16	11/3	Ix	7
2/17	11/4	Men	8
2/18	11/5	Cib	9
2/19	11/6	Caban	10
2/20	11/7	Etznab	11
2/21	11/8	Cauac	12
2/22	11/9	Ahau	13

BIRTHDAY	SOLAR GLYPH	TONE	BIRTHDAY	SOLAR GLYPH	TONE	BIRTHDAY	SOLAR GLYPH	TONE
2/23	11/10	Imix	1	4/16	Ben	1	6/7	Chicchan	1
2/24	11/11	Ik	2	4/17	Ix	2	6/8	Cimi	2
2/25	11/12	Akbal	3	4/18	Men	3	6/9	Manik	3
2/26	11/13	Kan	4	4/19	Cib	4	6/10	Lamat	4
2/27	11/14	Chicchan	5	4/20	Caban	5	6/11	Muluc	5
2/28	11/5	Cimi	6	4/21	Etznab	6	6/12	Oc	6
3/1	11/16	Manik	7	4/22	Cauac	7	6/13	Chuen	7
3/2	11/17	Lamat	8	4/23	Ahau	8	6/14	Eb	8
3/3	11/18	Muluc	9	4/24	Imix	9	6/15	Ben	9
3/4	11/19	Oc	10	4/25	Ik	10	6/16	Ix	10
3/5	11/20	Chuen	11	4/26	Akbal	11	6/17	Men	11
3/6	11/21	Eb	12	4/27	Kan	12	6/18	Cib	12
3/7	11/22	Ben	13	4/28	Chicchan	13	6/19	Caban	13
3/8	11/23	Ix	1	4/29	Cimi	1	6/20	Etznab	1
3/9	11/24	Men	2	4/30	Manik	2	6/21	Cauac	2
3/10	11/25	Cib	3	5/1	Lamat	3	6/22	Ahau	3
3/11	11/26	Caban	4	5/2	Muluc	4	6/23	Imix	4
3/12	11/27	Etznab	5	5/3	Oc	5	6/24	Ik	5
3/13	11/28	Cauac	6	5/4	Chuen	6	6/25	Akbal	6
3/14	11/29	Ahau	7	5/5	Eb	7	6/26	Kan	7
3/15	11/30	Imix	8	5/6	Ben	8	6/27	Chicchan	8
3/16	12/1	Ik	9	5/7	Ix	9	6/28	Cimi	9
3/17	12/2	Akbal	10	5/8	Men	10	6/29	Manik	10
3/18	12/3	Kan	11	5/9	Cib	11	6/30	Lamat	11
3/19	12/4	Chicchan	12	5/10	Caban	12	7/1	Muluc	12
3/20	12/5	Cimi	13	5/11	Etznab	13	7/2	Oc	13
3/21	12/6	Manik	1	5/12	Cauac	1	7/3	Chuen	1
3/22	12/7	Lamat	2	5/13	Ahau	2	7/4	Eb	2
3/23	12/8	Muluc	3	5/14	Imix	3	7/5	Ben	3
3/24	12/9	Oc	4	5/15	Ik	4	7/6	Ix	4
3/25	12/10	Chuen	5	5/16	Akbal	5	7/7	Men	5
3/26	12/11	Eb	6	5/17	Kan	6	7/8	Cib	6
3/27	12/12	Ben	7	5/18	Chicchan	7	7/9	Caban	7
3/28	12/13	Ix	8	5/19	Cimi	8	7/10	Etznab	8
3/29	12/14	Men	9	5/20	Manik	9	7/11	Cauac	9
3/30	12/15	Cib	10	5/21	Lamat	10	7/12	Ahau	10
3/31	12/16	Caban	11	5/22	Muluc	11	7/13	Imix	11
4/1	12/17	Etznab	12	5/23	Oc	12	7/14	Ik	12
4/2	12/18	Cauac	13	5/24	Chuen	13	7/15	Akbal	13
4/3	12/19	Ahau	1	5/25	Eb	1	7/16	Kan	1
4/4	12/20	Imix	2	5/26	Ben	2	7/17	Chicchan	2
4/5	12/21	Ik	3	5/27	Ix	3	7/18	Cimi	3
4/6	12/22	Akbal	4	5/28	Men	4	7/19	Manik	4
4/7	12/23	Kan	5	5/29	Cib	5	7/20	Lamat	5
4/8	12/24	Chicchan	6	5/30	Caban	6	7/21	Muluc	6
4/9	12/25	Cimi	7	5/31	Etznab	7	7/22	Oc	7
4/10	12/26	Manik	8	6/1	Cauac	8	7/23	Chuen	8
4/11	12/27	Lamat	9	6/2	Ahau	9	7/24	Eb	9
4/12	12/28	Muluc	10	6/3	Imix	10	7/25	Ben	10
4/13	12/29	Oc	11	6/4	Ik	11	7/26	Ix	11
4/14	12/30	Chuen	12	6/5	Akbal	12	7/27	Men	12
4/15	12/31	Eb	13	6/6	Kan	13	7/28	Cib	13

Mary Fran Koppa is an artist as well as a writer. She has channeled 43 paintings based on the symbols of the Mayan Calendar. These paintings carry the energy of the symbols. You may order reproductions of this wonderful art, and other related products.

ITEM	COST	UNIT	AMOUNT
Set of 20 SOLAR GLYPH ACTIVATION CARDS			
Full-color solar glyph painting prints with instructions	$29.95		
POSTER-of the 20 solar glyph paintings, 24 x 36	$19.95		
MAYAN CALENDAR COLORING BOOK			
Line drawings of the 20 solar glyph paintings			
by Mary Fran Koppa, for children of all ages	$8.95		
AUDIO TAPE on Mayan Calendar by Mary Fran	$12.00		
MAYAN CALENDAR BIRTHDAY BOOK			
Handbook for finding your solar glyph, tone and planet	$12.95		
T-SHIRT Solar glyph painting of your choice on			
white T-shirt, crew sizes L and XL	$22.95		
CANVAS TOTE BAG-approx 18"x16"x 7"			
with solar glyph painting of your choice	$22.95		
SOLAR GLYPH PAINTING NOTE CARDS			
Set of 20 different cards with envelopes	$39.95		
SOLAR GLYPH PRINT-choose 1 through 20	8" x 10" $12.50		
	11" x 14" $14.95		
YOGANANDA'S ANGEL ASPECT	8" x 10" $12.50		
Print of charcoal drawing by Mary Fran Koppa	11" x 14" $14.95		
		SUBTOTAL	
SHIPPING AND HANDLING			
up to $50	$4.00		
$50-$75	$8.00		
$75 to $100	$9.00		
$100-$130	$10.00		
$130-$150	$11.00		
$150-$175	$12.00		
$175-$200	$13.00		
over $200	add $3.00 per $100		
Canadian orders	add 10% to regular charge		
Overseas orders	triple the shipping charge		
		SHIPPING CHARGE	
		TOTAL	

ALL ORDERS MUST BE PREPAID
WITH CHECK OR MONEY ORDER
Please print your name and address and include your telephone number. Thanks!
MAIL YOUR ORDER TO: Mayan Calendar Art, P.O. Box 1833, Cottonwood, AZ 86326 Phone (520) 639-1146
Send for free catalog.
E-mail: ahau@verdenet.com   Homepage: http://verdenet.com/commercial/mayan